# PLOW PEDDLER

# PLOW PEDDLER

*The Plow Peddler
sold the plows
that produced the crops
that stocked the stores
that fed the people
with wholesome food
for a smaller percentage
of disposable income
than anywhere else in the world*

## WALTER M. BUESCHER

Glenbridge Publishing Ltd.

Cover Illustration
Patricia Hobbs

Copyright © 1992 by Walter M. Buescher

All rights reserved. Except for brief quotations in critical articles or reviews, this book or parts thereof, must not be reproduced in any form without permission in writing from the publisher. For further information contact Glenbridge Publishing Ltd., Macomb, Illinois 61455

Library of Congress Catalog Card Number: 91-72529

International Standard Book Number: 0-944435-18-1

To

PAUL CRITTENDEN

If he had not taken me with him to LaPorte, Indiana,
January 25, 1936, I would not have started to
work for Allis-Chalmers the next day.
There would have been no farm equipment career
to write about.

"Give us this day our daily bread."

> The Lord's Prayer

# CONTENTS

Foreword ix
Preface xi

## PART I: LaPORTE

1. They're Hiring! 2
2. Heads, LaPorte, Tails, Michigan City 20
3. Go West, Young Barrister! 32

## PART II: TOLEDO

4. A New Branch is Born 50
5. The Banting Company 67
6. They Made the Stuff Run 83
7. The WC, Our Workhorse Tractor 97

## PART III: CLEVELAND

8. Hello Affluence, Goodbye Poverty 122
9. The White Sheep of the Family 144
10. Deafness Can Be a Virtue 160

## PART IV: BACK TO TOLEDO

11. A New Swivel Chair 192
12. Some of the Guys 209
13. Live and Learn 224
14. Don't Try to Stop the Tide 247

## PART V: MILWAUKEE

| | |
|---|---|
| 15. Centralization In, Centralization Out | 262 |
| 16. The Indestructible Gleaner | 282 |
| 17. Carrot On a Stick | 295 |

# Foreword

In my line of work, I get to meet a lot of interesting people. We publish several country oriented magazines, and over the years, I've conducted in-depth interviews with all sorts of fascinating folks. A few of them have stood out and found a special place in my memory bank. Walt Buescher is one of them.

He's one of those people who can talk non-stop and keep the conversation interesting. He'll pepper his remarks with enough humor to keep you laughing while you're learning.

Most of his stories are about people he met in his line of work. When he ran across a character who was knee-deep in real history, Walt sat him down and drew all sorts of fascinating facts out of him, and then committed them to memory.

Walt is still discovering new things to do. This book is a good example. When he realized that nobody had set down the history and details of the people in the farm equipment industry, in which he worked for years, he set out to do it himself.

Walt will introduce you to many of the people he met over the years. You'll meet inventors who dreamed, manufacturers who gambled, executives who managed and mis-managed, salesmen who met quotas, and during hard times didn't, servicemen who made the stuff run, sometimes ingeniously, dealers who were the middle link in the chain, and farmers who put the products to good use.

While Walt's book reminisces long and lovingly on the farm equipment business, it's short on nuts and bolts. Instead, it's filled with "people stories," some mighty engrossing ones.

There's one people story to which he doesn't give proper emphasis. It's the one about Walt Buescher, who, while active in the equipment industry, was such a mover and shaker that he was named "Marketing Man-of-the-Year" by the National Agri-Marketing Association in 1974.

Quite a fellow, Walt. Quite a book, this. But don't start reading until you find a mighty comfortable spot and have more than just a few minutes to spend; you're going to be sitting a spell.

        Roy Reiman, Reiman Publications

# PREFACE

Did you eat yesterday? Do you plan to eat tomorrow? Are you a bit hungry right now?

After that incident with the serpent, God told Adam, "In the sweat of thy face shalt thou eat bread," and, as a caution, God warned Adam that his farming would be complicated by "thorns and thistles." Adam had a choice. He could either till the soil and sweat or he could look into a mirror and watch himself slowly starve to death. From that moment to this, agriculture has been the world's most important industry. There's a little country in all of us since our ancestors had to provide food for themselves in order to survive.

If we move near enough to the equator, we can dispense with clothes and shelter. We can walk around naked as a jaybird and use palm branches to divert the rain, but we can't live without groceries. Food and water are the only indispensable elements in the world. Daily bread is absolutely essential to the survival of mankind. Animals, too.

This book focuses on the years when I was one of millions in the food production business. Together we came up with the miracle of ample food. There probably wasn't one of us who realized that we ordinary people were writing the most notable chapter in world history, the chapter entitled, "From Hunger to Plenty." If there is hunger today, it is not because of a lack of food. It's either poor distribution, or some dictator is using starvation as a political tool.

We who worked in agriculture and agribusiness, didn't sense that we were on a crusade. We had no great and glorious leader who spelled out our goals, held a timetable before us, and measured our performance. We were part of a free market system that, by its very nature, strove for constant improvement.

People come and go. Since companies are made up of people, they come and go too. I was with one such company that came full turn in my lifetime—from glory days to disappearance—but in the fifty years this book describes, it contributed much to provide you with more, better, and less expensive food.

Had Moses returned to my grandfather's farm, he would have recognized most of the implements on that farm. The food revolution is quite recent. Hunger was standard equipment over much of the world for centuries. More change took place in the food production industry in my lifetime than in all the preceding centuries. That's the story that will unfold as you read on.

All of agribusiness helped the American farmer to make it happen—seed companies, fertilizer suppliers, chemical applicators, storage manufacturers, and a host of others. However, this is the story of the people who invented, manufactured, sold, serviced, and used the machines that made it possible for two percent of our people to provide enough food for the nation and many other peoples of the earth, with enough left over to create continuing political turmoil over surpluses. Without machinery, most of the other aspects in agriculture would be quite impotent.

*Preface*

Thomas Robert Malthus (1766-1834) was the English economist and clergyman who predicted that people would multiply geometrically while food production increased only arithmetically. He forecast mass starvation then, just as some doomsayers do now. This book is the story of the people who proved Thomas Robert Malthus and his present-day alarmist cohorts dead wrong.

In the writing of this book, your author found the occupational hazards of a historian to be very real. When several people saw the same thing happen, each had a different historical version to relate, some diametrically opposed to the others. When confronted with several versions of the same story, I used the one I found most interesting, the one I thought most likely to have happened. When embarrassment might occur, fictitious names were substituted for the ones on the birth certificate. As is the case with most twice-told tales, almost surely there is embellishment. Mark Twain said he had the ability to remember everything that happened, whether it happened or not. Your author has that same remarkable ability.

Mine has been an interesting lifetime. The reader will now sit back and enjoy. There's a 93 percent chance that the contents of this book are accurate . . . 87 percent of the time.

# PART ONE
# LaPORTE

# 1
# THEY'RE HIRING!

"Why don't you go out to Rumely's? They're starting to build Oil Pulls again. I hear they're hiring."

Mrs. Droege's statement was a combination of information and disinformation. It wasn't Advance-Rumely anymore. Allis-Chalmers Manufacturing Company had bought Doc Rumely's terminally ill Rumely Company in 1930. Further, the venerable Oil Pull tractor, affectionately known as "Kerosene Annie," had not experienced reincarnation. This giant power plant of threshing machine days had a secure place in farm equipment history books, but its days in the agricultural marketplace were long gone. Allis-Chalmers had begun to build a machine they called the All-Crop Harvester in the old Rumely thresher plant in LaPorte, Indiana.

Mrs. Droege was right about one thing, however. They were hiring! Even though he had written me a month or two earlier that there were no jobs open, this time Personnel Manager Doc Glassman said, "Go home, kid, and change clothes... bring some tools and go to work."

"I'm from out-of-town... we live in Bremen," I told him.

"OK, go home and come back tomorrow morning," Doc replied. "The whistle blows at eight. Come in here first ... at 7:45."

## They're Hiring!

Doc Glassman's manner was as warm and loving as a drill sergeant's bark, but as long as the news was good, what difference did it make how he sounded?

In 1936 jobs were as plentiful as balanced budgets in Congress are now. Dizzy Dean said, "there are two chances of changing an umpire's decision . . . slim and none." That described the 1936 job scene too.

Black Tuesday in 1929 was only the beginning. The economic slide kept sliding until it hit rock bottom in 1932. Franklin Delano Roosevelt promised a reversal of trends and was elected president by a landslide. Only Maine, Vermont, and my father dissented. The nation found that President Roosevelt's promised economic recovery was an elusive sort of thing. In 1936, one could hardly call the nation's economy dynamic. Collapse had come quickly. Rebuilding took time.

Those of us who graduated in 1935 read our share of want ads, pressed our share of doorbells, made our share of phone calls, wore out our share of shoe leather. Our verse was, "I'm looking for a job." The refrain came back, "We're not hiring."

But now there was a job. Hallelujah!

The trip to LaPorte happened this way: Paul Crittenden asked me if I wanted to go to LaPorte with him. Since there wasn't anything else to do, I told him I would be glad to go. Paul's mother wanted to visit Mrs. Droege, an old family friend. Mr. Droege worked at the bank. This kill-time trip was on January 25, 1936. On January 26, 1936, my thirty-nine years with Allis-Chalmers began.

The New Deal's blue eagle cheered because one more job had been created. My folks cheered because their free-loading son was gone, never to live at home again. The lady on Lincolnway cheered when the room that she had advertised in the *Herald-Argus* was rented for $1.50 per week.

Doc Rumely's Advance-Rumely Company had suffered the pains of obsolescence, national economic depression, and over-expansion. Finley P. Mount was appointed receiver in the bankruptcy proceedings. Now it was 1936! From the economic ashes of the Rumely operation there was innovation instead of obsolescence, and under-expansion instead of over-expansion. To hear dealers tell it, Allis-Chalmers just couldn't turn out its new All-Crop Harvesters fast enough. And I was caught up in this rising economic tide!

## BREMEN

My hometown of Bremen, Indiana, was a small town about twenty minutes below South Bend . . . by telephone. If you plugged in your toaster, the street lights went dim. B Street was the edge of town. If you found a cat in our town with a full tail, you knew he was a tourist. We had a beauty contest in Bremen one time. Nobody won. If you threw a dog a bone, he would signal for a fair catch. We had three dogs that were the fire department in Bremen. The biggest business we had in town was a 300-pound Avon lady. In those Depression days we didn't have much to do so we wrestled with the girls. That's when I found out that it isn't whether you win or lose, it's how you play the game.

Actually Bremen had 500 houses, twenty-two stores, two grain elevators, five churches, one foundry, two schools, a city hall, and a depot. My father taught in one of those two schools. He was the Lutheran school teacher in Bremen for forty-seven years.

## They're Hiring!

My first recollection of Bremen (or anything else for that matter) is the memory of whistles blowing and church bells ringing. "Papa, why is the foundry whistle blowing? Why are all of the church bells ringing? Why are they shooting all of those guns?"

"Son, the war is over!" he said. "The war is over at last. The Kaiser has surrendered." World War I was history.

The whistle that was blowing was the whistle that called people to work at the American Radiator Company plant in Bremen. Household and commercial steam and water radiators were built there. The bells that were ringing belonged to the Reformed, Lutheran, Evangelical, Dunkard, and United Brethren churches in town. The day was November 11, 1918. Armistice Day, coming as it did, had a special meaning for our family. Until then, Dad had not been drafted because he was both a father of a four-year-old boy and five-month-old girl, and he was a school teacher. The war's manpower requirements were great, and had the war continued for another month or so, Dad, too, would have had to go.

My father's face was a mixture of smiles and tears when he said, "Son, the war is over!" Dad and Mom embraced like I never saw them embrace again.

Dad taught in a one-room school where there were forty to forty-five students. Since teaching forty students was not a full-time job, he was also church organist and choir director at St. Paul's. And church and school janitor! Dad could be stubborn at times. After the Gospel reading, the hymn book called for a response from the congregation, "Hallelujah, hallelujah." Dad refused to play that hallelujah on Pentecost when the Scripture reading ended with, "Others mocked, saying, 'these men are full of new wine.' I'll be darned if I play 'hallelujah' for a bunch of drunks."

The other day, when I read what per-pupil costs are today, I did a little figuring on the back of an old envelope. Playing it on the high side, I couldn't come up with over $45 per-pupil cost in Dad's school, and that's both capital cost and operations.

In 1918, we lived in the "Mochel property" where the rent was seven dollars a month. On a winter evening, while doing homework at the dining table, a warm glow came from the base burner stove nearby. One could see the hard coal burn through the transparent little "eisen glass" squares on three sides of the stove. Our sanitary facilities stood in the back yard, a combination three-holer and woodshed. The bathroom was the kitchen floor on Saturday afternoons. Dad climbed into the washtub first, then Mom, then us kids. The Mochel property had running water . . . we ran to the pump in the yard. We had a cistern filled with rainwater, and that pump was inside the house. No need to go outside to wash hands or dishes. The two bedrooms were upstairs; an upstairs that was completely devoid of heat in the wintertime, except for the warmth that escaped through one register over the stove in the living room.

Dad hailed from a farm in Southern Illinois where his grandfather had settled when he arrived in this country from the Bielefeld area of Germany. My father was the scrawniest of the twelve children in the family. Since he would never have amounted to anything on the farm, he was sent to Concordia College in Addison, Illinois, to become a school teacher.

Mother came from St. Louis where her father was the night watchman at the Waltke Soap Works on North Broadway in Baden, where William Waltke made Lava Soap and Oxydol. Mom told and retold of the majesties of the St.

Louis World's Fair with its world's-biggest Ferris wheel that had to be dynamited down after the fair because nobody wanted to buy it. That was the fair that first sold hot dogs and ice cream cones. Grandpa Sperber, his bride and twenty-two dollars came from Ansbach, Bavaria, to settle in St. Louis. Just off the boat from Ellis Island, Grandpa met a sharpie who spoke German, a "landsman" who sold Grandpa a gun for eleven dollars that wouldn't shoot.

Translated, the huckster said, "When you get to St. Louis, you'll need protection from Indians and bears." That was Grandpa's first lesson in American capitalism, back in the days before "caveat emptor" disappeared.

After the Mochel property was sold, we moved into the "Dietrich property" where the fifteen dollars monthly rent took a big bite out of Dad's $100 per month salary. Finally, in 1926, St. Paul's built us a fine new home across from the church and school. We luxuriated in this modern eight-room house, complete with indoor plumbing, a bath and a half, kitchen cupboards, a gas range, a central heating coal furnace, and a coal-fired hot water heater.

When Paul Crittenden and I returned home on January 25, 1936, my old college trunk was hauled out of the attic and in it, I packed my work clothes and "good" clothes. A dinner pail that dated back to my summer vacation days in the peppermint marshes around Bremen came out of hibernation. Dad's work bench was relieved of a hammer, screw driver, wrench, and a pair of pliers. Mother fixed the first day's lunch and then Paul and I headed back to LaPorte.

My corporate career had begun! Pay in #2 Shop averaged eighty-eight dollars a month. That came to $1,056 per year. In 1936, lawyers averaged $4,000, doctors $3,000, school teachers $1,300, and coal miners $800. Sounds low today, but then in 1936, a "loaded" Chevy cost $600, Park Avenue hotels charged seven dollars a night for a room, and in Bremen, Billy Walters charged twenty-four cents per pound for sirloin steak. Henry Kiefer's horse-drawn milk wagon delivered milk to the door for eleven cents per quart. Store-bought bread at Foltz's grocery store was seven cents per loaf. Since that was a little steep for the Buescher budget, Mom baked her own bread!

**THE 1936 FARM SCENE**

In 1936 Mid-America, a 100-acre farm was a good sized farm. In fact, two thirds of the nation's four million farms had less than that, and that included the West where 100 acres was only enough land to pasture a few yearling heifers. Most farmers still had at least one team or horses and, obviously, the hay and oats field that it took to feed those horses. Everybody had a Fordson tractor, Henry Ford's agronomic Model T. A few of the bigger and better farmers had graduated to an International Harvester Company "Farmall." In all of International's corporate history, two innovations stand out—the McCormick-Deering binder and the Farmall tractor.

When I was born in 1914, fifty-eight farm equipment manufacturers built 15,000 tractors and the nation's barns housed 25.4 million horses. By 1936, the tractor population had grown to 1,174,889 units. Manufacturers built 194,000 wheel tractors in 1936. The horse population was down to a little over sixteen million. Farmers planted corn on land that had formerly been used for horse feed.

Standard equipment on the 1936 farm was at least one cow for milk for the family, a hen house full of chickens for eggs, and a few hogs, one of which could be butchered when the first cold snap hit. If there were several cows, the surplus milk, over and above the family's needs, went through a cream separator. Farmers sold the cream to the local creamery and the skim milk went to "slop the hogs." Cranking a DeLaval cream separator was hard work but not nearly as much work as washing all of those consarned discs that mysteriously separated the cream from the milk. At the creamery the cream was churned into butter. If there were surplus eggs, they were taken to town on band concert night in the summertime, or Saturday night the year around, to trade for groceries. "Give me two dozen egg's worth of sugar," was a common order in a grocery store.

The 1936 farm required neighborhood cooperation at threshing time and butchering time. Farmers traded work. When the grain was ripe, a steam engine pulling a thresher came into the barnyard. The engineer fired the boiler and set the thresher. The threshing machine had to set level, which often meant placing blocks under one wheel and digging a little hole for another wheel. Any deviation from level meant lost grain.

Wagonloads of bundles of wheat, oats, barley or rye came to the thresher from the field. Out in the field, the men pitched bundles, butts to the outside, onto a wagon that we called a hay rack. Horses moved from shock to shock with the same intuition that leads geese south in the fall.

For the uninitiated, the thresher process, step by step, was this: (1) Two men pitched bundles of grain onto the machine's "feeder" which carried the bundles into the threshing cylinder. (2) The cylinder, a rotating device equipped with teeth or rasps, separated the grain from the chaff from the straw. (3) The cylinder's momentum tossed the separated materials onto a "straw rack," a long slatted table that shook back and forth. Grain and some chaff fell through the slats. The straw rack's up-and-out action moved the straw to the rear of the machine. (4) The grain and chaff that fell through the straw rack, fell onto a "cleaning shoe" which was a unit of shaking sieves—the top one coarse, and the bottom one, sized for the crop being threshed. (5) A fan blew air across the cleaning shoe sieves, blowing the chaff to the rear of the machine. A set of "wind blinds" on the fan controlled the amount of incoming air.

Too much air could blow the grain out of the machine, so adjusting the wind blinds was the job for an expert. If there was a gusty wind from the west, the threshermen all but closed the wind blinds on the west side and opened the ones on the east side. He wanted a nice even flow of air across the sieves. (6) Do you remember seeing a long metal pipe on the back of a thresher? That was called the "windstacker" because it stacked the straw on a straw stack often behind the barn. A big fan blew the straw and chaff from the straw rack and the chaff from the cleaning shoe onto a stack. (7) The grain, separated from the chaff by the fan and cleaning shoe, was delivered to a chute and there the grain was bagged.

It was the stack man's job to build the straw stack so that it wouldn't tip or blow over, or take up too much room in the barnyard. The stack man on the straw stack wore a straw hat and had a red handkerchief around his neck to protect him from the blasts of straw, chaff, and lost grain coming from the windstacker. The stack man was sworn to secrecy by the engineer because only he knew how many lost kernels of grain were coming through the thresher's windstacker. The stack man was often pelted by the lost grain. The farmer's first clues of lost grain appeared in the spring when the straw stack sprouted. A water boy rounded out the crew.

Oh yes, the cooks! We surely can't forget them. Come dinner time the engineer blew the whistle and the threshing (we pronounced it "thrashing") crew headed for the house. They washed their hands and faces in a communal washtub on the back porch, then dried their faces and hands with a common towel. Inside the house, the dining room table was extended to accommodate a threshing crew of eight to twelve men. Kids ate at the "second table." The cooks were the threshing crew's wives. Threshers ate well!

The threshed grain went either to the granary on the farm or it was hauled into town, either to the flour mill or to the grain elevator next to the railroad track. In our area, about half of the grain that came to town went to the elevator located next to our aging B&O depot. Threshing was an every-farm experience since every farmer in our part of the world raised wheat and oats . . . sometimes a little barley and buckwheat too. "When everything else fails, plant buckwheat," farmers said. Buckwheat was a worst case scenario.

At corn harvest time a corn binder went into the field to cut the corn and tie it into bundles. The bundles were shocked to make the sort of pictures that painters love to paint even today. Fellow Hoosier James Whitcomb Riley said, "When the frost is on the punkin and the fodder's in the shock." Other farmers stripped the ears off of the stalks, "shucked" the ears with a husking peg that hugged the hand like a glove, then tossed the ears into a wagon, which moved along parallel to the men who did the corn picking. The far side of the wagon had sideboards higher than those on the near side. You've heard of the "symphony of the bangboards?" When the ear of corn hit the high sideboards on the other side of the wagon . . . BANG!

Full loads of corn went to the corncrib. Corncribs were narrow and the walls were slatted. Air blowing between the slats and through the narrow crib of corn dried the crop. At harvest time corn was too moist to keep without a lot of ventilation. Slatted corncribs provided the air conditioning.

At haymaking time, farmers took their horse-drawn mowers to the field to cut their alfalfa, timothy, or clover. After a few days of drying time, the farmer hitched his horses to a side delivery rake. The evenly cut hay was delivered sideways to what we called a "windrow," a row of hay. Today, tractor-drawn balers come down the windrow to bale the hay, but in 1936 the dried hay was loaded on wagons and taken to the barn. A hay loader, hitched to the rear of the wagon, carried the hay in the windrow to the man with a pitchfork who built his load of hay.

To get the loose hay on the wagon into the hayloft, you either pitched it up there by hand, or if you were more prosperous, you used slings. A sling (ropes with connecting wooden slats) was laid on the bare wagon. When the wagon was half loaded with hay, a second sling was thrown over the hay. Thus one wagonload of hay consisted of two sling-loads of hay. At the barn, the barn's hay ropes were fastened to the top sling on the wagon. As horses pulled on the rope, the half-load of hay went up to the ridgepole of the barn, and from there on a track to the hayloft on one side or the other.

When the sling-load of hay was centered over the mow, a man pulled the trip rope and the hay fell into the mow. Leveling hay with a pitchfork in a dusty haymow on a hot summer day was not an occupation of choice.

One day, when Uncle Carl was making hay, the truck came from Billy Walter's slaughter shop to pick up the scrub bull that he had sold to our local two-man packing house. "What is a scrub bull?" you ask. Let's just say that a scrub bull is not sought after by the better girl cows in the barnyard.

All efforts to get that critter into the truck failed. He was beaten with 2x4s and jabbed with a pitchfork, but resolutely the beast stood his ground. No ride to oblivion for el toro. Finally a light turned on in Uncle Carl's head. He placed a halter on the bull and led him over to the haymaking operation. There he placed a set of slings under the bull, thinking that he would raise the bull just high enough to slip the truck in underneath him.

It was a world-class idea, but Uncle Carl had not reckoned with the fact that this scrub bull had never been airborne before, and, as it turned out, the critter was scared of flying. When the fourth hoof left the ground, that bull let out a bellow that chased the pigeons out of the courthouse steeple eight miles away. The bellow scared the horses that were hitched to the hay rope and they took off. The bull shot up to the ridgepole of the barn like a rocket taking off at Cape Canaveral, then shot over to the south haymow. There, the bull's struggling legs tangled with the trip rope, and the bull fell into the haymow. Everybody in and around Bremen came out to look at that bull and give advice about how to get a bull out of a haymow. Finally, Uncle Carl asked Jack Annis to come from Billy Walters's slaughter shop to stun and stick the bull up in the haymow. Beef on the hoof came out of that haymow in quarters.

In 1936, every farmhouse had a kitchen stove that consumed wood or coal, like the houses in town. There was a fire box, the drawer for ashes, four cast-iron stove lids, a warming oven over the stove, a warm water reservoir beside the fire box, and an oven for baking bread and warming cold feet on a winter day.

Farms without electricity used coal oil lamps to provide light for all nocturnal work and pleasure. Water for animals and humans was pumped by hand, and there were no milking machines. Then Delco systems began to appear, a combination of windmills and batteries provided electrical power of sorts.

Grade schools were within walking distance of the farm. Farm kids who went to high school had to find a way to get there. There were no yellow busses. In Bremen, the Snyder kids drove a horse to town and parked the animal behind their grandparents' woodshed, then walked a few blocks to school. The Ellis kids drove a Star (yes, there was an automobile by that name). Everybody else walked. Today, we bus the kids to school, then provide a gymnasium next to the school to give them exercise.

In the '30s every farm that I knew of, had a Singer sewing machine (the sewing machines were manufactured in nearby South Bend). A good share of the farm family's clothes was "homemade." Mom bought her dress goods at Dietrich's store that sold groceries, dry goods, notions, and men's suits and shoes.

The farm garden and orchard provided food for canning. Most farms were all but self-sufficient. Since coffee, sugar, salt, and pepper didn't grow very well in northern Indiana, they had to be store-bought. Often they were acquired with tradein eggs from the farm henhouse. That's a short overview of the 1936 Midwest farm scene. Now back to that newly launched farm equipment career.

## IN THE BEGINNING

It was a long, long walk across that quarter mile of frozen tundra between the plant gate and the entrance to #2 Shop on January 26, 1936, as Allis-Chalmers's newest employee reported for work for the first time. Foreman Art Smith explained that the job would be, among other things, assembling header lift levers. My workbench was beside a door large enough to permit a Greyhound bus to enter . . . sideways. With disconcerting regularity, that door opened to permit one big truck and one big blast of Siberian air to enter.

Quickly it was discovered that my conservative work ethic did not fit this blue collar world. "Slow down, kid!" my fellow workers told me. I had no intention of setting new Guiness records, but my fellow employees told me, "They're only gonna build about five thousand of these machines this year and when they're built, we'll all be out of work. Slow down."

It wasn't hard to sympathize with men who were trying to postpone the inevitable layoff in those days before unemployment compensation and food stamps. When layoffs came, I could go back and freeload off of my parents again, but many of the men around me had large families to support. The eighty-eight dollar monthly pay check didn't leave a lot of room for under-the-mattress savings.

The company's position, of course, was diametrically opposed to this stretch-out-the-work system, so management decided to put all jobs in #2 Shop on a piecework basis. Those around me pointed out that it should take eight minutes to assemble a header lift lever. When the time-study man arrived on the scene, it took eight minutes to assemble a header lift lever. When the time-study man returned several days later, it took eight minutes to assemble a header lift lever. I not only tightened every nut, I retightened it and then retightened the retightened nut on the bolt.

A farm boy who was hired that morning was placed at my bench, and the time-study man came back for a third time. After the farm boy assembled the header lift lever in four minutes, I was placed back on that job. The proper assembly time should have been two minutes or less. When I began assembling header lift levers again, I had to loaf half of the time in order to preserve the piece work rate. Somewhere in this confrontation there is a powerful economic sermon.

Much has been said and written about the monotony of bluecollar work in factories. Monotony is rank understatement! The bluecollar work that I experienced in #2 Shop was mind-deadening. After two days on the job, I could have done the work with my eyes closed, my hearing turned off, and one hand in a sling. Not over one percent of a person's brain-power was necessary to do the work. The other ninety-nine percent was available to think about romance, automobiles, romance, world powers, romance, Saturday night bowling, romance, and payday.

In #2 Shop we were building a machine the likes of which I had never seen before. An assembly line of sorts started near my work place. Workers assembled a tongue, a frame, and two wheels and pushed it to the second station where additional parts were added, and so on down the length of the building until a completed machine appeared at the test block at the end of the line. A big electric motor revved up the machine, and if no parts flew off, it was disassembled for loading on a flatcar.

## They're Hiring!

I kept asking, "What are we building?" None of my fellow workers knew . . . or cared. Foreman Art Smith didn't know either. "It has something to do with threshing, but that's all I know," he said. This machine resembled a threshing machine like a kangaroo resembles an alligator. The logo on the machine, "All-Crop Harvester," indicated that Art Smith was at least on the track of the truth. But a threshing machine? Naw, can't be!

The cutter bar looked like the cutter bar on a haymower. Then there was a table that evidently carried the cut crop uphill to a rotating device . . . sort of like a hand-push lawn mower cylinder, except that the blades were not sharp and they were covered with rubber.

The separating area or straw rack of this machine looked a little like the one in a thresher, but this one was crossways to the rest of the machine. My common sense told me that fast tracks don't go around right-angled corners. Years later, C. V. "Brownie" Brown said laughingly that it was "Caesarean section." Delivery out the side!

I kept inspecting the finished machine during lunch hours. There were persistent hazy feelings that I had seen this machine before. Ah yes, it was at Chicago's Century of Progress World's Fair in 1934. I remembered seeing this machine sitting out in the open with a crudely lettered sign hung on it. The sign forecast one-man harvests. When I saw it in Chicago, there were a few farmers around the contraption, pointing and laughing. "A one-man threshing crew? Haw, haw."

I wouldn't give five cents to relive my experience in #2 Shop, but I wouldn't take ten thousand dollars for having had the experience. Work wasn't always one hundred percent monotony. A riveting crew, at a work station next to mine, always had some horseplay going. That is, until the life of the party got his hand caught in a riveting machine and severely crippled his hand for life. In those days there were no big lump sum payments to victims of such accidents, and the courts didn't provide multi-million dollar settlements. If you had an accident, you told yourself that you should have been more careful, and you lived the rest of your life with the reminder of your accident.

In #2 Shop, newly married men could expect an unannounced ride. At a date that everyone except the victim knew, the newlywed was seized just after the five o'clock whistle's echo faded away. He was placed into a crate and the crate was nailed shut. Metal bands were placed around the crate. Then, the crate was "hoisted" onto the bed of a pickup truck. A parade formed that drove through town, horns a-honking. Eventually, the parade ended at the couple's home where the crate was dumped off unceremoniously into the front yard. The dainty little bride had to uncrate her new husband with F. W. Woolworth tools, which wasn't all that easy since the crate was sealed about as secure as the front gate at Fort Knox.

The machine noise in #2 Shop was deafening, a little like a rock band concert in the '80s. In 1936 nobody counted decibels. There was one deaf worker on the assembly line, the only worker in our shop who could hear. When his dad or brother, who also worked for the company, came into #2 Shop, they could talk sign language with this man. Sometime handicaps are handy-caps.

After working at my no-skills-required job in the Rumely ex-thresher plant for several months, I revisited Personnel Manager Doc Glassman. "Do you realize that you have a university graduate out there in #2 Shop working at a job that a chimp could do?"

"Yes, I know," said Doc, betraying no compassion. "We like to get you college kids' hands dirty. We like to see just how bad you want to work. Your foreman tells me that you are doin' good work. One day . . . don't know how soon, but probably pretty soon . . . there will be an opening in the office. I'll be in touch when that happens."

"One day." How many tomorrows add up to one day?

# 2

# HEADS, LaPORTE, TAILS, MICHIGAN CITY

Thanks to a college classmate, a crack at an accounting job opened up at Crane Company in nearby Michigan City. Even though I had a degree in accounting, I hated it. I couldn't even keep my checkbook straight. But the Crane offer was a desirable white collar job. Decisions! Decisions!

I walked the streets of LaPorte that night, trying to decide. Finally I looked up and said, "Lord, this one is too big for me to handle all by myself. I'm going to turn it over to you."

"Heads, LaPorte . . . tails, Michigan City." Heads it was! And the very next week Doc Glassman called me in to tell me that I could have a job as assistant machinery clerk in LaPorte Branch.

The world mourned the loss of a potential accounting genius and thrilled at the prospects of a soon-to-be plow peddler.

### THE BOTTOM RUNG OF THE CORPORATE LADDER

Just offhand, can you think of a job any lower on the corporate ladder than assistant machinery clerk? But the food miracle came about just as much by the work of millions of little people like assistant machinery clerks as by the likes of Cyrus McCormick, John Deere, and Jerome I. Case.

What a relief it was to put those greasy overalls away, and what a pleasure to wear a white shirt once again. What a joy it was to have clean hands and fingernails once more. Best of all, on this job I had to think—no more mindless repetitive moves with a socket wrench. No longer did I need to fear fall layoff after the five thousandth All-Crop Harvester was built. I had a year-round job.

With this "promotion," came less pay . . . $80 per month, instead of $88, but that was a minor irritation. It was on an August day in 1936 that I walked into Branch Manager Ed Lanigan's office to start a happy thirty-seven year marketing career with Allis-Chalmers. Actually, I worked for Allis-Chalmers thirty-nine years, but two weren't all that happy. More about that later.

## OUR LaPORTE TEAM

In farm equipment industry parlance, the branch house was a company-owned, wholesale operation of whole goods and parts. The branch served the independent dealers in the branch's geographic area. Allis-Chalmers's LaPorte Branch was typical. Ed Lanigan, a genial, lanky, elderly Irishman was our branch manager. He was a past master of good management. He would come to my office to ask for a report.

"Mr. Lanigan, that's the very next thing I was going to do," I stuttered. He cleared his throat with a hrumph and left, expressing no displeasure. The next day he came in to ask for the Michigan tabulation.

"Mr. Lanigan, it's in this pile that I planned to get at yet this morning." Again he hrumphed and left without a word of criticism.

It took only about three or four of these alibis to teach me to anticipate his requirements. It was so much more pleasant to be able to say, "Yes, Mr. Lanigan, here it is!" The work discipline this man taught the people in our office, served us well for a lifetime. He got what he wanted and earned mountains of respect in the process. He had the respect of everyone in the organization from the best blockman to the poorest dealer, from the janitor to all of the home office personnel who called on him. He was not the kind of man you loved, he was the kind of person you respected.

The rest of the members of the LaPorte team were: Bookish Lou Drewes, our assistant branch manager; rough, tough, soft-hearted (an explanation of the paradox comes later); "Grat" Gratner, our branch sales manager; Thelma Wilson, Mr. Lanigan's maiden lady secretary. Maiden lady by choice, by the way. If Thelma had been male, she would have been a branch manager. Liz Henderson, Lou Drewes's secretary. A maiden lady too, but not by choice. At least, that's what she led us to believe; Ed Bradley, my boss, the machinery clerk. He carried himself as proper as a Britisher in Commons; Abe Nelson, our accountant. Abe bounded around the office like a halfback, just off the sick list; Bill Schultz, Abe's assistant. Bill later became a blockman in LaPorte Branch territory; Hank (the last name escapes me), a quiet sort who pored over his books in the accounting department; Amos Drinnen, our service manager. A serviceman's serviceman who educated and helped our dealers' servicemen; Paul Grimes, our other serviceman. Unique to the farm equipment industry, field salesmen were called "blockmen." They covered a block of territory.

There was one more person in our office. Joe Hanson wasn't on our branch payroll, but we shared our office with him. He was a leftover from Advance-Rumely Company. His job was to try to collect old Rumely claims . . . about as futile a job as trying to cash in Czarist bonds at the branch bank of Wells Fargo in Leningrad. Joe Hanson smoked a pipe as he typed. With disturbing regularity, his pipe ashes fell into the waste basket filled with one-shot carbons. It isn't every office that has a weekly fire drill.

## CONSTANT, RELENTLESS CHANGE

At the beginning of this historical account, there were 6.4 million farms in this country. At the end, there weren't over one million really productive farms. At the beginning, 25 percent of our people were on the farm. At the end, 27 percent lived in rural areas, but only two percent of our population were farmers. Criticize or thank farm mechanization for most of that change. If you're critical, would you trade places with the people of the U.S.S.R., China, or India where high percentages of the population are still on the farm?

## SOLD! ONE RUSTY DISC HARROW

At LaPorte, our implements were stored in what we called the Pinola Sheds. Pinola was the first little burg to the west and this warehouse was the westernmost the company had. In one of the sheds we had an old rusty disc harrow, half buried in mud. This old rusty hunk of iron should have been scrapped, but Allis-Chalmers believed that farm machinery inventory, like fiddles and fine wine, improved with age. Not only was this disc harrow not scrapped, there was no fire sale price on it to move it either. One day Grat caught one of our dealers off guard and the disc was finally sold. To sell it, Grat chewed the dealer's Red Man cut plug, almost choking in the process, but he got the disc harrow loaded on the dealer's truck. I was sent to Factory Machinery Clerk Al Neiss to get an order so that the truck with the rusty implement could get out of the plant gate as quickly as possible. Just in case the dealer regained consciousness and changed his mind.

 I routinely took my orders to Al Neiss, a gnome-like individual who was lord of the inventory books that looked like the deeds record books in the county court house. At LaPorte, unlike every other branch, our inventory was on the plant's books and in the factory's possession. That's why I had to work through LaPorte Works personnel. This time Al wouldn't give me an order. Consulting his big book, he found that the disc harrow I had on the order and had seen loaded, was really an illusion. There was no such disc harrow in inventory. His big book said so. Obviously something that does not exist cannot be shipped; so, no order!

 I gave Grat the news. He cussed, then whispered to me to keep the dealer occupied. "Walk him around the grounds," Grat told me, "so he won't look at that disc harrow." Grat told the dealer, "Wait here just a minute. I'll be right back."

 Grat bounded into the office of Works Manager Charley Hood. He slammed his plant pass on Charley's desk and shouted. He told Charley exactly where he could stick that pass. Charley sat there with his hat on, as was his custom. In and around the plant he never took his hat off. Without raising his blood pressure, Charley took his cigar out of his mouth and said, "What's the problem, Grat?"

Grat told Charley what the problem was, punctuating his remarks with an assortment of sizzling words. After Charley got Grat cooled down, he picked up the phone and called Al Neiss. "Bring an order for that disc harrow down to my office in two minutes, Al." Al was there in one minute flat.

## WHEELS

Now that this 1936 refugee from the Depression had a job that paid big money, $80 per month, he could begin thinking of acquiring some of the finer things in life. The first luxury that 99.9 percent of young men think of is an automobile. Young men don't consider a car a luxury, it's an absolute necessity. Boys may have trouble learning how to use a lawn mower, broom, spade and hoe, but no boy on record has ever had difficulty learning how to drive a car. No sacrifice is too great when one wants wheels!

Dad said that there was a dairy farmer near Bremen who had a 1929 Chevy four-door that was for sale for $50. He said that the car was in good shape except that two of the door handles were broken. No problem; that was a congenital disease of 1929 Chevrolets, as common as one-headlight cars in East Tennessee. Dad said that the farmer had removed the rear seat cushion and had hauled milk cans in the car, so the rear seat cushions were like brand new but the interior of the car smelled a bit like not-too-fresh milk. So what? The price was right and I could open the windows.

"Put a hold on that car," I told my Dad. "I have $25 saved and the next paycheck will provide the other $25."

Wheels! Now I had wheels. Wow!

But this new owner of an automobile had not anticipated the enormity of economic shock that comes with auto ownership. Gas, oil changes, license plates, insurance, grease jobs, and repairs. The budget tightened up. Breakfast cost ten cents and dinner twenty-five cents at an overgrown diner operated by an ex-Army man who had lost one eye in the service. Lunch was homemade in a brown bag. Rent took a whopping $1.50 per week. A picture show at the Premiere Theater was fifteen cents, thirty cents if there was a girl along. Bowling cost ten cents a line and a Coke and candy bar each cost a nickel. I had joined the middle-income, upper-outgo class. Ouch!

Without a car, my dates and I walked. During my carless days, I had money for an occasional date. Now I had wheels and wheels were supposed to attract a better class of girls. But there was no money left over for dates. Adults don't understand the complexity of life of a young single male.

**JONES & FARMERS**

My most poignant experience at LaPorte Branch was to watch Ed Lanigan, our branch manager, and Pop Jones, our dealer in Richmond, Indiana, embrace each other while both were crying tears of intermingled joy and sadness. Pop came into the branch one day in 1937 to pick up the last Advance-Rumely thresher. Former Rumely Branch Manager Ed Lanigan and former Rumely dealer, Pop Jones, were closing a history book that day. The binder-thresher era ended with the departure of that last Rumely threshing machine.

Pop's firm was known as Jones & Farmers. Can you think of a finer firm name? Under "Jones & Farmers" on Pop's building sign were the words, "The Farmers are all my Partners."

It's easy, too easy perhaps, to minimize the magnitude of this history-changing event. All of the binder and thresher manufacturers in the country had been laid low by a little $545 tin box called an All-Crop Harvester. As a boy, I served as water boy on my uncle's and grandfather's farm at threshing time. Now, a few years later, I was the casual, uncaring, and unthinking machinery clerk who wrote the order for the last Rumely threshing machine.

## CATALOG NUMBERS AND PRICES

It didn't take long to learn the catalog numbers and the prices. Dealers ordered their Model WC tractors either on steel wheels, air tires or "air front." Air front meant rubber in front, steel in the rear. Although Allis-Chalmers pioneered rubber tired tractors, there were a lot of farmers who still thought that if the good Lord had intended farmers to ride on rubber-tired tractors, he would have made rubber a crop that could be grown in and around Spencer, Iowa.

A good 99 percent of the WC tractors I wrote orders for were cultivating models, like International Harvester's Farmall with the two front wheels close together. We had a wide-front model, but almost nobody bought it. Today, nobody buys the tricycle type anymore. Fuel choices were gasoline and distillate. The distillate tractors had a one-gallon gas tank that was used to start the unit. When the engine warmed up, the driver switched over to less expensive distillate.

A belt pulley came as standard equipment on the WC tractor. Then there were two options: (1) a power-take-off (PTO), and (2) a mechanical power lift. Anyone who bought an All-Crop Harvester had to buy a PTO. Those who bought cultivators had to buy a power lift, or bust their backs lifting by hand.

The prices of 1936 are still imbedded in my mind . . . a WC on steel had a list price of $785 and the air-tired model was $960. The PTO sold for $50, the power lift for $35.

When it came time for me to write up an All-Crop Harvester order, a hitch had to be added. The "hitch" hitched the power-take-off of the tractor to the drive shaft of the combine. In 1936, the industry had not yet standardized power-take-off and hitch specifications, so we had to stock dozens of different types of hitches. The hitch inventory problem was a nightmare. In the late '30s, the American Society of Agricultural Engineers (ASAE) came to the rescue. They standardized PTOs and drawbars and separate hitches were no longer needed. Happy day!

All-Crop Harvester customers generally bought a straw spreader to scatter the straw coming out of the combine. They generally bought a pickup attachment to use when windrowed crops (clover seed, for instance) were threshed. The farmer paid twenty bucks for the spreader and thirty-five for the pickup.

Most of our combines were bin machines. But there were a few spots in our territory where there were no grain elevators. In those places a man had to ride the combine to place the crop into bags, then slide the bags down a chute to the ground. Later someone came along to pick up the full bags.

Farmers who harvested seed crops generally bought a Hart-Scour-Kleen, a cylindrical recleaning device. Clover seed was and is very small. It was easy to get something beside clover seed in the combine's bin. The more foreign material in a seed crop, the less seed buyers paid for it. When run through the Hart-Scour-Kleen, a very high percentage of the foreign material was removed, resulting in higher prices to the farmer.

The All-Crop Harvester called for two-plow power up front. A few farmers were so much in love with their smaller tractors that they bought a power unit and mounted it on the tongue of the combine. The tractor did the pulling and the power unit powered the combine. In Amish country, horses did the pulling.

There were occasions at harvest time when it was so wet that you had to wear boots just to look out the window. For conditions such as that, we had both dual tires and tandem wheels.

This is what the usual implement order looked like when I typed it up to take to Al Neiss:

| | |
|---|---|
| 1 LX1027 2-bottom, 14-inch plow | $110.25 |
| 1 LX1625 2-row cultivator | 127.50 |
| 1 LX1387 wheel track mulcher | 18.75 |
| 1 20035 power lift | 20.00 |

Some farmers added a seven-foot tandem disc harrow to their implement order, but I don't remember the catalog number and price.

It's hard to believe what happened to the numbers game in my lifetime. When I was a machinery clerk, the net price of a WC on rubber was $720. It would have taken one hundred of such tractors to equal the net price of our biggest tractor when I retired in 1975. As the old newsreel used to say, "Time Marches On!"

## WINNING SURE FEELS GOOD

In 1936-37, Allis-Chalmers was burning up the league with its WC tractors and All-Crop Harvesters. When I saw the first trainload (yes, trainload) of All-Crop Harvesters pull out of the A-C siding and onto the New York Central main line, I gave a snappy salute and tried to swallow the lump in my throat. It was like the sun coming up over the mountains after a week of rain. During 1937, my second year at Allis-Chalmers, we shipped half again more combines than the whole industry shipped in the disastrous year of 1985. The 1985 machines were much larger, of course, but the comparison is still startling.

The advantage that A-C had on the industry was that we had newly designed machinery in newly tooled plants, whereas our competition still had what was left over from the '20s. It was not unlike post-war Germany and Japan with their new plants and machinery. You've heard of Nissan, BMW, Sony, Siemens, and Mazda, haven't you?

It sure felt great, being on a winning team that was moving up on the competition daily. Little by little, during the late '30s, we edged up to the big boys in unit tractor sales. In the pull-type combine department, we started first in market share and were never caught. From beginning to end, we never had less than fifty percent of industry pull-type combine sales. Massey ran a poor second in combines. I climbed on board in 1936. Pearl Harbor was bombed on December 7, 1941. In those five years, we climbed to first in tractor market share, as well as combine sales. If you've ever been first in football, bridge, badminton or bowling, you know the feeling!

# 3

# GO WEST, YOUNG BARRISTER!

E. P. Allis, a New York attorney, came to Milwaukee in 1846. At the railhead, Milwaukee, he built flour mills and sawmill equipment for the hinterlands and the populated eastern states. As the business grew, other heavy-line items were added—steam engines, generators, turbines, stone crushing equipment, and pumps. Allis soon learned that capital goods manufacture is a cyclical business. When Allis's firm suffered pangs of receivership in 1913, General Otto Falk took over as receiver and president of the company.

Otto Falk had been born of a Milwaukee brewer's family. He attended a military academy, served in the Spanish-American War, and was head of the Wisconsin National Guard. He rose to the rank of brigadier general and was prominent in Milwaukee business affairs.

When Falk took over, he installed austerity. He ripped carpeting out of executive offices, disbanded the company's brass band, told his managers to ride streetcars instead of taxicabs, and told them to use the mail instead of the long-distance telephone.

Receiver Falk took the gamble of moving Allis-Chalmers into the tractor business. After all, A-C was building all other types of power. Why not an internal combustion engine?

Starting in 1918, Henry Ford built the Fordson, a 20-horsepower, 4-cylinder tractor that had two speeds forward and one in reverse. Ford's tractor had doubtful profitability. General Motors burned themselves in the farm equipment business to the tune of over $30 million. Sears tried farm equipment with a David Bradley line but soon made a hasty exit.

General Falk really stuck his neck out when he opted for the farm equipment business. People asked, "What does Otto Falk know that Henry Ford, General Motors, and Sears don't know?" At first, the proper answer to that question would have been "nothing." Profits were elusive, which is a polite way of saying that there weren't any. Then Harry Merritt arrived!

**WHO'S THE GREATEST?**

St. Matthew records that Christ's disciples asked him, "Who is the greatest in the kingdom of heaven?" Teachers ask, "Who's the greatest President the country ever had?" Baseball fans wonder, "Who's the greatest—Babe Ruth or Lou Gehrig?" Since we're considering farm equipment, it's logical to ask, "Who contributed most to the farm equipment industry?" You be the judge.

Cyrus McCormick gave us the reaper and captured the grain binder market. McCormick gets the credit, but an Ohio Quaker by the name of Obed Hussey patented a mechanical reaper before McCormick did and Benjamin Ott, John Appleby, and Hector Holmes came up with early twine-binding mechanisms. McCormick's successors moved

International Harvester Company into first place in the farm equipment industry.

John Deere, the blacksmith in Grand Detour, Illinois, gave the industry the steel moldboard plow. Deere said about his plow in 1837, "Scours in the foulest of ground. Wrought iron. Share of steel. Price reduced as a consequence of hard times last year." John Deere gets the credit for the steel plow, but Charles Newbold patented an iron plow in 1797. Newbold's plow went nowhere because farmers thought the metal would poison the soil, thereby causing mass starvation. Alarmists are no latter-day phenomena. Remember the critics that Noah and Columbus had? The successors of Blacksmith Deere built a company that surpassed Harvester after World War II.

By way of contrast, Jerome Increase Case brought to the American farm scene a host of machines ranging from steam engines to gasoline powered tractors, from threshing machines to combines. There was also a whole barn full of implements that bore the J. I. Case label. In 1915, there was even a Case automobile. An ad that year read: "Announcing the New Case 40, $1090." I would have no qualms about voting J. I. Case the greatest if it were not for Harry Merritt. "Merritt?" you say. "Never heard of him."

## HARRY MERRITT, MENTAL AND PHYSICAL GIANT

Merritt was a giant, a man and a half tall, a man and a half wide, and two men heavy. He was a mental giant as well. I used to see him walk around #2 Shop and in and out of the LaPorte Works office. When he climbed into his Buick, the car tilted to portside. Omar, the tentmaker, tailored his overcoats. He did not carry calling cards. His reason: "If a man doesn't make enough of an impression to be remembered, a calling card isn't going to rescue him." That reasoning is valid for giants, but not every Joe Klutz is a giant.

Harry Merritt was born in Vermont, Illinois, in 1881. His career included tractor sales and road building. Somehow, he was involved in the building of a road from Wichita to Wellington, Kansas. The specs called for a "road to be built with tractors." In the age of horses, mules, fresno scrapers, wheelbarrows and a lot of back-breaking hand labor, this was a departure from norm. Merritt came to Allis-Chalmers from Holt, one of the predecessor companies of Caterpillar. Otto Falk placed Merritt in charge of the tractor operation January 1, 1926.

After Merritt's arrival, the profit picture changed. The farm equipment business proved to be a financial lifesaver for the corporation. During the last years of the Depression and in all but the war years, it was the plow peddlers who put the bread on the table. From next to nothing in 1927, Merritt saw the percentage of farm equipment business go to just short of sixty percent of corporate sales.

Take your pick! Some say that General Falk pulled Harry Merritt into Milwaukee to liquidate the ailing tractor division. Others say that he was brought in to breathe new life into the moribund and unprofitable operation.

Even if the first appraisal is correct, the second proved to be the way it turned out. Merritt suggested to Falk that the price of the remaining Model 20-35s in inventory should be lowered from $1,950 to $1,295. At these discount-house, factory-outlet, wholesale-store prices, the tractors moved.

Then Merritt asked logically, "If we can make money selling tractors for $1,295 each, why don't we do it?" He stripped the 20-35 down, eliminating a half-ton of weight. He cut back on some of the frills, but added gasoline and oil filters, an innovation in the days of unprotected engines. Sales of the 20-35 were just over 100 in 1921, but by 1928 Merritt had the sales figures above 5,000 per year. By the way, when you see a tractor designated 20-35, that means twenty horsepower on the drawbar and thirty-five horsepower on the belt pulley. In other words, the tractor used about fifteen horsepower just to pull itself around.

Bill Roberts was a close disciple of Harry Merritt. Together they put this package together for America's four million small farms:

| | |
|---|---:|
| Model B Tractor | $518.00 |
| Single-bottom 16-inch plow | 67.50 |
| One-row cultivator | 50.25 |
| Five-foot disc harrow | 112.50 |
| Pull-type 40-inch combine | 345.00 |
| | $1,093.25 |

A fully mechanized farm for $1,000. Farmers, in the bargaining process, invariably insisted on even money. That took away the $93.25. Today you can't mechanize a garden for that kind of money.

Before his stint with Allis, Merritt worked for several other tractor companies. He sold 1-cylinder tractors because of "less service, less fuel." He sold 2-cylinder tractors because of "more power." Merritt laughed when he told of his experiences with a Mr. Campbell, a Missouri farmer. First he tried to sell Campbell his 1-cylinder tractor. Then, after Merritt changed jobs, he went back to sell Mr. Campbell a 2-cylinder tractor.

"But the last time you were here, you said that the 1-cylinder tractor was the best," the farmer countered.

Merritt, realizing that both 2-cylinder and 1-cylinder tractors of the day had horrendous service problems, said with resignation, "Mr. Campbell, there are times when I wish the blooming things didn't have any cylinders at all."

When Harry Merritt worked for Holt Tractor Company, he had a young salesman working for him by the name of William Hazlitt Upson. As the story goes, Upson was supposed to unload some crawler tractors from a flatcar and bring them into the branch warehouse. We're told that one of the tractors got away from Upson, sheared a fireplug and water geysered up through the tractor.

Upson disappeared, leaving his dinner bucket, coat, and paycheck. He was not heard from again until his articles about Alexander Botts, the demon tractor salesman for the Earthworm Tractor Company, started to appear in the *Saturday Evening Post*. In the *Post* story, Alexander Botts had the misfortune of running an Earthworm tractor over a fireplug. Warner Brothers made a movie of this story called, "Earthworm Tractors," starring June Travis, Joe E. Brown, and Guy Kibee.

Harry Merritt had a sense of humor that matched his size. The story was told of two salesmen who came to call on him in his Allis-Chalmers office in Milwaukee. Merritt faked near-deafness. Every time one of the visitors said something, he cupped his ear and said, "Wazzat you say?" The shouting match continued for some time with little communication taking place. Finally the visitors decided to give up. They began to put their papers away.

"He's deef as a rock," one said.

The other replied, "Yeah, but he's a big son of a gun, isn't he?"

That remark broke Merritt up. He burst out laughing. Then the communication started all over again.

Harry Merritt gave the North American farmer the rubber-tired tractor, the first tractor designed for rubber tires, the first one-plow rubber-tired tractor, the first one-man combine, bright colored paint on farm equipment, and a corn picker that did not shell corn. Even though Merritt had retired by the time that Allis's unique round baler and forage harvester were introduced after World War II, he surely had a hand in the early negotiations with the engineers who designed them.

Quite an accomplishment!

## SELLING TIRES TO HARVEY FIRESTONE

A Firestone salesman called on Merritt and suggested, "How about putting tractors on rubber?"

"How about it?" Merritt mused. "There are 3,000 patents on lug designs in the patent office so nobody has figured out the best way to get traction. Why do you ask?"

The Firestone representative told of hard rubber tires on tractors in the Deere & Company plant. "They use them to pull skid loads of parts around." He told how farmers in sandy citrus orchards in Florida took the spade lugs off their tractors and replaced them with truck tire casings, cut up and wired together. "They get better traction with that rubber than they ever did with spade lugs."

Merritt suggested they go to Akron to see Harvey Firestone. Firestone said, "I'm in the tire business, but I'm not stupid. Tires belong on highway vehicles."

The two did not give up. The Firestone man knew that the company had once built some airplane tires for a plane that cracked up. The molds were around the plant somewhere. Several big treadless tires were made, tires that were as bald as your author's head.

Back at the A-C plant in Milwaukee, Merritt had his engineers place two of these tires on a Model U tractor. Waddya know, they pulled a load faster, they pulled a heavier load and less fuel was used. Merritt and the Firestone rep returned to Akron with the data.

Harvey Firestone said, "I've been wrong before and I guess I was wrong this time too. Let's get going." Firestone began to build tractor tires. Firestone's competitors soon followed!

Albert Schroeder, a farmer who farmed near Waukesha, Wisconsin, did part-time work with A-C's engineering department. Some of the tire trials were run on Albert's farm. When it came time to return the tires to the plant, Albert said, "They stay here." So Albert Schroeder of Waukesha, Wisconsin, in October of 1932, was the first farmer to buy a rubber-tired tractor.

## THREE STRIKES AND A HIT

Production of an air-tired tractor was one thing. Selling the proposition was quite another chore. Harry Merritt tossed the job of sales promotion to his sales promotion manager, W. Ellzey Brown. Brown had three strikes on him before he got up to bat. (1) Customers didn't know Allis-Chalmers. They asked, "Alice who?" (2) Farmers knew that you couldn't pull the hat off their head with a rubber-tired tractor. (3) In the middle of a depression, Allis wanted an extra 150 bucks for the rubber. What to do?

Ellzey Brown placed truck gears in two Model U tractors, replacing the tractors' road gears. At state fairs, Ellzey plowed the infield, then had Barney Oldfield and Ab

Jenkins, two of the greatest race drivers of all time, race those two rubber-tired tractors around the state fair's racetrack. A world's record of 67.4 miles per hour was set.

Ellzey even set up some phony speeding tickets in towns when Barney Oldfield came speeding through on a rubber-tired tractor. That always made the paper.

Racing tractors had absolutely nothing to do with farming, but the stunt placed rubber-tired tractors in front of a lot of people. It generated plenty of lively conversation in rural America's news stands, pool rooms, elevators, and barber shops. When the Allis dealer in town received his first rubber-tired tractor, there was always one screwball there to buy it. More sensible farmers watched over the fence to see the screwball get stuck. But that didn't happen very often. Doubting spectators became believers, and they bought. By the time I got to LaPorte in 1936, A-C was 65 percent on rubber. The industry's figure was 15 percent.

## DOC RUMELY HAD WHAT MERRITT WANTED

In BHM (before Harry Merritt) days, marketing tractors at Allis-Chalmers was mostly wishful thinking. An early ad in the *California Farmer* told of the magnitude of A-C's marketing organization. The facts were that A-C didn't have a marketing organization worth a counterfeit three dollar bill. Deere & Company, International Harvester Company, J. I. Case, Hart-Parr, and others had picked off the choice dealers. A-C had a mixed bag of what was left over after the big boys had their choice.

Even though Merritt's tractors took off, people didn't beat a path to the door of the man with the better mousetrap. Merritt knew that he sorely lacked marketing backup, so he was instrumental in buying out Advance-Rumely. Doc Rumely's terminally ill Oil Pull tractor and threshing machine business was for sale. (The "Doc" came from university work and degrees at and from Notre Dame, Oxford, Heidelberg, and Freiberg.) There were production facilities in LaPorte, Indiana, but much more important, there were twenty-four branch houses scattered around the United States and Canada. And a few key people still inhabited each of the twenty-four branches. Rumely had 2,500 dealers. Merritt bought Rumely mainly to get those twenty-four branches and 2,500 dealers. Fifty years later Tenneco's J. I. Case Division bought International Harvester Company's farm equipment operation for precisely the same reason. Case wanted those IH dealers!

Lawrence Schultz was a superintendent in the shops at LaPorte. He told me that in the early Rumely days, workers received their pay in gold and silver. If a worker had $23 coming, he received one $20 gold piece and three silver dollars. The counting took place in the basement of a house that later turned into a personnel department . . . the building in which I was hired in January 1936 when I went to work for A-C. In the counting process, some of the coins fell through the slatted floors.

Schultz said that Works Manager John Klassen asked him to bring a crew over to haul all of the files out of that basement. They were wanted in Milwaukee. "We went through some of the files and found money . . . disputed claims that still had the money in an envelope." Later Klassen asked Schultz & Crew to remove the slatted flooring in the basement to see how much gold there was under that floor. Schultz told me that it wasn't the Klondike strike all over again, but there was enough of the glistening stuff to make things interesting. I forgot to ask, "Who got the dough?" Rumely heirs? Allis-Chalmers? Or was it finders keepers?

## THE PLOW WORKS

After Harry Merritt began to get the tractor situation in hand in Milwaukee, he realized that an implement line was needed to complement the tractor line. The LaCrosse Plow Company of LaCrosse, Wisconsin, was for sale. Allis bought if for $275,000. The LaCrosse plow was the first to use a mechanical power lift. It had cold-rolled steel beams that you could not saw with a hacksaw in a month of Sundays. If a farmer smacked into a rock hard enough to bend the beam, something that almost never happened, it could be rolled out cold again. Bend a hot-rolled plow beam and it's bent for good. "Junk yard, here I come." Tubular steel, which Republic Steel made out of old railroad rails in Elyria, Ohio, was used for structurals in some implements.

LaCrosse's plows and cultivators were good, but the grain drill was a strikeout, because it had no fertilizer attachment. The LaCrosse corn planter was nose-heavy, like an Arkansas razorback hog.

LaCrosse's line of disc harrows, field cultivators, spring and spike tooth harrows were well received. The plant's big problem was that they always shipped everything ten months early (translation: "two months late").

Implement production is different from that of tractors and combines, which are built as units. Implements arrived at our branch warehouse and at our dealers' places of business in bundles—a wheel bundle, an axle bundle, a planter hopper bundle, or a sickle-bar bundle. Implement A might be made up of six bundles. Implement B might have five bundles identical to those in Implement A, but one bundle had to be different to warrant a different catalog number. Had implements been assembled at the factory, there would have been a horrendous warehousing problem there, and the freight bills would have brought smiles to the railroad comptrollers' faces. Dealers assembled implements before delivery, sometimes with choice words added to the hard work that was involved.

LaCrosse Works had the bad habit of back-ordering one bundle per implement when they shipped us carloads of implements. An implement missing one bundle is as useless as a glass eye at a keyhole.

## INDUSTRIAL ESPIONAGE

Harry Merritt bought the All-Crop Harvester idea from Bob Fleming of Los Angeles. The original of the machine we were building in LaPorte was referred to as the Fleming-Hall combine.

Merritt brought the machine to the newly acquired Rumely plant in LaPorte, Indiana, for further engineering. There were a few Rumely engineers still around, and they were augmented by a few more from the defunct Avery plant in Peoria. These men knew threshing.

After several years of engineering and testing, Merritt asked his chief engineer if the machine was ready to go. He asked for one more year. Then Merritt turned to Charley Scranton, the assistant chief engineer. Charley said, "She's ready." Merritt fired his chief engineer and Charley became the top man in the engineering department at LaPorte. Charley, accompanied by his cigar, came often to visit Grat at LaPorte Branch to see how things were going out in the field. Over the years, Charley Scranton acquired a room full of trophies and awards for his work in harvester engineering.

Prototypes were built (I've heard of everything from two to eighteen) and were tested in varying crops and geographical settings. At the outset the combine was intentionally built flimsy light. Merritt figured that field experimental work would turn up the weak spots. When they were encountered, those areas of the machine were beefed up. At the end of the engineering work, and before the introduction of the machine, Merritt had the strongest possible machine with the least possible weight. Steel sells by the pound, so he had a price advantage over the competition, until the competition too began to build a one-man combine.

The combine started as the "Corn Belt Combine," then the "High Speed Combine," but when it was introduced, the name was "All-Crop Harvester." Originally the machine was designed to thresh oats, wheat, barley and rye. It didn't take long to discover that there were other crops that could be threshed—hence the name All-Crop. The final instruction book listed 106 crops that could be threshed with the machine.

In the farm equipment industry, it's hard to keep secrets from the competition. Experimental machines must be tested with various crops in various geographical areas. The word soon gets around and news of the All-Crop Harvester was no exception.

There was a persistent story about Harry Merritt and the All-Crop Harvester that I could neither confirm or have denied. Even if the story is fiction, it's too good to pass by without mention. Here's the way I heard the story:

With devilish motives, Harry Merritt invited the chief engineers of his competitors to LaPorte to see the machine work. The group went to a ten-acre field of wheat near

LaPorte. The combine operator was Barney Oldfield. We had used Barney, the famous race car driver, to race rubber-tired tractors at state fairs.

Merritt made his speech to the assembled throng. "This machine will change the harvesting habits of the world." At the end of the speech, Merritt motioned Barney to take off. Barney did and after twenty feet, he plugged. Too much crop and/or too little combine. Anybody can plug once, but Barney kept plugging. It took him over a half hour to go around that ten-acre field.

Merritt fumed. Blue smoke seemed to come from his ears and nostrils. Servicemen ran around wildly with their wrenches. Engineers tried to hide. Competitors enjoyed the show immensely. Then Merritt said, "I'm sorry. My engineers told me that this machine was ready to go. As you can see, it's not. Never take the word of your engineers. Check it out yourself. What can I say? I know that I will be the laughing stock of the industry. I'm sorry! Goodbye."

When the last of the competitive engineers left the wheat field, got on the New York Central club car and ordered a drink, Merritt told Barney to get off that tractor. "Let somebody up there who knows how to run a combine. Then let's get the machine out of the shed that we'll build next year. We gotta get this wheat cut." Buzz, buzz, the field was quickly cut. Merritt had staged that whole afternoon's performance! He gave as his reasons, "If that don't set the so-and-so's back five years, I'll kiss. . . . "

Whether the legend is true or not, that's the way it worked out. Our competitors' chief engineers remained complacent even though they knew that something was going on at LaPorte. They did not accelerate their engineering. The All-Crop took off like a hot rodder when the light turns green, and our competitors never caught us. During the days of the pull-type combine, we never had less than half of the total market.

## WHOOPS!

To say that business was conducted haphazardly in the early days of the Tractor Division is rank understatement. Charley Decker, Dealer C. C. Banting's assistant manager, liked to tell of the railroad station agent in Texas who sent a Western Union telegram to our home office in Milwaukee.

> HAVE HAD CARLOAD OF YOUR TRACTORS ON OUR SIDING FOR A YEAR STOP WHO DO THEY BELONG TO STOP SOMEBODY HAS TO PAY THE FREIGHT AND DEMURRAGE STOP

J. R. "Mac" McKnight, Allis's sales manager at the Kansas City Branch, told of the days when he worked with Merritt in Milwaukee. According to Mac, he was sent to Toledo to see if he could find out how much money The Banting Company owed A-C. Like the carload of tractors in the Texas oversight, somebody had lost track of the Banting account.

"Go down and see Mr. Banting," Merritt said. "See what you can find out, then collect what you can."

Mac went to Toledo and there met C. C. Banting for the first time. After pleasantries were exchanged, Mac said, "Mr. Banting, I believe you owe the company some money."

"Yes, I do," said C.C. "Charley, bring me the list." Charley Decker handed the paper to Mr. Banting and he handed it to Mac. Mac studied it with all of the concentration of a vaudeville memory exhibitionist. He wasn't studying so much as he was memorizing. He jotted a few notes in his notebook to reinforce his memory. Then Mac pulled a blank account book from his briefcase and faked an audit. Satisfied that he had a grasp of the situation, he looked up at Mr. Banting and commented, "Yes, your listing looks right. It jives with what we have. Do you suppose you could pay something on the account today?" C.C. wrote a check for something less than the full amount.

Mac told me that he then asked directions to the rest room where he wrote down a lot of the figures he had memorized. He said the rest of the money came in a little later. After the Banting incident, Mac said that Home Office was a bit more careful with its accounts receivable.

## MOVING UP IN THE WORLD

Late in 1937, Mr. Lanigan, our branch manager, and Grat, our sales manager, called me into Mr. Lanigan's office. "Allis-Chalmers will open a new branch house in Toledo, Ohio, before the year is out. Would you care to go to Toledo Branch as machinery clerk?"

"WOULD I?"

This assistant machinery clerk grabbed at the opportunity to jump up one rung on the corporate ladder. Grat was to be the first branch manager at Toledo Branch.

Bags were packed. There was a liquid farewell party with the gang from St. John's at the Zahrt home. After all of the goodbyes, my 1929 Chevy headed east.

The promotion brought with it a twenty dollar per month increase in pay—from $80 per month to $100.

Comin' up in the world!

# PART II
# TOLEDO

# 4

# A NEW BRANCH IS BORN

On November 30, 1937, there were no speeches of dedication, no ribbon-cutting ceremonies when the Toledo Branch opened for business. The mayor wasn't there, nobody from the Chamber of Commerce, not a soul from the Industrial Development Commission. We set right to work trying to make the old warehouse that had once housed the Willys-Overland crankshaft plant habitable. The order of business was:

1. Unpack desks, chairs and typewriters.
2. Fight off the cold; the building had no heat. The new ice age had come early.
3. Unpack filing cabinets and in them, store dealer records that came to Toledo from our LaPorte and Columbus Branches.
4. Fight off the cold by stomping feet and blowing on hands. No global warming in Toledo.
5. Meet with the blockmen of the new branch to establish policy and outline sales strategy. We had about as many blockmen in Michigan as we had dealers. We were starting to build from scratch.
6. Fight off the cold. We sure could have used some greenhouse effect.

# A New Branch is Born

7. Start building an office inside the warehouse, complete with heat. Brrrr, it's cold!

Before leaving LaPorte, I was handed my first expense book. Mr. Lanigan also gave me a $100 expense advance. What a thrill it was to have someone else paying my bills. We all checked into the Secor Hotel, a hostelry more palatial than anything I had ever inhabited before. The price of three dollars per night (hotel taxes hadn't been invented yet) indicated that it was indeed luxurious. Some meals in the coffee shop cost more than a dollar. I wasn't used to that sort of blueblood living, but when I ate with Branch Manager H. A. "Grat" and Regional Manager Barney Baker I entered one dollar and more in my Persian orange expense book without getting the shakes.

One evening I got away from the big shots. I sought out a restaurant more fitted to my economic stature. I selected one with a jeans/T-shirt appearance only to find out that this was Dyers, a quaintly non-plebeian fish house, the best there was in town. And the most expensive. Holy boly, the cheapest thing on the menu was swordfish for a buck five. With a ten cent tip, that was $1.15. My hands shook as I started to enter that war-debt size figure in my expense book. Then I hesitated and ended up entering twenty-five cents, swallowing the other ninety cent expenditure, because I figured it was my mistake. The company shouldn't have to pay for my mistaken restaurant choice. At this stage of the game, I couldn't give management the idea that this cornfield rookie was the last of the big spenders.

The managers at the new Toledo Branch were just as typical as those in LaPorte, and any other of the company's branch houses, for that matter. There was Grat, our branch manager, Frank Spilker, our assistant branch manager who came from Des Moines Branch. Our accountant came to us from Peoria Branch, Parts Manager Bill Jeffrey came from Billings, Montana, Branch; Service Manager Paul Grimes from LaPorte, and yours truly. We were the starting team.

Toledo was selected as the site for the new Toledo Branch because Toledo was the home of the Banting Company, the company's largest dealer. With The Banting Company less than a mile from the branch, the company could dispense with the services of a blockman, thereby saving his salary, expense account, and two percent commission. That more than paid the rent on the branch house.

Our branch territory was everything east of Lansing in the lower peninsula of Michigan and a pie-shaped slice of northern Ohio, one county deep on the east side and four counties deep on the west side of the state.

Two years after tiny Toledo Branch opened, only giant multi-state branches in Minneapolis and Memphis exceeded our sales volume. Only St. Louis Branch had a higher market penetration. We only had parts of two states, but still we nipped at the heels of branches that covered several states.

It sure felt good to be on a winning team!

## BUD & LUKE'S

There was an article about Bud & Luke's Restaurants in Colliers (or was it Saturday Evening Post?) before I moved to Toledo. The restaurants sounded like fun. When I arrived in town, glory be, there was Bud & Luke's Restaurant a mile from our office.

The magazine article said that Bud and Luke operated

## A New Branch is Born

a combination filling station and six-stool restaurant. Business got so good that the two of them couldn't handle it properly, but there wasn't enough extra business to justify the hiring of a third person. They decided that they would insult a few customers to get the load down to where the two of them could handle it. Instead of losing customers, the insults brought even more customers. Quickly the two sold out the filling station and opened two restaurants—one out our way and one near downtown. The stock in trade of the two restaurants was insults and hijinks. The cafés could have stood on the reputation and price of the food, but the insults packed the house.

I ate there several times before I told anyone at the branch. The food was good, the prices were right, the service was excellent, and the entertainment was terrific. Then I asked several fellow employees to go with me to lunch at Bud & Luke's. Finally we asked Grat, our branch manager, to go along. We didn't tell him what to expect, of course. Grat ordered bean soup. When the bean soup arrived, the waiter laid a rubber glove down beside the bowl of bean soup.

"What the h— is this for?" bellowed Grat.

"Sir," said the waiter, "your reputation for sloppy eating is well-known . . . we don't want you to get your wristwatch rusty when you dunk your crackers in your soup."

For once Grat was at a loss for words!

Home Office sent an accountant to us from Atlanta Branch to help our accounting people get the books set up. We took this rebel to Bud & Luke's one day. Quite naturally, he ordered in southern dialect. After that, all of the waiters and waitresses shouted their orders to the kitchen in southern dialect. Then all busboys, dishwashers—all of the employees of the restaurant. One looked under the table and said, "See, I told you he is wearing shoes." Then they all lifted the table cloth to see for themselves.

Another standard routine was an argument between waiters over a table.

"That was my table."

"No, it was my table."

"No, it was my table."

This kept up, the argument getting louder all of the time, and more sarcastic. Then a sledgehammer flew through the air—a *papier mâché* sledgehammer that weighed about an ounce and a half. But it sure made the diners scatter. Never failed! Wouldn't you move if you saw a sledgehammer coming your way?

When a female customer headed for the rest room, two waiters grabbed her by the arms to prance her back there, singing, "I know where you're going. I know where you're going." The two waiters would then abandon their tables to stand guard at the door of the ladies' rest room. If the lady did not emerge in two minutes, one of the waiters pulled on a bell cord that rang a bell over the women's can. "Honey, are you having trouble in there?"

For every customer that Bud & Luke's lost because of insults, they gained ten more.

Another standard routine was to bring a bottle of chocolate milk to the table. "But I didn't order chocolate milk," the diner would say. The waiter would look at his order pad. "That's right. You sure didn't." When he grabbed for the bottle, he tipped it over. That scattered people. But it wasn't bottled milk at all; it was just a milk bottle painted brown on the inside.

Then a waiter came through the dining room with a tray that held a cup and saucer and two rolls of toilet paper. "Who ordered the rolls and coffee? Who ordered the rolls and coffee?"

When the place was full of diners, the entertainment was kept to a minimum. But just let things slack down a bit and the hijinks accelerated. Waiters wore outlandish uniforms. Several had sailor straw hats with the top lifted like the top of a grand piano. The dining room was really a stage for actors and actresses. You could hire those kinds of people as waiters during the Depression.

When business slacked off considerably, the Bud & Luke crew staged a fire. A waiter wadded up several napkins, placing them in a soup bowl on a front table. Then he lit the napkins and shouted, "Fire!"

All of the help went to the kitchen where they donned firemens' helmets. They filled their mouths full of water and each had a siphon hose. While the cook cranked on the siren in the kitchen, the firemen put out the fire.

That "insult the customers" policy worked so well at Bud & Luke's in Toledo that I've wondered why someone else hasn't picked up the idea elsewhere in the country. When World War II came, both Bud and Luke went to war. One restaurant stayed open but the insult entertainment was no more.

I suspect nobody has done it lately because there would be one arrest and lawsuit after another. A customer who had a *papier mâché* sledgehammer coming at her could sue for "pain and suffering." There would be arrests for slander. Since movie actors, 60 Minutes, laboratory rats, and ambulance-chasing lawyers have taken over our government, life in the USA isn't the fun it once was. They've declared everything either illegal, life-threatening or fattening. Fun days are over as we worry about plugging the pipes with cholesterol and/or global warming.

## WHAT GOES UP MUST COME DOWN

When Harry Merritt bought Rumely with its twenty-four branch houses, he closed the original four A-C branches that weren't anything to shout about anyway. Allis-Chalmers had a typical assortment of field offices and warehouses. All of the full-line companies had such branches and we all had a few sub-branches. Typical of the industry, we had four regional managers calling on our North American branches. Each branch had a whole goods inventory of tractors and implements, as well as parts.

When Toledo Branch opened, everything was shipped by rail. Small shipments went LCL (less than carload). Then roads improved and truck freight stole all of the local business from the railroads, and much of the long-haul carload business, too. Travel time was reduced dramatically.

During the 1970s, companies began to close branch houses. Computerized inventory control and fax machines took over. There were fewer but bigger farmers, fewer but bigger dealers, and less branches. Parts depots opened. With overnight air freight, it was possible to receive emergency parts shipments in less than twenty-four hours. During agriculture's disastrous '80s, branch houses, as we knew them in the '30s to the '60s, all but disappeared. There were regional offices without warehouses attached, but, for all practical purposes, it was factory-to-dealer, with the wholesale function eliminated as the industry moved into the 1990s.

## GRAT

Before H. A. "Grat" Gratner signed on with A-C, he was a collector for International Harvester Company. Grat was big, rough, tough, profane, and obscene, but he built a team spirit not unlike that of Vince Lombardi's Super Bowl Green Bay Packers or Knute Rockne's Four Horsemen of Notre Dame. Grat's bravado was largely window dressing. When he thundered, "Look here, old buddy, you're either going to line up or line out," that meant that he would give the man another seventeen chances before lining him out.

Grat boasted about his collecting skills. After all, he had been a collector for the great International Harvester Company, of which there was no greater. When Saginaw Blockman W. D. "Cope" Coplin couldn't collect for a Rumely threshing machine that had burned up six years before, Grat chewed at him. Then one day Grat made the mistake of going to Saginaw. Cope told Grat that he wanted to see a professional collector at work. Foolishly, Grat took the bait. He should have come up with some fake excuse like, "I think I'm coming down with something."

The farmer with the cremated threshing machine towered over Grat's oversize frame by an inch or two. Grat came nose-to-nose with this giant and bellowed, "Are you or aren't you going to pay for your threshing machine?"

The farmer yelled back, "NO!" spraying Grat's face and gassing him with the odor of chewing tobacco.

Grat said meekly, "Just thought I'd ask."

When Grat returned to Toledo, he told Kenny Cummerow to cross that claim off of the books. "I don't think Cope will ever collect it."

There were no women in Toledo Branch. Grat said that women were all right in a kitchen or bedroom but they weren't worth a hoot in an office. Today's feminists would have conked him after that remark, but these were the days before Women's Lib and Affirmative Action. Kenny Cummerow and Milt Graham were our secretaries, both male as you can tell by the names.

With the approach of World War II, the sex barrier began to crumble. Grat had to hire women because there weren't enough men to go around. That meant that Toledo Branch, for the first time, had to install a ladies' rest room. It about killed Grat, but he went to Start's Drug Store to buy a Kotex dispenser. The folks at Start's never let him live that down.

Few managers can mingle socially with employees, then discipline them in the office. But Grat could. We would go to his house for a drink one day, only to be chewed out unmercifully the next day. And that was followed by, "How about going to the ball game tonight?"

**SELF-STYLED GOURMET**

F. A. Spilker, coming to us from Des Moines Branch, was our assistant branch manager. F.A. was a quick-witted man who originally hailed from Wisconsin, a fact which, he rationalized, qualified him as a gourmet. F.A. loved good things to eat and drink. He swooned over a block of Wisconsin cheese! He luxuriated over a bottle of Pabst Beer. Sheboygan sausage and bratwurst made him drool. He also respected the distillers of bourbon in Kentucky. And, of course, the Scotsmen.

With F.A. and his German background, and Wisconsinite Herb McCormack, a descendant from the ould sod, there was a constant flow of good-natured banter in Toledo Branch.

Said F.A. one day, "Those dumb Irish cops in Milwaukee. One of them found a dead dray horse on Kinnikinnick Avenue. He couldn't spell Kinnikinnick for his report, so he picked up the horse and carried him over to First Street, and made out his report there."

F.A. was also an amateur theologian. During a poker game at Sylvania Country Club, he asked one of the players, "Do you believe in a hereafter?"

"I'm not sure," said the man with three jacks.

"You're a lousy gambler," F.A. rejoined.

"Why do you say that?" the gambling poker player wanted to know.

"If you believe in a hereafter and there isn't one, you're home free . . . you haven't lost a thing. But if you don't believe in a hereafter and there is one, brother, are you going to need air conditioning and fire insurance! You're a lousy gambler, Joe, that's all I've got to say."

F.A. had a very subtle sense of humor. He was able to laugh at himself when someone pulled one on him. When something good happened that was not routine, he would say, "Even a blind boar will find an acorn once in a while."

Sales managers tend to find at least one scapegoat in the organization. Walt Burow was F. A. Spilker's scapegoat. Walt had the Flint, Michigan, block . . . got it after the previous blockman was lined out because he had his landlady send in daily reports while he was living it up for a week in New York City. F.A. noted that Walt Burow wasn't selling many Model 40 All-Crop Harvesters. Nor was anyone else, for that matter. One day F.A. sent a bulletin to all of our blockmen: "It has now been fifteen days since Walt Burow sold a Model 40 All-Crop."

The next day the bulletin read, "sixteen days," then "seventeen days," then "eighteen days." That went on until

Walt finally unloaded a 40 All-Crop. F.A. wired all of our blockmen:

STAND AND FACE FLINT AT 11 AM TUESDAY MORNING FOR A MOMENT OF SILENT REVERENCE STOP WALT BUROW HAS SOLD A 40 ALL-CROP STOP.

F.A. told Walt, "You're not selling them because you don't know your machine." F.A. lived to regret that remark.

At the next field day sales meeting, all blockmen were assigned a unit to "sell" to the rest of the blockmen. Guess what machine Walt Burow was asked to talk about. Right! The Model 40 All-Crop Harvester. We sat in the shade of a tent while the speaker and his machine were just outside of the tent. In the front row of this august assemblage were Grat, F.A., and Regional Manager Barney Baker.

Walt Burow, yardstick in hand, pointed out every bolt and nut on the Model 40 All-Crop Harvester. He gave us the size, the reason the bolt was there, and what would happen if it were not there. Just in case we missed it the first time around, Walt repeated the sales story. This insomnia-breeding monologue went on for an hour and a half. F.A., having brought this misery on himself, had to pretend that he was enjoying the performance. He had to sit still and listen to Walt's droning on and on.

Barney Baker and Grat could ill afford to complain about a man who really knew his machine. John Walker, in the back row, stood up, made faces, thumbed his nose, wiggled his fingers in his ears, all to no avail. Walt Burow could only think of the magnificent scientific marvel he had

## A New Branch is Born

in front of him. He never looked up. As it must at every filibuster, mercifully the end finally came.

F.A. allowed that Walt did indeed know his machine and that it would be well if the rest of the blockmen knew their sales stories as well. Walt's hour-and-a-half sales pitch had loused up the time schedule. We were running behind time, way behind time. Fortunately, Joe Turman, the next blockman on the program, got us somewhat back on schedule again.

Joe's assignment was the #8 disc harrow. Joe circled the disc harrow several times, tapping it with his yardstick pointer. Then he looked up at Howard Shireman and said, "She's a (expletive omitted) good disk, aint' she, Howard?" And sat down! We were back on time.

It was a favorite trick of Spilker's to pass a dealer's place of business late at night. At the witching hour he placed a note on the door: "Stopped by this morning and waited an hour but you didn't show up to open up so I left. (Signed) F. A. Spilker." Whatever time the dealer got to work in the morning, there was F.A.'s note. Several asked me when that scourge got up in the morning.

## HOW NOT TO SUCCEED IN BUSINESS

Our sales manager at Toledo Branch proved the old proverb, "There is good in all of us, even if we are only a horrible example for the rest." It was sad to see the man tangle up his life, doing all of the right things at the wrong time and all of the wrong things at the right time.

This man (we'll call him Joe) had once been a Chevy dealer, but the Depression took its toll, and Joe resorted to hauling a stud horse around the country from mare to mare. C. C. Banting, the company's largest dealer, fell on bad times too and his corporation became insolvent. C.C. was not the type to stay down long. When he got into high gear again, Joe became C. C. Banting's blockman.

When Banting's sales took off again, Joe started to earn money about as fast at the U. S. Bureau of Printing & Engraving could print it. He got the blockman's usual two percent commission on sales, and C. C. Banting and sixteen salesmen did all of the work. Joe's two percent added up to about as much money as General Manager Bill Roberts received in his pay envelope. Joe's big problem was that he thought he earned all of that money. He didn't realize that it was a windfall that would inevitably end—most likely sooner instead of later. Instead of squirreling the fortune away, Joe lived the life of Riley, and O'Sullivan, and O'Flannerty.

The windfall ended when Toledo Branch opened. The elimination of Joe's two percent was one of the big reasons that the new branch was located in Toledo. Joe was "promoted" to branch sales manager, which cut his income to something like twenty-five percent of what he had been getting. Joe spent little time in the office because bill collectors began to come in pairs.

Joe figured that the least Bill Roberts should have done for him was to demote him to branch manager. There were rumblings that Joe had begun to undermine Grat out in the field, hoping to get his job. The news of the behind-the-scenes activity filtered to Home Office, and Regional Manager Barney Baker came down to Toledo with his shirt tail sticking straight out behind him. "Get Joe in here!" he shouted. For Joe, it was all over!

After he was fired at our branch, Joe took a job with Minneapolis-Moline. M-M came out with a big tractor that they called UDLX, for ultra-deluxe. It had a cab, the first in the industry, hub caps, license plates, headlights, cigar lighter and a road speed of 40 miles-per-hour. Joe drove one of those tractors around to demonstrate it. Joe sold the tractor, one of 125 that M-M built in 1938, to the Toledo street department that was in the other half of our building. He figured that the sight of this Minneapolis-Moline tractor every day would be fit punishment for his dismissal.

After Joe left, he was not replaced. He didn't leave a vacancy. F. A. Spilker became both assistant branch manager and sales manager of Toledo Branch. We heard Joe died a pauper.

Sad. Very sad.

**I GOTTA HAVE A RAISE OR ELSE**

General Manager Bill Roberts came from Missouri, and he told all of us less fortunate folks all about it. He had a sharp, high-pitched, crackly voice and a bewitching smile. Most of the time anyway. When there was a frown, we knew he meant business.

He didn't believe in organizational charts and threatened to fire the man who drew one up. His door was always open. A-C people didn't need to go through channels to get to Bill Roberts. His door was open. He answered his own phone.

Roberts had a phenomenal memory for names, faces, and facts, particularly baseball facts. He could meet 100 people for the first time and then turn around and call them all by name.

Bill Roberts was a teetotaler, or pretended to be. There were those who said that his abstinence was to set an example to company people who had a way of sneaking booze onto the expense account. Roberts knew that hangovers made for a lot of lost time at company expense.

The reputation that, "anyone can talk to Bill Roberts" got through to the janitor at Dallas Branch. When Roberts was scheduled to visit there, the janitor waited at the door.

When the Dallas branch manager arrived with Bill Roberts, he introduced Mr. Roberts to the janitor. The janitor said, "Mr. Roberts, I hear that you talk to everybody." Roberts nodded assent. His message had gotten through, clear to Dallas.

The janitor said, "Mr. Roberts, I need a raise. I gotta have a raise or else."

Roberts bristled! "Or else what?" Roberts shot back.

"Or else I got to work for the same ole pay," replied the janitor. That year only one person in the division got a raise . . . the janitor of Dallas branch.

Roberts's life was divided two ways—work and sports. He was generally the first man in the office in the morning. Every once in a while, serviceman Slim Rockwell beat him by a few minutes. Roberts alibied, "If Slim had stopped to tie his shoes, he wouldn't have beat me."

When Bill Roberts played golf, he set speed records. Never a practice swing. Go to the ball on a half gallop and whack. No hip and shoulder adjustments, just hit.

Even though Roberts ran a tight ship, everyone respected the man. He inspired confidence and achievement in his people. By his own admission, he flew by the seat of his pants. He knew his successors wouldn't be able to do it, but that didn't cause him to change his method of doing business. The fact that sales skyrocketed when Bill Roberts was general manager of the division was proof enough that Roberts's system worked.

## THE PETER PRINCIPLE AT WORK

Our accountant at Toledo Branch, (let's call him Bill) was an import from Peoria Branch. Bill was a living example of the Peter Principle at work. If the accountants of 1937 had been judged on the basis of neatness, Bill's fine Spencerian hand in his ledgers easily would have won the blue ribbon. Bill's books were works of art, but were invariably about two weeks late. His desk drawers were stuffed with unfinished business, back in those days of TP-TP ('tis paid, 'tain't paid) accounting,

Bill took as much pride in his books as the Library of Congress takes in the original draft of the Declaration of Independence. At a stag party that Grat and F.A. threw for us one evening, some miscreant got into Bill's office and placed thin slices of Limburger cheese between the pages of his ledger. No bull entering the Plaza del Torros in Mexico City ever had more anger, vexation, and acrimony in his eyes than Bill had when he discovered that Limburger cheese the next morning.

Bill posted our blockmens' bonus checks, so he knew how much the guys out in the field were making. A good deal more than the accountant at Toledo Branch, that's for sure. So Bill hounded Grat and F.A. for a job as a blockman. Against Grat's better judgment, he gave Bill the job on the Napoleon, Ohio, block. Bill's days on the block were numbered from the outset when it was quickly discovered that he couldn't sell a lifebelt to a drowning man, couldn't tell a plow coulter from a battleship.

Bill's dealers said, "Get rid of him," so Grat got rid of Hank. Lined him out!

## THERE'S A FIFTY-FIFTY CHANCE

Complaints of blockmen about their dealers were common (and vice versa, by the way) in any company's farm equipment branch, and, I dare say in most other business offices as well. F.A. listened to the blockman's complaints without interruption, allowing each to get it all off his chest. "I'm gonna to get rid of that no-good blankety-blank," the blockman would say. "He ain't no good!"

F.A. then leaned back in his chair and mused, "So you're going to get rid of that no-good blankety-blank. Hmmmm! I'll admit that he has been no Marshall Field, but did you ever ask yourself if you are not a big part of the problem? What do you suppose your dealer thinks of you? Remember, if you start with a new dealer, you start over at square one in training. And also never forget, you have only a fifty-fifty chance of finding a better dealer the second time around, and there's a fifty-fifty chance that you'll find a *worse* one!"

Over the years, I've seen dozens of people sacked because of this or that real or alleged fault. After the sacking, I found that F. A. Spilker was right. The replacement was better fifty percent of the time and worse the other fifty percent of the time. Frank Spilker's advice was good then, and it's just as pertinent today.

# 5

# THE BANTING COMPANY

    C. C. Banting is a legend in the farm equipment industry. He was born and grew up in Woodville, Ohio, a small town southeast of Toledo. C.C.'s father ran a general store in Woodville, a general store that had one kerosene pump in the back room. Clerks were coached to always ask if the customer wanted high test or low test coal oil. C.C. explained, "Some people wanted price and some wanted quality, so we aimed to please. We gave the customer what he/she wanted." But all of the kerosene came out of that one pump.
    C. C. Banting built a threshing machine in Toledo, the Banting Greyhound Special. This rig was driven by a Banting Greyhound Special tractor, a basic tractor he bought from Allis-Chalmers and then rebuilt. He installed bigger pistons and painted the unit gray instead of Persian orange.
    At one time, C.C. built a cotton picker; one cotton picker, to be exact. But the cotton crop around Toledo wasn't so hot, so a second Banting Cotton Picker was not built.
    While C. C. Banting was a manufacturer in his own right, he was also an Allis-Chalmers dealer who laid claim to a block of territory about the size of the state of Connecticut. When Toledo Branch opened for business, we cut Banting back to a territory about the size of Rhode Island.

Even with less territory, his sales volume kept moving upward. Good salesmen always scream when you cut the size of their territory, but it doesn't take them long to do more business than they did before. Don't ask me to explain . . . that's just the way it is.

Depression and technological change brought The Banting Company to its fiscal knees in the 1930s, but C.C. pulled it back up again. When I was the assistant machinery clerk at LaPorte Branch, Banting's truckers came to LaPorte five days a week to haul two All-Crop Harvesters back to Toledo. C.C. became a better salesman of our line of small equipment than he had ever been of his own line of "big stuff."

After the opening of Toledo Branch, Banting covered the five counties of territory with sixteen salesmen, no two of whom were paid alike. "Don't want them to compare notes," C.C. said. He had remuneration agreements from straight salary to straight commission and everything in between.

C.C. coached his men to bring prospective customers to Toledo "to look around." When the salesman brought the farmer into C.C.'s office, an order pad lay open before C.C. on his desk. "Whatcha buying today, Joe?" C.C. would ask.

The salesman was rehearsed to interrupt at this point with, "Oh, he's not buying anything. He just came in to look around."

Then C.C. cut in with, "I know Joe here. He likes me and I like him, but he doesn't like me well enough to drive thirty-five miles just to look around. You're here to buy, aren't you Joe? Do you want a plow with your WC? How about a cultivator?"

C.C. simply took it for granted that anybody who came into his office came in there to buy. When a salesman sets up a proper buying atmosphere, most customers will buy. C.C. was a past master of that art. His order blank always lay before him. He would write the customer's name and address on the order blank during the obligatory discussion of the weather. He would have the tractor on the order before he looked up. That much was taken for granted. Now the selling started. What implements? How much for the tradein? When should delivery be made? How will it be paid for? That last one was critical. President Roosevelt hadn't quite brought a chicken to every pot as promised, and so some of Herbert Hoover's grass was still growing in the street.

Financing farm equipment was always a problem. Allis-Chalmers had money enough for brick and mortar and machine tools plus a little inventory if it turned over fast enough, but A-C didn't have lending money. It sure wasn't a branch of First Wisconsin Bank. C. C. Banting managed to finance some of his paper through the Production Credit Association, a New Deal government-sponsored farm lending agency. He did business with the Black Swamp PCA in Bowling Green, Ohio. Some banks in the territory would finance their customers. Former International Harvester Branch Manager John Hupman bought some paper from Banting, and Allis got what the others didn't want. We got the leftovers.

Charley Dunham was one of the best of C.C.'s salesmen. Charley Decker told this story about Dunham and C.C., dating back to the thresher days:

Banting: "Ch-ch-charley, when you c-c-call on a fa-fa-farmer to sell him a threshing machine, don't don't any of them ev-ev-ever invite you in for dinner?"

Dunham: "Oh, many times."

Banting: "B-b-ut you never fail to put the dinner on your expense book."

Dunham: "Mr. Banting, when they invite Charley Dunham in for dinner, they're inviting Charley Dunham in, not C. C. Banting."

Florence McKinnon was C.C.'s secretary. C.C. would say, "Florence, take a letter," and then he started to dictate. Florence would go over to sharpen her pencil, she would look to see who the letter was addressed to, and then she would write her own version of the letter. Her letters were better than C.C.'s.

C. C. Banting is gone now and so are his two sons. Where The Banting Company stood is now an interstate highway.

That's progress?

**COLONEL HINKSON**

Colonel Hinkson was C. C. Banting's service manager. He wore bib overalls, tennis shoes, and invariably he had a bag of gumdrops stashed away on his drill press. Pointing to his drill press, he would tell me, "At thar drill press is a goodun—plus or minus two." He didn't mean two millimeters; he meant two inches. The contraption rocked back and forth as it drilled.

Actually, Colonel was a service manager in name only because C.C. never had any intention of providing service.

We knew it and his customers knew it, but once in a while, a customer complained.

Grat would tell the customer, "When you bought that machine from Banting, you knew you wouldn't get any service, didn't you?" The customer would admit that he knew. "If you had to have service, why did you buy it from Banting?" Invariably the customer would say, "When C.C. sticks that hand of his out and says 'how are you?' you grab his hand and you know you've had it again." Grat and the customer would both laugh with a pained sort of laugh, and then we would send one of our branch servicemen out to see what could be done to make the customer happy again. Machinery was pretty simple in those days. Most crossroad garages could fix what was ailing.

Common sense dictates that it is the servicing dealer who will survive. I believed it sincerely at one time, but experience taught me otherwise. Banting always did well and so did Sam Wieland, our dealer just north of Bay City, Michigan. Any service a customer got from those two was purely coincidental. We had one dealer in the Thumb of Michigan who offered superb service, but his sales charts looked like something out of Mother Hubbard's poverty-stricken abode. Yes, I know it's not fair, but that's the way human beings operate. They buy from sales people, not service people.

Colonel Hinkson said he came from Hinkson County, Kentucky. When I looked at the map of Kentucky, I couldn't find Hinkson County, so it must be invisible like Lake Wobegone, Minnesota.

One day, with some of Banting's other employees gathered around him, the Colonel told about his Russian silk wolfhound that he had in Hinkson County, Kentucky. Freddie Klein, a Banting Company salesman, aged 82, said, "I got tired of listening to dot crap. I thought I vould shut the Colonel up vunce and fer all. I said, 'Colonel, did I efer tell you about my dog?' "

The Colonel didn't think so. Freddie then gave this word picture of his smart dog: "He vas a big dog, a cross between a pointer and a Newfounddoundland. Ve go hunting and he point and I shoot. Ve get a lot of game and ve start home again. Da game vas heavy and dere vas dot big lummox valking along aside of me carrying nudding. You know, I'm not a young man anymore, I'm 82 years old, so I climed on an rode. Den da dog point and I shoot. Da recoil knocked me off of da dog backward. But Colonel, to show you how schmardt dot dog vas, da next time it happened, he put up his tail to gif me a brace." Freddie told us, "Dot's da last time da Colonel ever talked about his dog."

## WHERE IS THE MONEY COMING FROM?

The company didn't have enough money to play banker so they discouraged us from sending customers' notes and mortgages to the home office. When Grat approved a loan request from a dealer's customer, that dealer knew that his Sales & Service Agreement said he would receive five percent less discount on the deal than if he had sent cash. Blockmen knew that their two percent commission would shrink to half of one percent. Even that wouldn't be paid until the customer's last note was paid. How's that for disincentives?

Blockman Willis Scholl had a banker in Adrian, Michigan, who took farm equipment paper. Since the business was a moneymaker for the banker, with few if any collection problems, and good interest rates, this banker talked other bankers on Willis's block into taking farm equipment paper. When Willis encountered a doubting banker, he laid several dollars on the banker's desk for a phone call.

"Call Fred Black over in Adrian. Let him tell you what his experience has been. There's the money for the phone call."

Willis piled up a lot of good banker-relation experience. He told me, "A bank is a store that sells money. Don't whisper like you're in a funeral parlor. Don't get on your knees like in a temple. Go into this money store just as you would any other store."

Blockman John Walker, down on the Van Wert, Ohio, block had several bankers who had taken a real licking during the Depression, handling IH and Deere paper. They were understandably gun-shy. John's fiancée worked in one of those banks, and John went to work on that bank's president. Instead of losing the five percent discount, John suggested to the banker that the dealer would place the five percent into an escrow account in the bank.

"Keep it there against the day that you need to use it to cover a past due. You make the first effort at collection, but if that first effort doesn't bring the money in, take it out of the escrow account and tell us. We'll collect the money and give it to you to rebuild the account."

The escrow accounts saw little or no use. A fine savings account began to pile up for Dealer Dale Wortman. After the escrow account stood idle for several years, the banker told Dale, "I've transferred it over to your checking account. I don't need it."

Uncle Sam's new Production Credit Association was another credit source, but PCA mortgaged everything that was loose, including the thread in mother's sewing machine, if that wasn't already mortgaged. Back then, getting financing was often harder than getting the order.

## JEFF, OUR BACK-ORDER SPECIALIST

Bill Jeffrey, our parts manager, came from Billings Branch where he operated a one-man parts department. Jeff, a bachelor, lived with his widowed mother, a grand dame of the old West who kept a loaded Smith & Wesson on her nightstand. We feared that one night she might mistake Jeff for a burglar and drill a couple of holes in her son. If she had shot at Jeff, she probably would have missed because Jeff wasn't much of a target. He was so thin he could stand in the shade under a washline. Either Jeff was allergic to calories or his mother was a lousy cook.

Jeff was a bit crotchety, and he always had a pipe in his mouth or somewhere nearby. The smell of the pipe was so strong that we didn't have to call Orkin or Terminix to keep the bugs away. A blind man could have found Jeff by following his nose to Jeff's pipe. Jeff's handwriting was so atrocious that Toledo was the only company branch that furnished a typewriter for its parts manager. Unfortunately, Jeff's typing wasn't much better than his handwriting. Jeff wasn't crotchety in the way that Dickens's Scrooge was crotchety. He was a fun person to be with, and his diligence in getting parts to dealers and customers was unequaled anywhere in the entire farm equipment industry in North America. Bar none!

Jeff, the original workaholic, came to work each morning, each evening, each Saturday, each Sunday, and each holiday. Grat threatened to take Jeff's office keys away from him, but that would probably have led to suicide or homicide. Jeff didn't have anything else to do. His work was all that he had in life.

For a time, Grat forbade Jeff to come to work on Saturday afternoons. Instead of parking his car in front of the office, Jeff hid it in the rear. Grat caught him at it and read the riot act to him. So Jeff didn't come to work on Saturday afternoon after that. He got a job with the parts department at Toledo Edison for Saturday afternoons.

Every evening, Jeff checked up on what his people had done during the day. He checked the paper work that Mart Rogan finished. He checked the inventory in the parts bins from which Jim Crawfis had taken parts. Invariably Jeff found a mistake or two that he reminded the boys about in the morning. This "looking over the shoulder" didn't exactly endear Jeff to his people, but his other sterling qualities made it impossible to get mad at him. Disgusted, yes, but not angry.

Before the days of computers, the whole equipment industry kept parts inventory records on what we called T-450 cards. Each card had a part number, a description of the part, the bin number, the price, a minimum inventory figure, and a maximum inventory figure. When a dealer's parts order came in, Mart Rogan checked each part off the T-450 cards before he sent the order out back. That way, if inventory was down to one and someone phoned in for that part, the card would show zero inventory even though there was still one in the bin tagged for the order that had come in earlier. We could tell in a moment if we had any given part in inventory. The maximum/minimum figures changed with the seasons. A maximum of 100 in the spring might only be ten in the winter.

At Toledo Branch we tried to achieve a 93 percent fill rate. Had we tried for a 95 percent fill rate, we would have had to have at least 25 percent more parts. Those last percentage points are killers economically. Back-orders were the plague of the industry. Jeff rated back-orders at the same level that he rated leprosy, malaria, and venereal disease. To be sure that dealers understood that it was the factory and not Toledo Branch that was responsible for not having what was ordered, Jeff showed his factory back orders to every dealer who came into the office. Bud Sailor, of Fisher Implement in Edgerton, Ohio, stepped one step inside the door one day and stopped. He cried out, "Jeff, as long as I've got to look at your (expletive deleted) back-orders, get them out and let's get that over with. I've got to get back to Edgerton yet today."

Since Jeff checked inventory daily, mistakes hardly cooled off before he caught them. When annual inventory time came, Jeff came within a small fraction of one percent of having a perfect inventory. That was unheard of anywhere in the industry. Jeff's inventory would have been 99.99999 percent accurate but for one thing: customers have a way of telling you about shortages in shipments but they're not always as vocal when the mistakes are in their favor. No home office thought it out of line if inventory figures were off three to five percent at annual inventory time. Jeff kept ours under one percent, way under one percent.

Over a beer, now and again, Jeff told us about his Big Sky Country experiences. Once Jeff and an Indian chief customer of his worked over a home office partsman who visited Billings Branch. The chief agreed to play the role of "dumb Indian." The Home Office man said,

"How! What partum you wantum, Chief? We gottum heap many parts."

Chief: (grunt)

"You gottum listum parts, Chief, that you wantum?"

Chief: (grunt)

"You wantum me to helpum you find partum in bookum, how?"

Chief, in perfectly good Harvard English: "Cut the crap. Get me the parts that I ordered over the phone yesterday."

Jeff's grammar and pronunciation didn't exactly match Daniel Webster's. He could get Jones and Smith right, but beyond that, he prided himself on being able to mispronounce peoples' names almost every time. Wortman came out WOORT-man. Mis-CIS-sin came out Mis-KISS-kin. Schluckebier came out Sch . . . mumble.

## MOVE OVER, CASEY JONES

Warehouse Foreman Pop Whalen came from Milwaukee where he had been the engineer (translation: janitor) at Regional Manager Barney Baker's apartment house. Barney took a liking to Pop; then when Toledo Branch opened, he offered Pop a job in Toledo and Pop accepted.

Pop, at one time, had been an engineer for the Illinois Central Railroad, but had lost out when increasing barge traffic ate into IC's freight business. The Illinois Central tracks pretty well paralleled the Mississippi River.

Pop had the delightful habit of adding fiction to history in a way that would make any historical fiction writer blush with envy. When Pop regaled us with his tall tales of his days as engineer for the IC, Servicemen Paul Grimes and Floyd Walker rolled up their pants legs to avoid high water.

"Don't you believe me?" Pop would shout in agonized disbelief.

"Oh, certainly we believe you, Pop. But the water was getting a little deep."

Pop told us many times how he herded "old 97" toward the Mississippi River bridge from Illinois into Iowa. According to Pop's story, he noticed too late that the bridge had been washed away. Here's Pop's narrative of heroic bravado:

"As I rolled 'old 97' up to that bridge, I had a gut feeling that everything was not right. And then, sure enough, I see it. *The bridge was out!* Washed away. Gone! Just a pile of twisted steel. When I see it, I set the air to 'old 97,' but didn't quite make it. The engine, the tender, and one freight car went over the brink. Luckily the couplers held and I was able to crawl out hand over hand without a scratch."

Casey Jones, move over! You've just been topped.

## MY $50 CAR HAS DONE COME AND GONE

Slim George was Pop Whalen's assistant out in the warehouse. He was a functional illiterate out of the Kentucky hills, but no more accommodating individual ever wore shoes in Kentucky or any other state. Slim and Pop made a great team!

As I had done two years before, Slim bought himself a car for fifty bucks. Slim's car received valet service daily . . . he treated his automobile as royalty treats the family jewels.

At the stag party that Grat and FA threw out in the warehouse, some miscreant cut an inner tube, wiring one end shut and wiring the other end to Slim's tailpipe. Going home, Slim got as far as the Firestone station, a block up the street, when the balloon stretched as far as it would go, and BANG!

Slim stopped his car, sat there and moaned, "My new car has done come and gone!"

That's life! No, I was not a party to the despicable action.

## OLÉ!

Louis Aleman, a Mexican national, was our other warehouseman. Aleman means "German" in Spanish. It's not an uncommon name in Mexico; fact is, one of Mexico's presidents was named Aleman. Louie said that President Aleman was a distant relative of his. Could be.

Louie's widowed mother worked in New York City in the Mexican Consulate. Louie had guts enough to enter Father O'Donnel's box at the Army-Notre Dame game in Yankee Stadium to ask him for a scholarship to Notre Dame. Louie got his scholarship all right, but it took him six years to graduate. He had to do a lot of work to pay for the other expenses of his college education.

During Louie's Notre Dame years, he fell madly in love with a girl going to St. Mary's across the road. You've heard of "the boys of St. Mary's," haven't you? The girl's father was a Milwaukee industrialist, and papa wasn't thrilled with the romance between his daughter and a Mexican national.

After graduation, Louie went to Milwaukee looking for work. He hoped to get a job there that would keep him in close proximity with his dear heart before wedding bells chimed. Louis called on Allis-Chalmers, hoping to get a job in the export department. He knew Spanish and Spanish is spoken over much of the world. Or maybe he could land a job with Allis-Chalmers in Mexico City; then he could take his bride there and live happily ever after.

Louie's prospective father-in-law told the folks at A-C, "Hire him and ship him as far away from Milwaukee as possible. I want him out of our hair."

Toledo Branch needed extra help like a mule needs floppy ears, but we got Louis Aleman! Grat, thinking that Louie would consider warehouse work too demeaning, assigned him to the warehouse under the surveillance of Pop Whalen, who hadn't graduated from Notre Dame or Central Teachers' College or Barber College, or anywhere else for that matter. Slim George, the functional illiterate from the Kentucky hills, had seniority over Louie. Grat figured that with Louie's Notre Dame degree, he would soon be on his way and our cost of operation would go down to pre-Aleman days.

Grat was wrong! Louie stayed. He didn't like it but he stayed. The salary of an assistant to the assistant warehouseman wasn't great, but Louie managed to save enough money for a weekend bus trip to Milwaukee each week. A week's noon lunches consisted of one twelve-cent loaf of bread. On Monday, Louie ate two slices of bread, then put the rest of the loaf beneath my typewriter. On Tuesday he ate two more slices and on Friday, before he caught the bus for Milwaukee, he ate what was left of the twelve-cent moldy loaf of bread.

It became quickly evident to Padre that Allis-Chalmers had not shipped Louie far enough from Milwaukee. Louie showed up every weekend, freeloading at his dear love's home. Since A-C had goofed with this Toledo business, the girl's father tried another tack. He sent his daughter on an extended South American cruise. Now Louie didn't have to go to Milwaukee once a week, but he had to buy two airmail stamps each day which cost, in a week, about what the bus fare to Milwaukee had cost. Twice a day he sent his cherished one an airmail letter, and airmail didn't come cheap in Juan Trippe's Pan American Clipper days. As you can tell, this was real love!

All good things must end, and finally the South American cruise ended too. The bus trips to Milwaukee started up again. The girl's father's mistrust of Louie was misplaced because he was a handsome, intelligent, and personable young man.

One weekend, the girl's mother brought her daughter to Toledo in the family convertible. The mother didn't share the father's antipathy for Louie. She loaned the couple the convertible on Saturday, and the two sweethearts drove to Napoleon and were married.

Then papa had the marriage annulled and Louie departed for parts unknown. None of us ever heard from him again. I've often wondered what happened to Louie. With his guts and persistence, he surely should have succeeded in the world. Perhaps Louis went back to Mexico City and the girl followed. Maybe, when the grandchildren came, the grandfather in Milwaukee thought they were the cutest, smartest, brightest, finest, loveliest kids in all of the Western Hemisphere and parts of Bangladesh as well. Who knows? Louie might have even become his father-in-law's Latin American representative and sold one million dollars worth of "el widgets" a year.

Louie's stay in Toledo was a prime example of man's inhumanity to man. Louie was a personable sort, very cheerful and friendly, but he was Mexican, and to some Anglos, Hispanics were and are a threat. Especially if the Mexicans are better educated. The boys out back nailed Louie's coat to the wall, and when he grabbed it, the nail tore a hole. They put Limburger cheese in his hat band. They tortured the guy, giving him all of the jobs that nobody else wanted to do. But still Louis Aleman smiled and tried to get along.

Olé!

# 6

# THEY MADE THE STUFF RUN

Branch servicemen in the farm equipment industry had a hot spot job not unlike the job of Shadrach, Meshech, and Abednego. They were called in when the farmer was broken down and exasperated, when the dealer had tried to no avail to fix things and stood there frustrated. "This blasted thing ain't no good!"

The first lesson that servicemen learned was to listen. "Let 'em get it out! Let 'em spill their venom and get it all out of their system. Then go to work."

If our servicemen were successful in getting the machine running again, they were instant heroes and miracle men. With experience from all over the branch territory, odds favored their having heard of the problem before. There were occasions when our men were stumped too. When that happened, they called the Home Office service department. There was a good chance that someone there had run across the problem once before somewhere in North America.

When some one machine's service problems multiplied, there was no profit left in that machine, but we knew that customers must get what they paid for. If we wanted to stay in business, we had to make the machines that we sold work.

Periodically, Home Office servicemen held schools for branch servicemen. Our servicemen, in turn, held schools for dealers' servicemen. To the credit of our dealers, we had near 100 percent attendance.

Floyd Walker was one of our servicemen. Floyd was well-accepted by our dealers because he stayed with a machine until it was running again. He didn't just give advice and run. Floyd had few callbacks. When he fixed something, it stayed fixed! Our servicemen generally didn't do the work themselves. They had a wrench in their hands, but they wanted the dealer's serviceman to get hands-on experience. The dealer's serviceman did most of the work.

Floyd worked, but that's not all he did. He played. In Saginaw, Michigan, after a few beers, he and his brother kept looking up at the roof on a downtown building and an invisible girl on that roof. They yelled, "Don't jump, little girl. Don't jump." That drew a crowd that eventually included a policeman. Taking Floyd by the shoulder, the cop said, "I'll jump you if you don't get out of here. You're snarling traffic."

Floyd told us of his former boss. "He traveled Eastern Michigan and another man traveled the western half. One day, when the two rode together, they stopped at a restaurant. My former boss went inside while the other man fiddled with road maps or something. My boss told the girl at the cash register in a stage whisper, 'I'm a doctor and I'm taking a patient to Eloise. He's not a violent type but I believe it would be best if you seated us in back. The only time I saw him go berserk, it was over a knife and a fork, so I would recommend that you do not serve him a knife and fork.' "

"The head waitress did as she was bidden. The two were seated in the back of the dining room. Where else? The table was set with a knife, fork, and spoon on one side, one spoon on the other. The man from Western Michigan politely asked for a fork, which was not forthcoming. He asked again, in a little louder voice. The louder his requests for more proper implementation, the more the waitresses hid in the kitchen. Finally he burst out with, 'Nuts to it. I'll eat with my spoon,' and proceeded to do so. He grumbled between bites. He grumbled when he handed his money to the cashier. He kept complaining as the two drove away. Finally a light lit and he turned to my boss and said, 'You so-and-so. You had something to do with that. What did you tell those people?' "

Ed Elgin was another of our servicemen, a tall man with hands the size of dinner plates and feet the size of home plate. When Ed grabbed the steering wheel of his poor Ford, that car couldn't possibly escape.

When Ed pressed down on the foot pedals of his car, it was a tribute to Ford engineering that his feet did not go down through the floorboards. The local Firestone station did the service work on Ed's car. They did it over and over again. If Firestone stockholders had known of all of this free warranty service, they would have sold their Firestone stock and bought Goodyear.

Paul Grimes, our senior serviceman, unlike the other two, was disgustingly normal. Paul got more callbacks than Floyd or Ed because he had the habit of telling the dealer's serviceman what to do, and then he left. "Telling them" was what our service schools were all about, and at that, Paul was a past master. But most of the time it took more than "telling them" to solve problems in the field.

If the reader has the impression that Toledo Branch's service department was like something out of M*A*S*H, the reader would not be far wrong.

### GO AHEAD AND SHOOT!

Cleo Etter was The Banting Company's blockman. Actually Cleo wasn't a blockman since he didn't get a commission.

Cleo looked a little like his name implied, at home in the lingerie department or in housewares. Looks, in this case, were most deceiving. Grat got to know Cleo when he was a desk clerk in the Secor Hotel at the time we moved to town and stayed at the Secor. Cleo hit Grat up for a job and Grat gave him the job of working with The Banting Company. Collecting pastdue notes, for instance.

One time Cleo called on a pastdue out in the country in Wood County. The delinquent came to the door with a shotgun. He said, "Now git, y'hear?" Cleo got. But he didn't got very far. He snuck around the house and through an open window. He saw the shotgun propped up against a living room chair. He edged himself through the open window far enough to take the shells out of the shotgun. Then he knocked on the door again. The farmer returned to the door, shotgun in hand and said, "I tole you to git! Now (too hot to quote), git, y'hear?"

Cleo replied, "Go ahead and shoot." He held out his hands with the shells in his hands. The two began to talk business after that and eventually Cleo collected. What else was the farmer to do? Anybody who is crazy enough to crawl through a living room window and take the shells out of a shotgun is also crazy enough to repossess.

## THE LATE HOWARD SHIREMAN

Pronounce that Sherman, not Shire-man. When we saw Blockman Howard Shireman, we could count on two things:

1. He would be impeccably attired, looking like a Hart, Schaffner & Marx ad. 2. He would be late. Just as a sales meeting or service meeting was about to begin, Howard would pull his Buick to a screeching halt in the parking lot in front of the branch. He would come in all out of breath and say, "Sorry I'm late folks. I had to make a few calls on the way in."

Howard Shireman was a brown-noser who tried to impress Grat and F.A. with his phony rapt attention. When a serviceman stooped over to point at a feature underneath one of our pieces of equipment at a service school, Howard stooped over too, keeping his nose two inches from the end of the yardstick pointer. On one such occasion, when Howard's posterior pointed heavenward, Blockman John Walker thought it just too tempting a situation to pass up. John placed an open book of matches in Howard's hip pocket, then lit the matches. Howard came up with some choice expletives as he pounded his rear end to put out the fire.

Howard and John Walker had adjoining blocks. It was quite natural that there would be phone calls between the two men. John said that Howard's phone calls began to be a nuisance because he couldn't ever get the guy to hang up. John decided to cure Howard of his long phone calls. The next time Howard called, spending his nickel, John allowed him to talk for half an hour. Then, when Howard thought the phone bill about as high as one dared put on the expense book, he tried to sign off, but John wouldn't let him. John had "just one more thing" to talk about. Those "just one more things" added up to an hour and a half of phone call. Howard's telephonitis was cured!

    Clad in his uniform of Hickey-Freeman suit and Florsheim shoes, Howard offered to help Dealer Herb Fisher place water and calcium chloride solution in a tractor tire. To get added weight for traction, at first farmers added cast iron wheel weights to their tractor's rubber tired wheels. Then someone discovered that water in the inner tubes of the tires would provide much less expensive ballast. Water, however, has the bad habit of freezing, so antifreeze had to be added. Calcium chloride was found to be the best antifreeze.

    This calcium chloride thing was quite new, and Howard didn't know the physical nature of calcium chloride. He knew that it wasn't corrosive, but he wasn't aware of calcium chloride's undesirable facets. In the process of pumping the water and calcium chloride into the tractor tires' inner tubes, some of the water spilled on the floor and Howard walked in it. The next morning, Howard's Florsheims were each in two pieces, the Flor uppers and the Sheim soles and heels. The calcium chloride had eaten away the stitching that fastened the sole and heel to the upper part of the shoe.

    Howard was an aviator who flew most of the day and then would burst into a dealer's place of business about four o'clock in the afternoon saying, "Let's get busy. We've got a day's work ahead of us. We've got to go out and sell some equipment." This went over with dealers like the proverbial cement balloon.

    Despite the hijinks, Howard Shireman and John Walker were good friends. One year we had a factory tour sales contest. Dealers and blockmen could both win a trip on a special train to all of our Midwest factories. I don't remember what they had to do to win. John and some of his dealers had won their berths on the special train. John wanted Howard to go too, so John shunted a few of his deals through Howard's dealerships; on paper, that is. That bit of philanthropy backfired because when World War II started, machinery was scarce and all machinery rations were based on past sales records. Throughout the war, Howard's dealers got the benefit of John's shunted "sales" that had been rerouted through Howard's dealers. John escaped the wrath of his dealers because the coward escaped to the relative safety of Rommel's North Africa, then to Mussolini's Anzio.

## HOW TO AVOID WINNING FIRST PLACE

Frugality was standard equipment in the U.S.A. during the Depression 1930s. At our place, it was even more so. In 1940, we carried frugality to ridiculous extremes. General Manager Bill Roberts announced a cost-of-doing-business contest. The branch house in the company that had the lowest percentage cost of operation compared to sales would be declared winner and would receive a trip to Milwaukee for all employees and their spouses.

Second prize was $5,000 in cash, to be divided pro rata to salary. Grat paraded around the office saying, "Nothing would make me more proud than to take my entire branch organization to be feted and honored by our company executives and to receive the plaque from Mr. Roberts." And he meant just that!

We understood Grat's desire for brownie points, but if we wanted a factory tour, we could go next door to the

Willys-Overland plant. Willys's drill presses and lathes looked just like those in Milwaukee. Our collective eyes were on that five thousand smackeroos. But how to win second place without winning first. That was our problem!

We had always had a low cost of operation, something in the neighborhood of five percent of gross, plus or minus a few bucks, so we definitely had a shot at the prizes. However, we certainly didn't want to carelessly win first prize and miss second. Those of us who were single (and that was about half of us) had no spouse to take to Milwaukee. The married employees couldn't all have found baby sitters for the better part of a week, so they weren't excited about a trip to Milwaukee either. We just didn't dare win first place! Out of the question. Absolutely not! No, sir! No, ma'am!

None of us wanted to win bad enough to ask for a cut in pay, but we did every other thing to economize. We worked in the dark to keep from burning lights. We worked at Antarctica thermostat levels to save on the heat bill. We wore pencils down until our hangnails scratched the paper. We utilized the backs of old envelopes. We recycled paper clips and straightened nails. No blockman was allowed the luxury of forty-cent expense book meals. Blockmen were told to sleep at home and not run up hotel bills. We used two-cent postcards instead of three-cent letters, and Alexander Graham Bell might just as well not have invented the telephone. Long distance calls were verboten! Typewriter ribbons were worn until holes appeared in the ribbons, and the typing became invisible. Parts packages had two bands instead of four. We reused cardboard boxes and twine. We economized! We recycled far ahead of our time. Frugality with a capital F.

We held our collective breath when the prizes were announced. "Toledo has won . . . (gulp) . . . SECOND PRIZE!" Some other branch, I don't remember which one, won first. They had either sold more machines or they found ways to economize that we missed. Glory, glory, hallelujah! Regional Manager Barney Baker came down from Milwaukee to present the checks. We locked up the branch and went downtown to the Secor Hotel to have lunch. After lunch, Barney made a laudatory speech about dedication and loyalty and all of the other sterling virtues that people in a corporation should have. Midway in the speech, a bellhop stuck his nose in the door. "Mrs. Whalen and Mrs. Melzer are down in the lobby. They are waitin' for their husband's checks."

Hank jumped up and shouted, "You tell that greedy wife of mine to get back home again . . . Now!" It took a little while to restore order, but F.A.'s laugh was a dead giveaway that he was guilty of the hoax. F.A. had tipped the bellhop to come up to our luncheon room with the fictitious message.

Our checks amounted to something more than a month's salary but not quite two months. None of us had difficulty finding ways to spend the money.

## BELIEVE IT OR NOT, LONGER IS SHORTER

Branch machinery clerks had their problems too. (1) Factories that ship the wrong things to the wrong dealer. (2) Factories that ship incomplete machines. (3) Factories that are always late with their shipments.

LaPorte Works was real good at shipping combines. Milwaukee's tractor shipments were tolerable. LaCrosse's implement shipments were impossible. Carload tractor shipments from Milwaukee to Toledo should have been a fast run. Two hours, Milwaukee to Chicago. A belt line switch from Milwaukee Road or Northwestern Railroad to New York Central overnight. Chicago to Toledo, 200 miles, an easy four-hour run. What should have taken two or three days, took two weeks. The railroads dug their own grave with such service.

Then one day, for unexplained reasons, the factory's shipping clerk routed a carload of tractors to us via Green Bay. The carload pulled up to our dock on the third or fourth day. The tractors had pulled out of the yards in Milwaukee one afternoon, had gone north to Green Bay instead of south to Chicago. In Green Bay the car was loaded on the Lake Michigan ferry headed for Ironton, Michigan. At Ironton the carload was hitched to the once-a-day train on Henry Ford's Detroit, Toledo & Ironton Railroad that went down to Toledo. In one day's DT&I running time, the carload arrived in Toledo where it was switched to the New York Central for delivery to us at our NYC siding.

Hey, we've hit on to something! I ordered a few more cars with that routing and predictably had a visit from the New York Central sales representative. Railroad sales reps don't have much love for short hauls. The Green Bay routing gave the NYC only the revenue from their yards to our dock a few miles away. "What in the world are you trying to do, routing tractors via the North Pole, giving us the short haul?" the rep wanted to know. My explanation fell on the deaf ears of a railroad rep whose job it was to get freight, not lose it. I promised that I would order two carloads of tractors, one via Chicago, one via Green Bay, and we would see which got to Toledo first. The bills of lading were to be noted each time the car changed hands. The Green Bay routing won again, hands down! The rep's dispirited comment was, "I guess you can just get too big to be good."

The debacle wasn't New York Central's fault. It was the fault of the belt line railroads in Chicago. It was their business to switch cars from one railroad to another, but their yards stacked up with freight cars, and that meant delay. During World War I, shippers found that they could bypass the Chicago railroad beltway debacle by buying trucks that drove straight through Chicago. Because of beltway railroad pileups, the trucking industry was born.

I was not the only person who gave railroad sales reps a hard time. Do you remember the record-breaking snowfall in Chicago in the mid-70s? To clear Chicago's railroad yards of snow, men with front-end loaders desperately dumped some of the snow into hopper cars. Children in Florida read about this and asked that a carload of snow be shipped to them, so that they could make snowmen. The railroad's PR department went all out to get a carload of snow to Florida in two days. Then shippers started to scream. "How come it takes you two weeks to get a carload of our merchandise to Chicago, when you can get a carload of snow down here in two days?" You can't win!

## THE MODEL B TRACTOR

Harry Merritt's streamlined, rubber-tired, one-plow Model B tractor was aimed straight at those three and a half million small farms in the country. He firmly believed that the Model B would remove the last horse from the farm.

Merritt's dreams of the $495 price quoted in a *Fortune* article didn't quite come true. The first price tag I saw was $518 with another $35 for a combination belt pulley and power-take-off. By the time that we began selling the Model B, it was priced at $525 list price, and that price held for years. The Model B was sold on rubber tires only and had a wide cushion seat, the first in the tractor business. Don't get carried away with that cushion seat business though. A wooden frame was covered with canvas, and a few zigzag springs were fastened underneath. Factory spec cost was probably about $2.17. There was comfort only when compared to the stamped steel seats that had been standard equipment in the industry to that date.

Companion tools for the 1939 Model B were a 16-inch, 1-bottom plow, a 1-row cultivator, a 5-foot mower and a 5-foot disc harrow. Starter and lights soon were standard equipment on the Model B. Merritt had made starter and lights standard equipment on the WC in 1939, the first such offerings in the industry. The year before, 90 percent of our WCs had been sold that way, so he just made it unanimous.

The new and revolutionary Model B went into production about the time that I moved to Toledo Branch. It would be hard to forget the first carload of Model B tractors that arrived in Toledo. Someone in the office spotted the car going past the branch, hitched behind a New York Central switch engine. When the switch engine shoved the car into place at our dock, the whole office and warehouse force was out there to witness the memorable occasion. All but me! I stayed in the office to call the ten dealers who were to get the ten tractors on the car.

When I got out to the freight car, half of the people there were in tears. The rest stood there silently, shaking their heads. It looked like a funeral coming back from happening. Vandals had gotten to that carload before it arrived at our dock. Every tire was slashed; not just some small superficial cuts, but deep slashes. Every gas tank cap and radiator cap was missing. The cushion seats were all slit open. All the spark plug wires were gone. All oil filters had been removed and thrown away. We suspected sand in the gas tanks.

I hurried back into the branch to call the ten dealers back. Five of them had already left. When those five arrived, they stood there in disbelief too.

This had to be the work of some adults who had a big gripe against the company or the Model B tractor. Surely it wasn't a bunch of ornery kids who caused this disaster. Kids wouldn't have worked so hard to do all of that damage. You don't put deep cuts in tractor tires with a pocketknife. "Who did it?" And "Why?" Those were the questions everyone asked, but no one provided answers. We were told to ship the carload back to Milwaukee "as is." West Allis Works, our tractor factory in the Milwaukee area, rushed a replacement car to us immediately. This time a railroad detective sat in a boxcar with a peephole to see if the scoundrels would repeat their vandalism. It never happened again.

Harry Merritt and Bill Roberts saw the Model B tractor as the machine that would take the last horse off the farm. But how were we to convince farmers of that fact? Jim Hardgrove, our sales manager at Columbus Branch, hit on the ideal method. He hired four young couples to square dance at the Ohio State Fair on eight Model B tractors. A fiddler and a caller rounded out the cast. These eight young people went through all of the gyrations of square dancers, but they used wheels instead of feet and legs. There was no commentator to explain the maneuverability of the tractor. That was obvious. Jim had come up with a commercial that had no words.

When that square dance of ours started up about four times a day, we pulled the crowds to the arena behind our tent. You could have shot a shotgun down Machinery Row, and you wouldn't have hit anything but a Case tractor and a Deere blockman while our square dancers performed. People climbed over anything and everything nearby to get a good view. After they filled our lot, they climbed all over machines in neighboring lots. Jim was invited to have his square dancers do their routines in front of the grandstand. The next year other State Fair managers asked the square dancers to come to their fairs. They offered to pay the tab for freight and honorariums. It would be hard to envision a bigger public relations plum than this.

Then someone at Home Office thought that the act was beneath our dignity and canceled the show. International Harvester allowed the idea to lie dormant for a few years and then they picked it up and made hay with it. We had rescued failure from the heights of success.

The innovative Model B brought quick response from the competition. International came out with their A, a tractor the same size as our Model B. The engine rode on the left side and the operator rode on the right, where he could see where he was going. In '41, Deere came with their Model L. The Model L had an engine about the size of the East German Trabant car, a little bigger than a washing machine engine. The IH A and A-C B are still around, selling for more than they did in 1940. Deere's Model L, if it's around, is a museum piece.

# 7

# THE WC, OUR WORKHORSE TRACTOR

The two-plow WC tractor was our mainstay, even after the introduction of the Model B. With Merritt's direction, C. E. Frudden and Walter Strehlow engineered the WC, the first tractor designed for rubber tires. Merritt was price conscious. He knew that air tires would add to the list price, and that the Depression was still with us. He wanted the price of the air-tired WC to be as low as possible. Frudden and Strehlow came up with a bull gear and pinion drive that would reduce the size of the drive wheels, thereby economizing on rubber. Less rubber, less cost. I used to say, "Small diameter drive wheels—like the drivers on a freight train engine."

The WC tractor engine was 4x4, four-inch stroke, four-inch bore. Square. The first such engine on the market. Earlier tractors had long strokes, chug, chug, chug. There was a snappy governor on the tractor that seemed to sense a heavy load, even before the load arrived. The WC designation meant Model W, with C for cultivating. But WC stands for "water closet" all over the world except in the United States. Surely the company must have given it another name when it was shipped overseas. Maybe not. After all, Chevrolet sent their Novas to Latin America. Nova, in Spanish, means "won't go."

While the WC was light-years ahead of the competition at the time, there were quirks. Sometimes, instead of the clutch going in, the seat went back. When you applied the brakes, you held the individual brakes on the wheels with two hands and steered with your third hand.

**SIFTING OUT THE RIFFRAFF**

When Toledo Branch opened, we had but a handful of dealers. It was absolutely essential that we add dealers, but the requirements for a new dealer were stiff, and so new dealers weren't all that easy to find. Here are some of those stiff requirements that we, and most of our competitors, laid before dealer prospects:

1. New dealers had to carry a $150 parts stock, even before they sold a machine that needed a part. In 1940, $150 was a young fortune.

2. New dealers had to place a three-dollar company sign on their building.

3. New dealers had to have enough money to pay the freight on the first carload of tractors or combines. That meant another fifty to seventy-five dollars.

4. New dealers had to have something just a bit larger than the proverbial hole in the wall out of which to do business. Often this meant an expensive $3,000 building or choking twenty dollar per month rent.

5. New dealers had to buy a dollar-and-a-half sales manual. Price books, order blanks, and catalogs were furnished free.

Those who met these stiff standards went on to mechanize the North American farm. There probably isn't an urban housewife alive who realizes what contribution our industry's dealers made to provide her with low-cost, high-quality food.

## THOSE IRREPLACEABLE MIDDLE LINKS IN THE CHAIN

Most of our dealers were just plain, garden variety, good citizens of their communities, so average that they didn't generate front page stories. No one handed them a trophy for the part they played in the U.S.A. food miracle, even though they deserved it.

We had a few unusual dealers too; not exactly budding Marshall Fields, but the kind who bring nostalgic smiles from farmers who did business with them.

Take Fred Rempert, for instance. Fred was our dealer in Tawas City, Michigan. A Pennsylvania Dutchman said his wife wasn't "so hot for purty, but she's heck for stout." Iosco County wasn't so hot for farming, but it was heck for tourism. There were a few farms in the county, and Fred knew them all. He sold two or three tractors each year, and one or two combines. Fred had a bucket full of tools in his garage and fixed everything with them. If the automobile, truck, or other machine couldn't be fixed with the tools in that bucket, it was unfixable.

W. D. "Cope" Coplin was Fred's blockman. F. A. Spilker kept gnawing at Cope because Fred wasn't selling more machinery. Way ahead of his time, F.A. did market research. He worked on demographics before the word was coined. F.A. showed Cope the farm income figures from the most recent United States Census. "See there. There's the farm income in Iosco County, and we're not getting enough of it. What are you going to do about it?"

Then F.A. made the mistake of going to Tawas City. Fred asked F.A., "Would you like to take a look at the territory?" Certainly F.A. would like to take a look at all of that farm land listed in the U. S. Census that turned out all of the agricultural wealth listed in the document. Fred knew the county like the back of his hand. He knew every farm in the county, every road and every fire lane. F.A. and Cope climbed into Fred's Model A Ford, and the trio set out to inspect the territory. Once in a while Fred would stop long enough to shoot at some animal through the car window, then continue onward. Since Fred knew the territory, he knew how to duck every last farm in the county. The three drove for two hours and didn't pass Farm Number One. Fred went up this road, down that fire lane, back on this road. When they got back to the shop, F.A. was heard to mumble, "I don't know how in the world you sell the few things you do sell." With that, F.A. climbed in his car and headed for Toledo. After that excursion, Cope never heard about the demographics of Iosco County again.

Ruth Farmers Elevator was a farmer co-op in the town of Ruth in Huron County, Michigan. Huron County is the tip of the Thumb of Michigan, one of the most, if not the most fertile county in the state. Ruth Farmers Elevator was our dealer in the eastern part of the county. To the west of Ruth, the farmers were German, and to the east, they were Polish. One year genial and accomodating Roman Booms, the president of the co-op, asked me to come up to show company films at the co-op's annual stockholders' meeting. That's the meeting where the president announces that there will be no stockholder dividend this year because the board of directors bought another business in town and that took all the cash there was in the till.

Toward the end of the meeting, Roman told the stockholders, "Dis vinter ve gonna haf some edjucatshunal meetinks. How many vould like to come to da edjucatshunal meetinks?" One fellow held up his hand. Roman continued, "Dese meetinks vill be about how ve vork togedder in da cooperative vay of life. How many vould like to come to da edjucatshunal meetinks?" Even the previous volunteer held back this time.

Roman tried a third time. He said the meetings would be "mit beer." Now all of the hands went up. Roman told me afterward, "I doan know about peepul. You can't get dem to come to meetinks if you don't haf beer. It's dere own money dey're sopping up, but if you doan haf a keg of beer, nobody comes." I told Roman that Washington and Lansing politicians knew all about this free beer business. They had the same problem!

Then there was Ray Savery at Ann Arbor. Ray looked like a corporate president from Fortune's 500 or #139 in Forbes' "400 richest." Distinguished face, three-piece suit, tie, a protruding potbelly draped with a gold chain and an elk's tooth. Ray was a personal friend of Henry Ford. When Henry Ford needed a spool of barbed wire or a pane of glass for the hen house, he called Ray. Ray sold Ford about a dozen All-Crop Harvesters a year. Ford had an 11,000-acre farm near Tecumseh, Michigan, another in the Upper Peninsula of Michigan, and still another in Georgia. Cherry Hill Plantation had about 1,800 acres. There was another huge Ford farm in Brazil.

When we received Ford's parts orders in the branch, they were on Henry Ford's personal high-grade linen, gold-engraved stationery. The fine linen bond had a simple

"Henry Ford" in gold engraved at the top of the sheet; nothing else.

Willis Scholl was Ray's blockman when Toledo Branch opened. In fact, Ray was his one and only dealer. During the day Willis looked for new dealers, and at night he and Ray went out into the country to sell machinery. When the annual contracting time came around, Willis twisted Ray's arm to sign factory orders for two carloads of tractors, a carload of implements, and five carloads of All-Crop Harvesters. Willis said he did a lot of arm twisting on Ray because, up to that point, Ray had never ordered even one carload of anything. He had hauled everything piece by piece from LaPorte Branch. In this battle of wits, Willis won, or thought he won. His one concession was that the five carloads of combines would be shipped at one time so Ray could get some free publicity in the local papers. The moment the carload orders that Ray signed arrived in Toledo, Ray canceled them. Dummy that I was, I did the canceling without checking with Willis first.

After a time, Willis asked me when Ray's carloads would be shipped. I told Willis that Ray had canceled the orders. Breathing fire, Willis told me over the phone, "Ray Savery doesn't cancel orders. I do. Reinstate those orders and ship immediately. I'll handle Ray." Willis told me the next time I saw him, "I went straight to Ann Arbor and told Ray that the equipment would soon be on the way. The air turned blue. Ray told me to stick my contract up my you-know-where. I told him that I couldn't do that but I would tear it up if he wanted me to. That calmed him down. He went on to make more money that year than he had ever made before in his life. It made him feel good to be a high-volume, big shot dealer."

The five carloads of combines all came at the same time, as promised, on a snowy, blowy day in February, *not* as promised. Willis told me, "I drove past the siding where they sat and there were Ray and Bill Elfring getting ready to unload. I knew what they were saying about me, so I drove on. A block from the rail siding, my car was still vibrating from Ray's invective."

Willis tells this Savery story on himself: "We were driving through the country when Ray hauled up in front of a business establishment in town. We walked in and I was properly introduced. Then, out of the blue, Ray said, `This guy is from the company and he's hounding me for payment of your bill. When are you going to pay up?'" Willis was dumbfounded, but he said it was vintage Ray Savery.

Dale Wortman operated out of an old streetcar in Van Wert, Ohio. Electric trolley cars had once been the sole mass transit in our cities, when the masses used mass transit instead of Toyotas and freeways. Dale bought one of those non-polluting trolley cars that some city discarded when they changed over to diesel-belching buses. Dale was everything a branch manager could expect of a dealer, except for that streetcar. Somehow, John Walker, Dale's blockman, kept Grat from ever seeing that abandoned mass transit conveyance. Eventually the streetcar gave way to a new and modern Stran Steel building. Dale had taken on the Stran Steel franchise.

Gary Schmidt operated out of Continental, Ohio, in the middle of Ohio's "jack wax" clay country. That jack wax was so tough that a farmer could hook onto a furrow with a chain and pull the entire furrow up to the barn. The Banting Company was our highest sales volume dealer, and Gary Schmidt was second.

Gary signed on when he was eighteen years old, at least that's what he said. When Gary signed on, he had a very modest financial statement, and later there seemed to be evidence that the bottom line was red rather than black. We had Gary on C.O.D. That was a handicap, but not enough of a handicap to slow Gary down. He loved sales volume!

Dealers around Gary accused him of cutting prices. "He's going to go broke if he doesn't break all of us around him first," was the constant cry that we heard.

When confronted with this "going broke" prediction, he would pull his 1040 out of his desk drawer. "Please show me where I'm losing money. Last year I had to pay a $5,000 income tax and I don't like to pay a $5,000 income tax. If I'm actually losing money, I won't have to pay all of that tax money," Gary countered. Gary retired at age thirty-nine, owning several farms and business blocks in town. The dealers who followed Gary did about as well as he did. Almost certainly, Gary had the best market penetration that the company had anywhere.

That jack wax soil around Continental was something else! It refused to be plowed. When farmers tried to plow, huge chunks of sod would go flying through the air. One could walk across a plowed sod field stepping only on the bottom of the furrow, in spots that the flying pieces of sod had vacated. We had a constant stream of complaints about our plows in that territory. The only consolation we had was that competitors were hearing the same sad tale of woe. Theirs didn't work any better than ours.

Gary Schmidt hated tradeins. When he took something in on trade, he rang doorbells until he had that item sold. His tradein lot was almost always bare. Gary sold equipment

## The WC, Our Workhorse Tractor

with the least amount of words of anyone I know. "Whatcha buyin' today, Charley?" Then he listened. If the customer didn't buy in fifteen minutes, Gary would say, "He's not ready yet," and he would move on.

Gary's price-cutting was developed to an art. Let some farmer come in from far away and Gary would slip him a hot deal. Then the farmer's neighbors, like obedient sheep going to be shorn, came in and went home with what they only thought was a hot deal. That's why Gary had to pay that much income tax. Those faraway customers drove right past their local dealer who would have given them a better deal. Try to explain that to neighboring dealers! I learned that you do not need to be a price-cutter to get the business. All you need is a reputation of price-cutting. It isn't what something is that is important. It's what people think it is.

Schmidt Implement Company was spotlessly clean. One could eat off the service department's workbenches. A mezzanine office at the rear of the showroom-parts area of the store was where Gary did business. Each evening he sat in that mezzanine office talking business with farmers. At the same time he ran a motion picture machine that projected company pictures (plus comedies that he rented) on a screen pulled down over the show-window at the front of the store. Those free picture shows brought nightly store traffic.

George Bokerman was our dealer in Napoleon, Ohio. We never tired listening to George tell of the building of the canal that linked the Ohio River with Lake Erie. George said the entire canal was dug by men with shovels and wheelbarrows, by mules and scrapers. The canal had to cross land from Delphos to Waterville. From Napoleon to Waterville, the canal paralleled the Maumee River with its rocks and rapids. Eight-foot wide canal boats were towed by mules trodding the tow path.

Marshall Lintemuth at Fowlerville, Michigan, sold at home more than any other dealer we had. Marshall saturated the farm market around Fowlerville with orange paint up to the five-mile limit, but seldom went beyond that imaginary boundary. Marshall was the most pessimistic talker and most optimistic doer that I ever knew.

Don Horton was our ex-Chevrolet dealer who operated out of Plymouth, Michigan. Don's General Motors connections, from his Chevrolet days, stood him in good stead. Many GM executives had farms. Some were near Plymouth but others were scattered all over the country. Don sold them all. This brought complaints from branches in other parts of the country, but Home Office ruled that business could be done either at the location of the farm or at the location of the owner of the farm.

I'll never forget the day that Sam Wieland came into the branch for the first time. He showed Grat and F.A. a picture of his cement block building in Kawkawlin, Michigan, the next little town north of Bay City. Sam had seen our Model B tractor and, rightly, he figured that it was made to order for his territory. Sam had a sort of threadbare financial statement. Despite the lack of great sums of cash, Sam wanted an A-C contract in the worst way. Grat and FA wanted a dealer in Kawkawlin in the worst way too, but they played hard-to-get. They knew from the moment that Sam opened his mouth that they would sign his contract, but they coaxed him on to promise more and more. Sam sold Model B tractors in bunches like bananas. He had sized up the market just right!

## The WC, Our Workhorse Tractor

One day Sam came to Toledo to buy one of the last of the used threshing machines The Banting Company had in inventory. Going home, through the edges of Detroit, Sam turned a corner a little too fast and the thresher fell off of the truck, landing in the middle of the intersection on its side. When the police arrived, he told them to call the nearest junk dealer. Sam sold the junk dealer the thresher "as is, where is."

Another time, at about the same intersection, he asked his son Merle, "Car coming?" Merle said, "No." Sam pulled out into the intersection and was hit by a truck.

"I thought you said there wasn't a car coming," Sam barked. "That wasn't a car, Dad. That was a truck."

Just north of Kawkawlin, lies Standish, Michigan, where Miscisin Brothers were our dealer. Newly minted MBAs would be interested in this firm. If prospects wanted arm-swinging rhetoric, they talked to Joe Miscisin who could fling his arms and shout with the best of them. If it took quiet boring-in to get the deal, Sam Miscisin took over. Both brothers could sell in a half dozen different foreign languages. Oh yes, English too.

### HENRY FORD, REVISITED

As has been mentioned, Ann Arbor Dealer Ray Savery supplied Ford with his All-Crop Harvesters and other items for the farm. Understandably, Henry bought all of the rest of his farm machinery from the Ford Motor Company.

Mel Partridge, our dealer in Tecumseh, Michigan, told us about Ford Farms.

"Ford has his Macon farm, 11,000 acres of it, close to Tecumseh. At the big house on the farm, there's lunch for twelve on the table at noon five days a week. If Ford doesn't show up by 12:30, the help eats the food. The farms are immaculate. Men walk around picking up chicken feathers. Smoking and drinking on the farm are strictly prohibited. Ford grows soybeans on his farms because he feels that soybeans can be used both for food and for raw material for commercial products that he can use in his factories."

Each of the small towns just north of us in Michigan had a small Ford factory located on the river. A waterwheel furnished power, power which probably cost Ford three times as much as the power he could have bought from the Illuminating Company. Henry Ford's biographer, Robert Lacey, called it "waterpower mania." Farmers worked in these factories part of the day and farmed the rest of the day.

Henry Ford, perhaps more than any other industrialist, took a good look at the industrial potential for farm crops. Soybeans for horn buttons, for instance. He saw the ethanol potential of Jerusalem artichokes, but concentrated instead on the soybean. He was interested in Vitasoy, a soybean drink that outsold Coca Cola in Hong Kong in the early 70s.

**NO MAN IS WORTH THAT MUCH**

This farmer came to my machinery clerk's desk madder than a Airedale with a docked tail. I asked what was wrong.

He explained, "I had a field of red clover out behind the barn that I was gonna plow under. Then my neighbor, who has one of those tin combines of yours, come over and said that he would like to thrash that clover before I plowed 'er down. I told him that there wasn't any seed in that clover field, but he said he would take his chances on that. He said he'd cut it on halves—fifty-fifty. I couldn't lose on a proposition like that so I took him up on his offer. You know what? That neighbor of mine combined that clover and got $100 of clover seed out of that patch that I had planned to plow under. He got half of the seed, that's fifty dollars worth, just for cutting it. And it only took him two hours."

I asked, "What are you so het up about? You got fifty bucks too."

"Him making fifty dollars for two hours work, that's what's got me hot under the collar. No man is worth that kind of money."

Historical update: Henry Kissinger gets $20,000 for a thirty-minute speech. And outfielders get . . . aw, you know what they get.

## McCORMACK WITH AN A, NOT AN I

Herb McCormack explained the importance of an "a," and not an "i," in McCormack, but I have long since forgotten what that earthshaking difference was. Something about lace-curtain Irish and shanty Irish, as I recall.

Herb's father was works manager at West Allis Works, our tractor production facility in the Milwaukee area. Herb had a degree from Marquette, which would have qualified him to work at Toledo Branch, but the fact that his dad was one of the big shots of the company, cinched the deal. Herb was a bean counter in our Toledo Branch accounting department.

Herb's dad was plant superintendent back in the days when men were men and women were glad of it. The McCormack family was like something out of a novel.

Charley McCormack was 100 percent Emerald Isle in an American insular environment of Germans and Poles. He fared well with both groups, and they with him.

Herb told us that one of his sisters had minor parts on the Broadway stage and the other was married to an itinerant artist who moved around the world painting portraits of the rich and famous, the high and mighty. The Milwaukee McCormacks could never find this daughter when a family emergency arose without checking roundabout through Long Island, Monaco, Presque Isle, and Naples, the most recent portrait locales. Herb said that his brother screamed. He had been in an auto accident, and when atmospheric or emotional pressures hit a certain point on the scale, he screamed. The McCormacks were a real-life lovable family that closely resembled that delightful fictional family in "You Can't Take It With You."

Herb graduated from Marquette (class of 1938), as did all good Catholic boys who lived in Washington Highlands in Wauwatosa. Rosemary Clancy was in Herb's class, and it was known from their freshmen days that the two were meant for each other. Rosemary's dad was a fighter of lost causes. He represented the ice company when Frigidaires came in. He represented the streetcar company when buses came in. He represented coal stoves when furnaces became popular.

In school, Herb had an unlimited expense account that permitted him to buy drinks for the Marquette football team at the Schroeder bar or at Mama Maria's Italian Gardens. When Herb left Milwaukee for Toledo, his father told him, "I've financed you all I'm going to. You're on your own now, Buster. Understand?" When Herb came to Toledo, oblivious of his father's words of financial abandonment, he brought his free-spending habits with him. The habits outlasted the money. For the first time in his life, Herb was broke. In fact, it was worse than that. He borrowed a few bucks from our sales manager, F. A. Spilker, and paid him back by beating him in poker. Each month Herb had about twenty days left over at the end of the month's money. And there was no Mama McCormack to bail him out. A mailed plea brought some results, and after that, mama's letters always contained a few five spots out of the McCormack's sugar bowl grocery money to help Herb out. She realized, as his father didn't, that it was not possible for a young man to live a good Catholic life in Toledo on what Allis-Chalmers paid.

Frank Spilker, a fellow Wisconsin Catholic who got to mass about as often as the sun is eclipsed, of Germanic (not Irish) background, ribbed Herb unmercifully about the Irish, but Herb could hold his own. Except on bowling night.

Each Tuesday night the gang from the office went bowling. Herb was a born gambler at cards, but when it came to bowling, he took leave of his senses. F.A. would sucker Herb into one bet after the other. When Herb's first ball left a 7-10 split, F.A. said, "Bet you fifty cents you can't make it."

"What kind of odds you give me?" Herb would ask.

"Odds? Who needs odds? You're a bowler, aren't you?"

Herb always fell for this malarkey, and of course, he always lost. There aren't many professionals who can make 7-10 splits with any regularity.

Herb's one other soft spot was Marquette. Spilker would say, "Marquette (that's when Marquette still had a football team) plays Notre Dame Saturday. How you betting, Herb?"

Of course Herb was betting on that citadel of academic excellence on Milwaukee's Wisconsin Avenue, named after Father Marquette.

"What kind of odds you gimme?" (Here we go again,)

"Odds? Have you lost faith in your alma mater?

The Marquette bets invariably ended up even bets, which is another way of saying that F.A. always won. But when Herb could get F.A. in a poker game, he would win all of that bowling and football money back again. Herb did so well at poker that he would occasionally revert to his Marquette ways, "Set 'em up for the boys, bartender."

When Herb married Rosemary Clancy, they lived in Toledo for a short time. Then Herb transferred to our home office in Milwaukee. Herb and Rosemary had five children. The last one was born when Herb was on his deathbed with lung cancer. Rosemary died of cancer a few years later. The five kids were on their own. Both of the McCormack grandparents were gone. With the help of the Clancy grandparents, Herb and Rosemary's kids made it.

People at Home Office didn't take Herb seriously. His Irish banter and occasional soft shoe made him look a bit like a clown, and people didn't listen to what Herb had to say. What he had to say was that the company was operating with an antiquated inventory system that badly needed updating. The system was updated just as Herb had recommended, but long after Herb was gone. The poor guy never even had a chance to say, "I told you so."

## CHARLEY McCORMACK

Three of us roomed with the Steve Talapkas, in a lovely home just off of Berdan Avenue, and only a few blocks from Toledo Branch. There were Herb, Ray Morris who worked for a glass company, and me. The Talapkases were a fine Bohemian couple. Steve was retired. They lived on a modest pension and the room rent we paid them. Steve tried to augment his income by playing the numbers. He kept telling us, "Vun day I hit da nuuumber." The "vun day" never came, at least while we lived there.

One weekend we three singles drove to Milwaukee. We stayed with the McCormacks. Herb wanted to see his fiancée, Rosemary Clancy. They had not yet married. Herb got Ray a date, and I went out with a high school classmate, as we made the rounds of Herb's Marquette haunts.

While in Milwaukee, Works Manager Charley McCormack regaled us with stories of the old days in the A-C shops. Charley's feifdom included the Erection Shop, where the big stuff was assembled. On the south end of the Erection Shop, there stood a boring mill that had a forty-foot table. Allis millworkers could drill a thirty-five foot hole, twenty feet deep in one solid casting sitting on the boring mill table. There was a lathe that could handle a fifty-five foot long bar, one foot in diameter.

Charley McCormack told us that Allis-Chalmers had a number of firsts in America's economic history books. The company started a student training program in 1903. Before graduation, students interned in our Milwaukee shops. One of the graduates of this training program was Walter Geist, a man who later became president of Allis-Chalmers. Geist patented the Texrope Drive, a multiple V-belt drive system, used in textile plants. In old textile mills, an overhead line shaft with pulleys and long flat belts, drove the machinery. This system generated static electricity which raised havoc with the thread.

The first attempt at improvement moved an electric motor to the floor beside the machine. When one V-belt couldn't drive the load, Geist suggested a series of V-belts running parallel to each other. Appropriately, Geist called this drive a Texrope Drive.

Another Allis innovation was an employees' dining room, the first in the country. White-collar types didn't need to carry a dinner bucket anymore. A third innovation was an in-house program for alcoholics. "The company wanted to salvage its people, not fire them," Charley said.

Another Allis innovation was post-prom parties. I don't know that we were first in the nation, but we certainly were first in our geographical area. After a group of high school seniors were killed in an auto accident after a prom, the company offered to work with local civic groups to hold post-prom parties in the A-C clubhouse following six different high school proms in the area. On three weekends in a row, there were parties after Friday and Saturday night proms. After the young people left their proms about midnight, they came to our dining rooms where they were given red carpet treatment.

One year there would be a French theme, the next year, Polynesian. Local service clubs and company employees dressed in costumes to fit the occasion. There were soft drink bars, and our company orchestra provided music for dancing. No one left the party until dawn. Then the exhausted kids were driven home. That ended the alcoholic

## The WC, Our Workhorse Tractor

highway deaths after high school proms in our part of the world.

When we stayed with the McCormacks, Charley told us of the "old days" in the shop. There was a story about Thanksgiving turkeys that went something like this:

Each Thanksgiving, two shop workers wrapped some wiping rags in butcher paper, then hung a turkey head out of one end of the paper and turkey legs out of the other. The two, laden with their "turkeys," passed a new employee working at his machine. When the rookie employee saw two fellow employees carrying what surely looked like Thanksgiving fare, curiosity was aroused and questions were asked.

"Where did you get the turkeys?" the recently hired employee asked.

"Haven't you got your turkey yet?" came the reply.

"No. Where do you get them?"

"Oh, the company always gives turkeys away every Thanksgiving. Just go down to the tool crib."

The freshman employee wiped his hands, turned off his machine, then headed for the tool room. At the tool crib, a man behind the counter set the request for a turkey down on an order blank. "Single or married? How many kids? How old are the kids? This boy who's eight, is he a big eater?" Enough questions to make a bureaucrat blush with envy.

"Now take this order blank over to the treasurer's office and get it countersigned. After all, the treasurer has to pay for the turkeys.

The new employee trudged blocks and blocks to get to the treasurer's office. There a clerk countersigned the turkey requisition and told the newcomer, "Now take this to the general manager's office and get it signed. It's his idea to give away these turkeys, so he wants to see all of the orders." The general manager's office was way off in another direction.

After a clerk in the general manager's office signed, the rookie trudged back to the tool crib to get his turkey. "Aw, isn't that too bad? We just gave away our last turkey. Better luck next year."

Charley McCormack told us that this charade went on for several years before management stopped it. The hoax was time-consuming and costly.

Then Charley told us that after World War I, there had been an influx of German immigrants to Milwaukee, a good many of whom went to work for Allis-Chalmers. A constant heated argument raged in the shops about the relative quality of the German and American army and navy. Charley told us:

"They decided to find out once and for all which navy was the best. A rowboat race was arranged to take place on the lagoon in Juneau Park one Sunday afternoon in June. The navy vets from Deutschland were to race the navy vets from the U.S.A. But the U.S.A. navy vets didn't fight fair. They got to the German rowboat the night before and hung window weights to the bottom of the German rowboat.

"When the race was about to begin, the shores of the lagoon were lined with spectators. The starter fired his gun, and the race was on. Both boat crews started to pull on their oars. No crews on the Thames or Charles ever worked any harder. Soon the American rowboat outdistanced the German rowboat. The Yanks let up long enough to light cigars, then started to row again, coming across the finish line a block ahead of the Germans.

"One of the Kaiser's finest came to me the next day and said, 'I vouldn't haf beliefed it if I hadn't seen it mit my own two eyes.' "

## GLENN LAMB AND THE MIRACLE SOYBEAN

Glenn Lamb traveled our Northeast Ohio block from his farm near Wellington, Ohio. Our sales manager, F. A. Spilker, always accused Glenn of being only a part-time blockman. "You're spending too much time on that farm." Glenn insisted that his sons did all the farming. It is hard to imagine that anyone living on a farm wouldn't grab a pitchfork now and then, but Glenn probably spent less time working his farm than F.A. spent out at Sylvania Country Club knocking a little white ball around each Saturday and Sunday. Followed by a few hands of stud, of course.

F.A. continued to make life miserable for Glenn. Then Glenn discovered a soybean that would set as many as 500 pods on a stem. This miracle crop would certainly mean a pot of gold for someone, and Glenn couldn't think of a more deserving person to get that gold than Glenn Lamb. Glenn told Allis-Chalmers goodbye, only to find that the miracle bean didn't have the proper oil or meal content. It was a fluke! The bubble burst and Glenn Lamb became a full-time farmer.

## RUMORS CONFIRMED

Glenn Lamb left the Northeast Ohio block about the same time that Cope retired from the Saginaw block. Two blocks were opening up. Two new men would be needed. A rumor circulated around the office that I was to get one of those two blocks. The rumor was a little hard to believe since the company had never had a blockman as young as twenty-five, and I was twenty-five years old. I most certainly had never lobbied for the job.

Of course, I hoped the rumor was true. A blockman's income was three times what I was earning at the time, even if the block was one of our poorer blocks. If I got the job of blockman, I could finally afford to get married, and I had just met the most wonderful girl in all of the world at a church young peoples' convention at the Mayflower in Akron. At $110 per month, marriage was out of the question, but . . .

If the rumor was true, I figured I would get the Saginaw block since it was heavily populated with Germans and I spoke a halting Deutsch-verderber German, enough to get by anyway.

The rumor proved true all right, but instead of getting the Saginaw block I was assigned to Glenn Lamb's old block in Northeast Ohio where there were about three German-speaking farmers. Instead there were Hungarians, Bohemians, Finns, Liths, Estonians, Slovenians, Croatians, Bulgarians, Ukrainians, and Italians. During the next two years, I learned to speak broken English in a dozen dialects.

Two years to the day from the time I came to Toledo, I moved to the Cleveland block. A month later I proposed to the girl I had met at the Mayflower in Akron the previous May, and she accepted. We were to be married after my first bonus (commission) check arrived. I figured that would be June, at the earliest.

Once again the divine invisible hand moved in my direction. A flip of a coin had kept me in the farm equipment business in LaPorte. Now I was headed for the Cleveland block.

# PART THREE
# CLEVELAND

# 8

# HELLO AFFLUENCE, GOODBYE POVERTY!

When my 1929 Chevy arrived in Cleveland at the end of 1939, I stayed one night with a classmate. By the second night, I had found a room in Shaker Heights.

Having had dealer contact on a daily basis for four years, there were few illusions that I had to overcome as I started my work in northeast Ohio, in Lorain, Cuyahoga, Lake, Geauga and Ashtabula Counties. I knew before I started that the average farm income in Ashtabula County was around $600 per year per farm and in Geauga County it wasn't that good. I knew, without being told, that I would have to find farmers with more than average income if I was going to sell those expensive $525 and $960 tractors, and $545 combines we had in the line.

Every company in the industry had blockmen on the road, doing what I was about to do. We got up early and came home late. They had good dealers and poor dealers just as I had. We used our persuasion to get farmers to add to and improve on their mechanization. International Harvester Company, the leader in the industry at the time, not only had blockmen on the road, they had specialists too. IH had cream separator specialists, canvassers, and collectors. One luxury that International men didn't have was an automobile. They had to drive those IH pickup trucks that they just loved (grrrr) to drive.

Lorain County was my best county. I knew it and my competitors knew it too. They had built good dealer strength there. Earlier, Glenn Lamb had mixed a lot of nothingness in Lorain County with a dash of disaster. His dealer in Grafton had great sales ability, but Barney used that ability to sell Chevrolets and not Persian orange farm equipment. Glenn's dealer in Wellington had both farmers and bankers yelping, which predictably brought on an economic disease now called Chapter 11.

Cuyahoga County was mostly Cleveland with few parcels that could really be called farms. The big farm income in Cuyahoga County came from some five hundred acres of greenhouses where tomatoes and cucumbers were grown for the winter market. Greenhouse owners do not buy many tractors and even fewer combines. Lake County was heavily dotted with nurseries—Wayside Gardens was the big one. Nurseries have high per-acre income but they don't buy the dollar percentage of tractors to income that other farmers do, and they don't buy combines.

Geauga and Ashtabula Counties were almost solid dairy country. Milk brought from ninety cents to a dollar ten per hundredweight. The nice thing about dairy farmers was that they received monthly milk checks, not the once-a-year checks that Kansas wheat farmers received. Geauga county also had a thriving maple syrup business. There was a settlement of Old Order "hook and eye" Amish in Geauga County who were wonderful people but they bought no power equipment.

None of this came as any surprise to me for Glenn Lamb had documented it for me several times. There were minor irritations on the block, to be sure, but the job of blockman was one of the most envied in the business. Compared to other jobs, blockmen made money, lots of money!

The pay plan of a blockman in our company was a bit complicated, so pay attention. First, unlike a machinery clerk's salary of $100-110 per month, a blockman received a munificent salary of $131.25 per month. Don't ask me how they arrived at that figure. Then, there was a $13,000 "nut to crack." Translation: The first $13,000 of sales were non-commissionable.

After the $13,000, there was a two percent commission, based on net and not list price, paid quarterly on all cash sales. Since farmers did not buy much machinery in the wintertime, and since there was that $13,000 nut to crack, there seldom was a bonus (commission) check in the first quarter of the year. In the years when we had only tractors, implements, and grain harvesting machinery, the big bonus check of the year arrived about July 15. Later, when corn harvesting machinery and other items were added to the line, there were healthy bonus checks in the fall too. Still later, Uncle Sam offered investment credits to purchasers of capital goods. That brought the industry sizable business in December. Before investment credit though, December was as barren in the farm equipment business as ten acres of Gobi Desert. The 1986 Tax Deform & Simplification Act, 2,239 pages long, did away with that incentive for capital investment. It did away with the December bulge in farm equipment sales, and a lot of other capital goods sales as well.

Almost all blockmen in Toledo Branch did over $100,000 sales volume. A blockman who sent in $113,000

## Hello Affluence, Goodbye Poverty! 125

net received his salary of $1,575 per year, plus nothing for the $13,000, plus two percent on $100,000 or $2,000, a total of $3,575. In 1939, believe it or not, an annual income of $3,575 placed a person in the top ten percent of income earners in the country.

Beside salary and bonus, there was an expense account. We received a thirty dollar per month car allowance. I traded Chevys annually for $300, so I had sixty dollars left with which to pay for grease jobs, insurance, and license plates. That sixty dollars didn't quite pay the bill, so I was out-of-pocket about twenty-five bucks per year for my car. Gas and oil went on the expense account. Later, and before blockmen drove company cars, there was a per-mile car allowance.

Since the folks at Toledo Branch were always conscious of cost-of-doing-business figures, our expense accounts were not lavish by anyone's standards, dollar and a half hotel bills and meals that cost twenty-five and thirty-five cents were acceptable. Three dollar hotel bills were OK in big cities like Toledo, Detroit, and Cleveland. If an expense book went over $100 per month, we could expect to hear about it.

The last year Glenn Lamb was on the Cleveland territory, he had a sales volume figure of about $125,000. There was no good reason why I couldn't do as well, or better. In 1990, it was not unusual to see a tractor or combine priced $125,000. One machine, $125,000! In the 1940s, I had to build my $125,000 sales volume in $400 and $700 bits and pieces. Model B tractors and All-Crop Harvesters were about $400 net and WCs about $700.

Now let's look at dealer income in 1940. The year before I came to the Cleveland block, as was said before, block sales were about $125,000 or $12,500 per dealer on the average. That $12,500 is what they had to pay Allis-Chalmers. What a dealer could get over and above that $12,500 was his gross income. Theoretically, the dealer should have gotten a little over $4,000 gross income from sales of whole goods. List prices in 1940 were as fictional then as they are now. No sane and conscious farmer ever paid list price for anything, so chisel that $4,000 down some.

If there was a tradein involved, and invariably every tractor sale had a Fordson tradein as part of the deal, the remaining gross could not be realized until the tradein was sold. There were a few bucks to be made in the parts department, but the service department was invariably a loser, so those two departments tended to balance each other out. Allis was the only long-line company that did *not* give dealers a volume discount. Some of our competing dealers virtually gave their machinery away during the year, figuring that their end-of-the-year volume discount check would be a good yearly income.

Most of my dealers had some short line sales volume. They were hooked up with New Idea, or New Holland, or Surge Milkers, or Dunham Cultipackers, or a combination of these. New Idea had corn pickers, manure spreaders, rakes, and hay loaders that we did not have. George Delp's New Holland had hay machinery that we did not make. We did not produce or sell milking machines or dairy barn equipment. Dunham made cultimulchers and cultipackers, specialized tillage tools the likes of which we did not have in the book. There was a small firm in Bellevue, Ohio, that made Blackhawk corn planters. Most of my dealers sold those corn planters. So, add it all together, and there was a fighting chance for a dealer to make $5,000 per year net before taxes, a quite satisfactory income in 1939.

Farm equipment sales in the late 1930s and early 1940s wasn't exactly a get-rich scheme, but compared to most other activities, it wasn't bad either.

## THE STORE THAT SELLS MONEY

The success that Willis Scholl and John Walker had with bank financing of farm equipment sales has been mentioned before. When I left for Cleveland, Willis Scholl gave me good advice in this area. He told me, "You won't have all that much trouble selling machinery. Farmers all want to mechanize. It's money that's the problem. It may be harder for you to finance a machine than to sell it. Remember always, a bank is a store that sells money. It's not the Taj Mahal or St. Peter's. You need not genuflect. You are a customer. The bank cannot exist without customers. Place your hand on the president's door confidently. You are there to bring him business. He must have business to exist. After introductions and a brief discussion of the weather, ask the bank president for the bank's financial statement."

"A bank statement?" I asked.

"Yes, the bank's previous year's financial statement. That will shake the banker a bit. He'll wonder where a plow peddler ever learned to read a bank's financial statement. He'll wonder what information you want. But, because bankers are inordinately proud of their financial statements, he'll get one for you. When you look at the statement, look for two numbers—local loans/discounts and deposits. They will be called different things in different banks but they'll always be there.

"Once you've located those two figures, divide. Find out what the percentage is. If the bank is loaned out twenty-five percent, you can leave quickly. That banker only lends money to people who don't need it. He's only in the bank in order to stay away from his wife a few hours out of the day. You'll never do business there. If, on the other hand, the bank is loaned out sixty-five percent, you can leave quickly too. That banker loans money to every Tom, Dick and Harry who walks into the bank, provided that there's money to loan. If money is short, that banker will turn down J. P. Morgan."

Willis continued, "If the statement shows a bank that has a thirty-five to fifty-five percentage, dig in and *start selling!* That banker will say "no" at first, but he won't really mean no. He's just testing you to see if you've done your homework. He'll take all of the good deals you can give him, but he won't take junk. That banker will be a hard sell. He wants to be convinced that you're convinced, and that's good."

Willis had good advice about recourse too. "When a banker says that he will take the deal, but 'with recourse,' he wants your dealer to sign with the customer. If the customer doesn't pay, the dealer must. In other words, the banker wants to shift his risk to your dealer. If the customer skips town, the dealer is stuck. There are enough risks in the farm equipment business, so why should a dealer assume the banker's rightful risks too? Bankers should be big boys, big enough to judge a credit risk. That's their business. Our dealers should not have to double-guess them. Slip a couple of junk deals into the bank and the banker will require recourse on the next paper you bring into the bank, and rightly so. If you play fair with the banker, most will be fair with you."

All of this was good advice. I don't know what I would have done without it!

## THE GREATEST CRIME OF ALL—STOCK SHORTAGES

In the late 1930s and early 1940s, Allis-Chalmers and the farm equipment industry generally granted fifteen to eighteen-month no-interest terms on whole goods. No other industry was so liberal. Stupid might be a better word. The curse of the book publishing business was return privileges. The curse of the seed business was free seed to people whose crop froze or drowned out. The curse of the grocery business was no-profit sugar. The curse of the farm equipment business was those ungodly long terms. But what else could the industry do? Farming is a seasonal business, and farm equipment sales are just as seasonal. There's but one corn or bean or wheat crop each year, and, generally speaking, one crack at machinery sales for those crops each year. Dealers, emerging from the Depression, didn't have the resources to finance the iron in their warehouses and yards. The industry expected prompt payments for parts shipments on a monthly basis, but terms for whole goods went on and on and on.

We blockmen took inventory of tractors, combines, and implements in each dealership on a monthly basis. The steel might be in the dealer's possession, but it was company money that was tied up in it. If a machine was missing from inventory, it was due for payment *now*! The Dealer

Sales & Service Agreement said that machinery was due for payment the moment it was delivered. But that was easier said than done most of the time. A good 90 percent of the industry's dealers didn't have the money to pay for a machine that was out of inventory if the customer had not paid for it. Banks and Uncle Sam's PCAs took a little time to process time deals, so there were some gaps in the enforcement of the duc date rules.

At inventory time, if a machine was out of inventory and the money was not forthcoming, we were obligated to report that fact on our inventory sheet that went to the branch. This was typical: "WC, serial 12388, out of inventory—sold to John Dewey, Route 3 Box 44, Matin, Ohio—being financed at Matin State Bank—money expected Tuesday 5/4/40."

The company overlooked minor crimes like bank robbery, murder or rape, but it did not forgive stock shortages. Ironically, it was often the smartest man on the payroll who got caught in the stock shortage web. Dummies like me were just dumb enough to tell the truth. Brainy types often figured they could work around a shortage with a little temporary cover-up. Invariably the shortage pyramided. The dealer who knew that his blockman had covered-up on the inventory sheet had the blockman over a barrel. Soon there was a second stock shortage, a third and a fourth. Once begun, using A-C's funds to pay other bills became contagious.

There always came the day when the stock shortage was discovered and then, quicker than Liz Taylor saying "goodbye husband, hello friend," out the blockman went on his ear. Blockmen were all bonded, but I don't recall that the bonding company ever called the sheriff. Most stock shortages were eventually settled with proper funds.

By the time a blockman was promoted to sales manager of the branch, he could smell the signs of stock shortages a hundred miles away. When unreported stock shortages were suspected, the sales manager rushed out to the dealership, and if a cover-up was discovered, the guilty blockman was fired, and the sales manager took a mortgage on everything that was unencumbered in the establishment.

Only once did I have a persistent stock shortage on my block. It was properly documented, but that didn't make it go away. I had a dealer who also sold coal and coal stokers. I presumed that he had used my money to pay his coal bills. A local nurseryman had bought a tractor and paid for it, but I didn't get my money, just a bad check. I kept the bad check at the bank, hoping that one day it would be covered.

When the shortage dragged on, Sales Manager F. A. Spilker, came out to help me. He huffed and puffed and wrote up a document. He slammed it on the desk and said to the dealer, "Sign here." F.A. handed the note to me for collection. Then F.A. got in his car and went back to Toledo again.

I may have been a corn field rookie, but before the hour was over, it dawned on me that a note without a mortgage is worth just exactly what a bad check is worth—zilch, zero, big fat nothing! I wasn't one second closer to collection of that money. What to do?

Our Dealer Sales & Service Agreement had a clause that said that the company held title to a piece of machinery until payment was received by the company. The company lawyers who wrote that in the contract knew that it was 100 percent bluff. They knew very well that no judge in the country would take a paid-for tractor away from a farmer to satisfy a dealer's obligations. Those were still the days when the Supreme Court and lower courts were on the side of the people.

I knew the nurseryman who bought the tractor. I visited him, showing him the clause in the contract. I told him that I knew that he had paid for the tractor, but the dealer had not paid me. He predictably blew his stack. I told him, "Simmer down. I have no intention of trying to use that clause. I'm telling you because I want you to know what's going on. It won't hurt the dealer to think that I am going to bring the sheriff out here. Here's what I propose to do . . ."

After handing the nurseryman a box of cigars, I continued. "Today I will mail you a letter, threatening you with that clause, only you'll never see the letter. The original will go into the waste basket, but a copy of it will go to the dealer. He gets his mail about nine o'clock in the morning. About ten o'clock tomorrow I'd like you to call him and read the riot act to him, really raise the roof. I'm going to guess that we'll get action. At eleven, I'll go to the bank to see if my dealer made his bad check good."

The customer agreed to do as I had outlined. When I went into the bank at eleven, the banker said, "What in the world did you do to that dealer of yours? He came in here like a nudist who spilled hot coffee in his lap, nervous as a hog on ice, as if you had given him the turpentine treatment. He made his bad check good. Here's my bank check to cover the payment." I told the banker what the nurseryman and I had done.

He smiled. "Never heard that one before, and I thought I'd heard them all," the banker said as I left the bank.

It only takes one such episode to make a blockman wary of stock shortages. Burned once, a blockman will swear, "never, never, never again!"

## THE PEACEFUL CHAGRIN VALLEY

Going to work in the morning meant forty-five minutes of driving through no-customer country. If I drove west, I had forty-five minutes of cross-Cleveland driving in days before freeways. If I drove east, I had to cross the Chagrin Valley. The Chagrin Valley enriched the heart and soul, if not the bank account. We sold a little machinery there, but not much. The Chagrin Valley was sheer natural beauty interspersed by the once-great estates of Cleveland's wealthy citizens. They sat there like aging movie queens, dignified, but years past their prime.

The luxuries of a pre-income-tax age had provided beautiful big houses, lovely barns, and beautifully arranged outbuildings. One barn even sported a clock tower. These estates thrived in days of low-cost field hands and house servants. Few of the estates were maintained in their original splendor when I traveled the valley.

The publisher of the *Cleveland Plain Dealer* had a working farm in the valley. We sold him some equipment. Near Willoughby, Ohio, we visited a beautiful estate that had grown up in weeds. The man who farmed the farmland bought a small tractor from us. The big house on this estate was built of terra cotta and crystal. An earlier time patio deck on the east side of the house faced a million-dollar formal garden with statuary and fountains. One day, it must have been very beautiful, but now it was full of overgrown trees, hedges, bushes, and weeds. It was enough to make a person cry. The man who farmed the farmland told us, "The man who built this place was a powerhouse in the Republican Party. I remember political rallies out here when there were a dozen steers roasting on spits. That one-room log cabin over there is chinked in lead. It cost $20,000 to build. When the boys had a little too much to drink, they went back there, played cards, and slept it off."

At another estate we sold a Model B tractor to the gardener. This man lived in a ten-room house on the estate. His job was to place flowers daily in the rooms of the estate, the town house in Cleveland, and the New York City apartment. He shipped flowers to New York daily via air express. One greenhouse was devoted to orchids only, for the ladies' corsages.

As we entered the estate, we drove through an arched and turreted entrance. The arch was thick enough to provide room for a gatekeeper's small apartment above the entrance. Just inside the turreted entrance, there was a cobblestone area, surrounded by coach houses, harness makers' shops, coach builders' shops, carpenter shops, and other services needed to keep the place functioning. There was even a private four-hole golf course.

The estate belonged to one of the sons of Mark Hanna, the Republican kingmaker. *Forbes* said that Hanna was the "dollar mark" power behind William McKinley and James Garfield, both of whom had the misfortune of being assassinated. Marcus Alonzo Hanna found that if enough money was spent, a candidate could get elected. Hanna and his Republican friends had reasons to spend money to elect their candidate. Beginning in 1892, the opponent was William Jennings Bryan, the orator from the Platte whose silver tongue pleaded for "free silver," something the moneyed powers in the country believed spelled financial chaos.

Hanna orchestrated an unusual campaign for McKinley. While 1,400 orators worked the hustings, McKinley sat on his front porch in Canton, Ohio, and the people came to him. It was called the "front porch campaign."

Still another Hanna estate in the Chagrin Valley specialized in purebred dairy cattle. We donned white coats and white boots to enter the cow barn, and had to walk through a pool of disinfectant before we got to the cows. The farm manager asked us if we would like a drink.

"Which will it be, whiskey or milk? They cost about the same on this estate."

## LEWIE LIPPS, WEST VIRGINIA TRANSPLANT

Lewie Lipps was my highest volume dealer. This West Virginian, my dealer in Williamsfield, Ohio, was an ace salesman and a topnotch mechanic. During those late-Depression years, Lewie helped farmers scrape together enough money for a down payment on an All-Crop Harvester. Then he helped those customers to line up custom work at three dollars per acre. More often than not, the custom work paid for the combine in the first year of operation. This economic fact of life was not lost on custom work customers, many of who bought All-Crop Harvesters to duplicate the procedure the next year.

Lewie and all of my other dealers met plenty of sales resistance when they tried to make All-Crop Harvester sales. First it was the "wheat has to go through a sweat in the shock, you can't cut it from the standing crop" prattle. Then it was "I gotta have my straw." The threshing machine piled the straw behind the barn. Our combine left it in the field. Back then, farmers knew of no other bedding for cows and horses than straw. Today's farmers use everything from sawdust to shredded newspapers for bedding. To satisfy his customers and prospects, Lewie tried to get the straw in with a hay wagon and hay loader, but after about two feet of straw had accumulated on the wagon, both Lewie and the straw slid off of the wagon.

Then Lewie heard of a new one-man pickup straw baler that George Delp and his New Holland Machine folks in New Holland, Pennsylvania, had just placed on the market. Farmers in Lancaster County, Pennsylvania, had the same straw problem that we had. Three Pennsylvania Dutchmen in Lancaster County cobbled up a machine that used the header and pickup attachment off of an All-Crop Harvester to gather the straw, a bale chamber from a J. I. Case stationary hay press to compress the straw, a McCormick-Deering knotter to secure the bales, a couple of wheels, a tongue and a power-take-off and they had the world's first one-man pickup straw baler. Of course it baled hay too.

The folks at New Holland Machine Company built a one-lunger gas engine. When New Holland's George Delp saw this prototype one-man baler, he bought it. He added some more sophisticated engineering, then began to produce the machines. Lewie signed a New Holland dealer's contract the first year the New Holland baler was on the market. That ticked me off. Almost certainly this meant that Lewie would spread his meager finances still thinner. Any time he spent selling New Holland machinery was time that he would not devote to selling my products. It wasn't long, however, before I discovered that I had cried before I was hurt. When Lewie began to sell New Holland balers, that solved the Ashtabula County straw problem, and we began to sell a lot more All-Crop Harvesters. Thanks to Lewie and my other Ashtabula County dealers, we reached a ninety percent combine market penetration in that county. That figure held as long as I was on the Cleveland block.

Ashtabula County, by the way, was once part of the Connecticut Western Reserve. Yankee surveyors had it divided up into one mile squares. Eastern farmers mined the land which wasn't too good to start with and then departed. When the wave of Eastern European immigration came, those hardy people worked long hours in Cleveland to make enough money to place a down payment on an Ashtabula County farm. Some of them made it. Some of them didn't. Ashtabula County was a bittersweet sight—fine farms interspersed with land grown up in thorn apple trees and weeds.

Another thing that boosted All-Crop Harvester sales on our block was the soybean. My Indiana experience with the soybean told me that it was a lousy hay crop. Then I heard that grain elevators paid cash for beans. I asked at several places and was told, "Sure, we'll buy beans." We began to sell soybeans like mad. There was a reason for our soybean sales pitch. If we could get a farmer to plant soybeans, we knew we had a combine sold since the beans couldn't be harvested by the binder/thresher method. If a farmer planted soybeans, we had him painted into a corner.

By asking around, we gathered enough information about soybeans to be able to pose as experts, more expert than those farmers who had never heard of the crop, anyway. Nonchalantly we asked, "Do you plan to plant any beans this year? I understand they're paying pretty good prices over at the elevator in Andover."

Our soybean campaign eventually proved to be beneficial to all, but you couldn't have predicted that from first-year experience. Come harvest time, it rained and rained and rained. Frog-strangling, gully-washing rain!

Somehow we had to mud those beans out of the field. We tried tandem wheels on the combine. We tried duals. One farmer mounted barrels across the back of the machine to get the combine to roll over the mud. One farmer mounted mud boat floats beside the wheels and pulled the combine with a small crawler tractor. Fortunately, the next fall the weather was good, and more farmers planted beans.

Lewie Lipps wasn't the easiest man in the world to get along with, but the two of us hit it off famously. I learned rather early in the game how to get Lewie to do something. I would verbally presume in his presence that he couldn't or wouldn't do it. He would then break his back getting it done. I would say, "There's something that I would like to see happen. Naw, I better forget it. You can't do it."

"What can't I do?" Lewie shot back.

As I described the prescribed action, I continued to insert "naw-you-can't-do-it." The more I said that it couldn't be done, the more Lewie wanted to do it. It was a reverse type of selling, but it worked. It was like the salesman who says, "Let me show you something that your neighbor says you can't afford to buy." That works every time too.

One day a junk dealer pulled up to the store in a truck that was loaded with batteries. "I buy battreys, Meester. Gif you good price," he told Lewie.

"How much you gimme?" Lewie asked.

"Twenty cents apiece," the peddler said.

"You're trying to steal them," Lewie shot back.

## Hello Affluence, Goodbye Poverty!    139

"No, I'm not. Dot's da goink price. I sell you all da battreys on da truck for twenty-five cents," the itinerant battery purchasing agent protested.

"SOLD!" Lewie jumped at the opportunity.

The peddler immediately realized that he had made a pricing blunder. He hurried to his truck, but he was too late. Junior Lipps had taken the keys out of the truck and the boys from the shop unloaded a truckload of batteries. When the truck was unloaded, Lewie counted the batteries, multiplied by twenty-five cents and paid off the peddler.

Madder than an airline passenger who is in Baltimore and his bags are in Calcutta, the peddler threw the money to the ground. Just then Jess Crawford walked up. "What's going on here?" he asked.

"This man offered to sell me all of his batteries for twenty-five cents apiece," Lewie said. "I bought them and paid him, and then he threw the money on the ground."

Jess picked up the money, pocketed it, and walked away. "If he doesn't need it, I can use it," said Jess with remarkable candor.

Now the blue smoke came out of both the peddler's nostrils and ears. Junior Lipps handed him his truck keys, and the itinerant headed straight for the sheriff's office.

It wasn't long before Lewie had a visit from a deputy sheriff of Ashtabula County. "This man says you stole his batteries," the deputy said. "What happened?"

Lewie explained what had happened. "He offered to sell me his truckload of batteries for twenty-five cents apiece and I took him up on it." The peddler objected, but there had been too many witnesses.

"Nothing illegal about that," the deputy explained.

"But I didn't get da money," the peddler protested.

"Is that true?" the deputy sheriff asked.

"No, it's not true. I gave him the money, and he threw it on the ground. Jess Crawford over there picked it up and put it in his pocket."

"Nothing illegal about giving your money away. Not against the law to pocket unclaimed money," the deputy said, looking at the battery buyer when he said it.

The battery merchant left in a rage, but almost certainly he never ever offered to sell his whole load of batteries for twenty-five cents apiece again.

Lewie was shrewd. When he called on a farmer, he permitted the farmer to take him anywhere the farmer wanted to go to talk. "Where can we go and talk?" Lewie asked.

The farmer invariably took Lewie to a spot in the cow barn where he had talked to competitive dealers too. Casually, Lewie looked at all of the doorpost and doors to see if the previous dealer had left some telltale arithmetic behind. More than a few times, previous dealers left no-longer-secret figures where Lewie could memorize them. That gave Lewie an opening to make a little better deal with the farmer than his competitor offered.

One day I rode with Lewie in his "van," making farm calls. You would call it a van today, but actually it was a ten-year-old panel truck that had a grain sack for guest seating.

"Hey, there lives a guy who owes me some money that I haven't been able to collect," Lewie told me as the truck bounced along on Ashtabula County's washboard gravel roads. "Let's see if we can collect some money. You don't need to say that you're an attorney, but I'll pretend that you are."

The delinquent farmer didn't have cash with which to pay the past-due account, but he said, "I got a calf you can have." We went to the barn to look at the calf. Lewie asked my advice on this collection-in-kind proposal, and I said it was legal. He asked the value of the calf, and I disclaimed all knowledge of the value of veal-on-the-hoof. Lewie agreed on a figure, and the farmer helped us load the calf into the van. We headed for the store and as we bounced along, the calf backed up against me, lifted its tail and let go, all over my freshly cleaned and pressed suit.

Instead of getting sympathy from Lewie, he roared with laughter. He didn't even offer to pay for cleaning the suit. I didn't think it was funny.

Early in the game, Lewie taught me how to sell rubber-tired tractors. I was steeped with air-tired tractor enthusiasm, but farmers didn't share that fervor. Lewie said, "Sell 'em steel, that's what they want. Don't waste time sellin' 'em rubber. They're not gonna buy rubber. You could kill the deal."

So we sold steel wheels and got tractor orders. But Lewie didn't order any steel wheeled tractors from the factory, he ordered all rubber. When the tractors came in, one by one, he went to his customers and said, "Charley, your tractor ain't come in yet, but I got a load of rubber in this morning. Tell you what I'm gonna do. I'll bring one of them out and you go ahead and start plowin'. When your tractor comes in, I'll come out and switch wheels with you. Is that OK with you?"

Always it was OK.

Lewie delivered the rubber-tired tractor to the farm. After the farmer had plowed with it a few days, he would come into the store with a sheepish look on his face. "I think I'll just keep that rubber-tired tractor, if it's all right with you, Lewie. How much more do I owe you?"

Lewie said to me, "See, they sell themselves. You couldn't sell one of those guys in a hundred years, but they can sell themselves. Works every time. I have yet to have one man come in to ask when his steel wheels are coming in."

Pause here, you professional salesmen, and check back to see what Lewie did. He not only sold the customer what he wanted, but he sold the customer what he *thought* he wanted. He thought he wanted steel wheels, but what he really wanted was rubber tires. You just can't beat that sales technique.

Shrewd as Lewie was, one day we both flunked Marketing 101. A farmer near Andover asked, "How much for a WC without starter and lights?" We explained that, starting that year, starter and lights were standard equipment. We explained that since 90 percent of our customers had opted for starter and lights the year before, the company had just made them standard and had not raised the price. "You might say that you're getting the starter and lights free."

"Shoulda left 'em off and lowered the price," the farmer editorialized. "Look here, I may be getting older but I'm still strong enough to crank a tractor and I'm a good enough farmer that I can get my work done in the daytime. I don't need no (sizzle) starter and lights, y'hear?"

Had either of us been endowed with the brains that the Good Lord gives bird dogs, we would have said, "You are so right, Mister. The world is going nuts with these new-fangled ideas. We'll take off the starter and lights and lower the price thirty-five bucks for you." We could have thrown the lights, starter, wires and battery into the parts bins and come out way ahead on the deal. But we didn't have that much common sense. Neither of us.

Believe it or not, that farmer bought an International tractor *without* starter and lights and he paid eighty-five dollars more for it than the price we quoted, a price that included those frivolous options. The man was willing to spend an extra nine percent more money to prove to his neighbors that he could crank a tractor and that he could get his work done in the daytime.

Lewie and I laughed over our stupidity many times after that. A Pennsylvania Dutchman described us to a T when he said, "Ve get so oldt fast and so late schmart."

# 9

# THE WHITE SHEEP OF THE FAMILY

Barney Rothgery was my dealer in Grafton, Ohio. He was the white sheep of the Rothgery family. While the rest of the family had its trials, tribulations, and assorted difficulties, Barney became a millionaire in days when a million bucks was a lot of money instead of small change in a senatorial campaign.

When I speak of Barney as a dealer, I use the word dealer loosely, since Barney did very little dealering for me. His calendars read: "Cadillac, Hudson, Studebaker, Chevrolet, Allis-Chalmers, and Horses Too."

Barney was the most congenial man I ever met. He had a permanent smile on his face. He was always there "with the encouraging word." Even though he was not a young man, he always ran up the stairs to his mezzanine office two steps at a time.

Barney knew the auto business like the proverbial book. He had started as a Ford auto dealer selling the $345 Model T cars that Henry Ford began to build in 1917. Despite Barney's encyclopedic knowledge of the auto business, he never did learn to find his way through a farm equipment price book. When he had a prospect, he would call me for catalog numbers and prices.

It was impossible to get mad at the man, but I did get frustrated when he sold so little. I told him, "Barney, you're not worth a hoot to me." He then placed his arm around me, smiled and said, "I know it. I know it." Next came a final pat on the back, and he would bound up to his mezzanine office two steps at a time.

Barney loved horses. Most dealers shied away from horses as if they were carriers of a deadly virus, but not Barney. He had the facilities on his farm to care for them. Other dealers didn't have barns and pastures for tradein horses, nor did they have the mentality of a horse trader. Most of the business that Barney gave me was horse tradein deals.

One day Barney sold a Model B tractor and took two hogs in on trade. While Barney had plenty of room for horses on the farm, he was not equipped to house hogs. He told the farmer to keep the hogs at home. "If I don't get them sold right away, you can have one of the hogs for your trouble." One day the farmer came into the store with a funereal face.

"Barney, I got some bad news for you."

"Oh?" Barney wondered.

"Your hog died," the farmer exclaimed.

"Think nothing of it. Those things happen," Barney consoled the customer.

Afterward Barney told me, "I got to wondering how he knew it was my hog that had died, and not his." When I recall Barney's dead hog story, I also recall the Arkansas farmer whose mule died. He exclaimed, "Funny, it's the first time the critter ever done that."

Although Barney was a wealthy man, unquestionably the wealthiest man in Grafton, he could make little use of his money. He spent at least twelve hours a day in the store. His wife had emotional problems that incapacitated her. She called Barney every few minutes over the most trivial things. His answers over the phone were always courteous.

"Yes, I know, Cora. That's all right, Cora."

Barney never left town. He would not leave his wife with anyone else, even for overnight. He imprisoned himself in Grafton but he never showed a smidgen of regret. Never an unkind word. Never a complaint. "Kinder and gentler," George Bush would say. Barney Rothgery gave me one of life's richest experiences, even if he didn't give me much business.

## PLOWMAN'S FOLLY

Ed Faulkner posted a letter in Elyria, Ohio, addressed to our home office in Milwaukee. They bucked the letter to Toledo and Toledo sent it to me.

I visited with Ed on a rainy April morning in 1941. We stood in the open doorway of Ed's garage and talked as the rain played a tattoo on the roof. Ed envisioned the disappearance of the plow. Ed's observation, "No one has ever advanced a scientific reason for plowing," was widely quoted as Blacksmith Jack Deere and Plowman J. P. Oliver turned over in their respective graves. Ed wanted Allis-Chalmers, a plow manufacturer, to finance his no-plow experiments. That was like asking General Motors to pay for research aimed at eliminating the family car.

Ed told me that the American plow had built an impenetrable hardpan that did not permit the water to come up or the roots to go down. Ed believed in plow-down cover crops, oops, make that disc-down cover crops, to build tilth in the soil. Ed's tillage tool was the disc harrow, not the plow. He was on the track of no-tillage, but was not quite there. Ed's detractors said that the disc harrow would cause as much hardpan as the plow.

At the time I visited with Ed Faulkner I still felt the plow was ordained by God and was therefore sacred. To put it mildly, there was no meeting of the minds in that open garage door in Elyria, Ohio, that day. I can be as closed-minded as the next guy.

If Ed Faulkner could not convince me and others like me, he did convince Louis Bromfield, author and lord of the manor at Malabar Farms near Mansfield, Ohio. When I lived in Cleveland, I finally discovered the Cleveland Farmers' Club, an adjunct of the Chamber of Commerce. At the first luncheon meeting I attended, Bromfield was the speaker, and there he supported Faulkner's no-plow farming. It was widely rumored that it was Louis Bromfield and not Ed Faulkner who wrote *Plowman's Folly* despite the fact that Ed's name was on the cover.

Ed told me about his experiments on Barney Rothgery's farm, something that Barney had not mentioned to me. Ed promised Barney the first 300 bushels of potatoes per acre from a small plot on the Rothgery farm. He would take what was left over after Barney got his 300 bushels.

I asked how many potatoes were left over. Ed replied, "The operation was a success but the patient died." He said he didn't come close to 300 bushels, but insisted that his theory was as valid as the dew. Capsuled, Faulkner's theory was this: Disc down the fall residue and plant wheat. In the spring, disc down the wheat to add tilth to the soil, then plant corn or soybeans. Never use a plow.

In every century since the plow was invented, there have been detractors who pointed out the folly of picking up millions of tons of topsoil, turning that topsoil over and dropping it again. No-plow theory runs headlong into the inescapable fact that farmers like to plow! Or at least they did in 1941. When the first warm days of spring arrived, there was nothing as soul-satisfying as getting on a tractor and turning over the good earth to form a seed bed for crops to come. During my days on the Cleveland block, farmers took pride in perfectly plowed fields, not a weed or stalk uncovered by soil. They took pride in perfectly straight plow furrows.

Since Ed Faulkner, Louis Bromfield, and *Plowman's Folly*, field cultivators and chisel plows have come to the tillage scene. Midwest farmers began to dig deep to bust up the hardpan just as California farmers had done for many years. Slowly but surely, a little trash on the surface was a sign of wisdom instead of sloth. Farmers began to count the toll that soil and water erosion took each year.

Later, I too became a convert to minimum-till and no-till, but in 1941 I was still firmly in the cheering section for plowmen. After my visit that rainy April day in 1941, I never met Ed Faulkner again. He and Bromfield caused quite a flurry with *Plowman's Folly*, but the flurry quickly subsided. They had come to the farm scene twenty years too soon.

## GILBERT MEYERS

Gilbert Meyers operated a small grain elevator and feed store plus a slaughter shop and retail meat market when

## The White Sheep of the Family

I got to know him and signed him as my dealer in North Kingsville, Ohio. Glenn Lamb had willed me a dealer in Ashtabula who had no parts and said he did not ever intend to stock parts. I parted company with that man quickly, then found Gilbert. Gilbert's long suit was that he could take livestock in on trade when he sold a tractor or combine. Livestock or grain. The cow, pigs, or wheat added up to a nice down payment. Livestock traded in went through Gilbert's slaughter shop and retail meat market. Grain traded in went through the elevator and into the grain trade.

Gilbert had the uncanny ability to guess a cow's weight on the hoof, give or take five pounds. He always asked the farmer to select the cow that was to be traded in. Gilbert told me once, "I do it this way because they almost always unknowingly give me their best cow."

The business office of the firm was the dining room behind the meat market, where Mrs. Meyers held forth as business manager. She kept the books, and I mean that literally. Time after time, we sat late into the night trying to reconcile a sixteen-cent discrepancy. Gilbert and I would have flipped a coin to see who should pay the sixteen cents, but not Mrs. Meyers. She did not countenance easy outs. She operated as if Price Waterhouse was looking over her shoulder twenty-five hours out of every twenty-four.

Each time I called on Gilbert, we went to the country to call on prospects. The moment we got into the house and Gilbert was seated, he fell asleep. I did all of the talking, waking him when it came time to discuss tradein prices. Staunch Republican that he was, Gilbert joined others on the special train from Cleveland to Elwood, Indiana, to hear Wendell Willkie's acceptance speech in 1940. Willkie never mentioned it, but it's my guess that Gilbert fell asleep during the acceptance speech.

Gilbert Meyers wasn't long on service. In the feed and meat market business, there is very little mechanical service, so he did not have the kind of background that would qualify him for farm equipment service. One day Gilbert told me that he had sent a serviceman to a farm near Geneva to answer a complaint on a tractor for which I had received payment, but for which he had not received his money.

Gilbert unfolded this sad tale about the tractor: On a Saturday, just before noon, a farmer and the farmer's neighbor lady came into the store. They wanted a Model B tractor and a 16-inch plow delivered in two hours, in order to surprise the lady's husband who was coming home from work from the Perfection Stove Company in Cleveland. Gilbert's men took the new tractor out of the barn, assembled the plow without first removing the warehouse grime and pigeon droppings. Gilbert's delivery man headed for Geneva and met the deadline. After he dropped off the tractor, he loaded the cow that had been traded in and took it to Gilbert's hamburger factory, where the animal was promptly butchered.

Gilbert told me that after he got a call from the lady in Geneva, he sent a serviceman over to see what could be done. He told me, "That woman is crazy. She threw my serviceman's tools out into the alfalfa field. She belongs in the loony bin." I paid little attention until I received a letter that this woman had written to our home office in Milwaukee. Those sorts of letters get filtered back to the man on the territory. I told Gilbert to give me a serviceman and we would go over to see what could be done. The letter spoke of "No-good spark plugs, no-good radiator, no-good tractor" and there were unkind four-letter remarks about Gilbert, accusing him of selling a secondhand tractor.

We found the woman (let's call her Clara) and her husband in the chicken coop, where they were performing some clean-up functions. "Did you write this letter?" I asked sternly. Yes, she had written it. "Clara, you claim that Meyers sold you a used tractor. I happen to know that the tractor was brand new. It went from the railroad car to the barn to your farm. It may have looked used, but you insisted on two-hour delivery time so there was no time to clean up the tractor. If you tell people that Meyers did not sell you a new tractor, you are slandering his good reputation. Slander is illegal. Meyers could make trouble for you."

I told Clara, "Let's see the tractor." When we arrived at the barn, the serviceman drove the Model B out into the open. He drove it around in a circle several times and then I motioned the driver to head for the road. The tractor was not paid for. Possession is nine points of the law. Clara, guessing what we were doing, tried to throw herself in front of the tractor but failed. Then she headed for the serviceman's tool box and started to throw his tools out into the hayfield. She pounded the fender of the truck, shouting, "No-good tractor. Meyers cheat the poor people. No-good radiator. No-good spark plugs. Meyers gyp the poor people." There were some choice four-letter words.

The discussion about "used tractor" continued. Clara's husband said, "I didn't say it was used, but the neighbor said it was used." He meant the neighbor who had accompanied his wife when she bought the tractor.

"Which neighbor?" I asked.

"That farm over there," the man pointed north.
"Let's go over and see that farmer," I suggested.
"He's not at home," the lady said.
"Yes, he is," I interjected. "He's over there tying up grapes."

The discussion at the neighbor's house was about the shabby appearance of the tractor. The neighbor told us what the lady meant by "no-good spark plugs . . . no-good radiator." It seems that the porcelain on one of the spark plugs cracked and the radiator had sprung a pinhole leak. We were getting nowhere, so I suggested, "Let's go over and do some plowing. If the tractor plows OK, let's go to the bank and get the money for the tractor."

Just as the demonstration began, rain strted to fall and my new clothes were drenched. That rain was as welcome as flowers in May because the land was terribly dry, and we consequently plowed up clods the size of boulders.

After we had all satisfied ourselves that the tractor worked like a tractor should work, we headed for the bank. At the bank, Mr. Searles, the president of the bank, said, "Clara, I thought that you had given up the idea of buying a tractor. I put the deal away. It's in the back room. I'll have to go to get it out." Mr. Searles returned with the file. He filled out the papers, had them signed, and asked who the check should be made out to.

Just then Clara popped her lid again. She pounded Mr. Searles's desk, shouting so everyone in the bank could hear, "No-good Meyers. No-good tractor. Cheat the poor people. No-good radiator. No-good spark plug." Mr. Searles looked as if he was in a slight stage of shock. I said, "Make the check out fast. I'll be back to explain."

In front of the bank, I proposed, "You now have a good

tractor and we have our money and everybody should be happy. Clara, I think it's time for a drink. I'll buy." We headed for the nearest watering hole.

The four of us were seated around a table. Clara's husband ordered a beer and so did the serviceman and I. Clara ordered a boilermaker and a helper. It appeared that she had mellowed. Clara told me, "You good guy. You make tractor work. We need hay loader. You come sell us hay loader." And then fortissimo, "Meyers, he no good. Cheat the poor people. No-good radiator. No-good spark plug. Gyp the poor people." Clearly, this woman was of the impression that Gilbert Meyers did not love the poor people in the same way that Lyndon Johnson did, when he eliminated poverty for all time.

I tossed the money for the tip and the bar bill on the table and got out of there! I hoped that one of our nice competitors would get that hay loader deal.

Gilbert seemed to attract female problem customers. I got a buck slip (that's a memo from the boss) that told of a lady near Ashtabula who had trouble with the planter she bought from Meyers. A serviceman and I went over to check the planter. She had come to Ohio from Georgia, was engaged as a janitress at a local theater. I looked into the seed cans of the planter.

I asked, "What's this you have in the seed can?"

"Ah jess found me some corn and beans an decided Ah was gonna plant me some succotash," she explained. Planter plates were sized to seed. To that time, nobody had invented a succotash plate.

Then there was a Finnish lady who bought a tractor. The tires were checked. Back in the days of natural rubber, all tires checked with very small hairline checks once the tire was in the sun for a few hours. I tried to explain this to the farm wife, but she wasn't convinced. Like our friend in Geneva, she figured that Meyers had sold her a used tractor.

In desperation, I took a gamble. We had just received a carload of tractors from the factory. They sat on the siding and had not yet been unloaded. I told the Finnish lady, "We got a carload of tractors in this morning. Come with me and I'll show you that the tires are checked on those tractors that just came from the factory." I kept my fingers crossed as we drove to the railroad siding. "Please, Lord, decorate those tires with checks." Sure enough, all ten sets of tires were checked. The customer was satisfied!

### WHO WAS THAT NUT IN OUR TOWN SQUARE?

It was one of those evenings in North Kingsville when Mrs. Meyers and I tried to reconcile our accounts after Gilbert and I made a couple of after-supper calls on farmers. The hour grew late before I headed home. When I came through Thompson on my way home, about three inches of snow covered the ground.

In the middle of the town square, Thompson, Ohio, had a maple syrup camp surrounded by majestic maple that were tapped just before the annual Maple Syrup Festival.

I remembered coming into Thompson, but I remembered nothing more until moments later when I found myself inside that town square, making three-inch tracks in the snow through the maple sugar camp area. Miraculously, I had missed all of the big maple trees. Since I had arrived at the point of no return, I kept right on driving through the square.

Almost surely the good merchants of Thompson said to each other the next day, "What kind of nut do you suppose it was who drove smack dab through our town square? He must have been drunk." I wasn't drunk. Worse than that, I was asleep. I was the kind of nut who doesn't pull over when he's sleepy. A drunk has some control over a car, but a driver who's asleep is a time bomb waiting to go off.

Since then, if I'm sleepy, I pull over and sleep, regardless of the time of day or night or the location. I recommend the same to you. You may not be lucky as I was. You may hit those maple trees in the square. Folks will walk slowly behind you and the pastor will have kind things to say.

## FARM SUPPLIES & POWER EQUIPMENT COMPANY, INCORPORATED

Say that fast five times and you'll never need nasal decongestant again. Write that tongue-twisting firm name a couple hundred times and you will wish your dealer would have called himself Ace Supply. At least something more abbreviated than Farm Supplies & Power Equipment Company, Inc.

John Balazs (pronounced Blaze) operated on the south side of Cleveland. His big sales volume came from vegetable farmers who bought our small tractors, Planet Jr. garden tractors, plus all of the other equipment that market gardeners use.

John's used machinery lot was a rusting fairyland of vintage equipment arranged in random fashion, interspersed with ragweed and other obnoxious vegetation. Even though the war (World War II) effort called for every bit of scrap iron that could be found, John resolutely kept his junk yard intact. His jewels continued to rust down. Most dealers entered World War II with used machinery on hand. Since there was a high demand for anything that would run, used lots were cleaned out pretty fast. But not the used lot at Farm Supplies & you-know-what. Farmers weren't desperate enough to buy John's rusty debris. It was older than they were.

Johnson (I don't recall that I ever heard his first name) was John's salesman; a little fellow, with a bewitching friendly smile frozen on his face. Johnson would have been a good salesman but for one fault. He was always late. I wish I had a buck for every time I heard, "You said you would be here last Tuesday. Since you didn't show up, I bought something else." I should have kept track. No, I'm glad I didn't.

Johnson's strong point was that he could get a farmer into the cab of his pickup and while he talked, he wrote up the order on a clipboard that he leaned against the steering wheel. Before the farmer knew what was going on, an order was all written up awaiting signature. Johnson tore up a lot of unsigned orders, but he got a lot of signed ones too. He was a good salesman.

**HONOR AMONG THIEVES**

When I made my first rounds of my new territory, I found a #56 cultivat-or in stock at Farm Supplies & Power Equipment Company. I knew the history of this antique. Our engineers designed a cultivator heavy enough to grub stumps in the Mississippi Delta. When I was assistant machinery clerk at LaPorte Branch, three orders for #56 cultivators crossed my desk. The #56 cultivator would narrow down to 27-inch rows, something our standard cultivator would not do without bending the hangers. The Thumb of Michigan had sugar beets and navy beans, all in 27-inch rows. Grat thought that just maybe the #56 cultivator would be the answer to our problems in the Thumb. Somehow, dealers managed to peddle two of the three cultivators that were shipped there. A third remained in inventory and was transferred to a new dealer every time the due date came up in the dealership it last inhabited. When Toledo Branch opened, the Thumb of Michigan was part of our territory. We not only inherited the Thumb, we inherited that bewhiskered #56 cultivator.

Now this ancient piece of bent and rusted steel had migrated clear down to Cleveland, Ohio. I asked John Balazs how he ever managed to get the thing that was in even worse shape than I dared to anticipate. John said he had asked Grat for a narrow-row cultivator for vegetables. Grat, obligingly, shipped the monstrosity to Cleveland, where it started our 18-month terms all over again. Allis had the despicable habit of never charging anything off, so inevitably there would be a due date, probably before John could find some blind, deaf, and dumb vegetable farmer, who had taken leave of his senses, to take it off his hands.

I asked Grat about the transfer, but he gave me no consolation. "John wanted a narrow-row cultivator, so I shipped him one," Grat said.

"Yes," I shot back, "he wanted a narrow-row cultivator for radishes and carrots. He sure didn't need something heavier than the anchor on the Titanic. That's like sending a semi to the post office to pick up the latest Book-of-the-Month." Grat just laughed. To me, it was no laughing matter. I could not in good conscience ask either a farmer to buy the wreck or ask John to pay for it, even if he had the money, which he did not.

The Children of Israel had the good fortune of having Moses open the Red Sea to let them pass through on dry land. John Walker was my deliverer. John's territory included the jack wax clay of Paulding County. Jack wax calls for *heavy* machinery. The #56 cultivator was heavy. At a sales meeting, John mentioned that his dealer, Gary Schmidt, had spotted the #56 cultivator in the price book and was impressed by its weight. He thought it might be the answer to Paulding County clay. John asked me if I knew anything about the #56 cultivator.

"Sure do! Waddya wanna know?" I told him. I lied through my teeth, "We use 'em all the time. Don't tell me you're not selling 'em." John asked if I had any in inventory. He said that Gary had a retail order for a #56 cultivator. I told John that I had just one left; that since we were such good friends that I would be glad to ship the cultivator to Continental, Ohio, because we had another carload order for #56 cultivators in the hopper. For the record, lightning did not strike me dead on the spot for telling those big fat lies.

"Would you ship me that cultivator of yours?" John requested.

"Be glad to," I told him. He never knew how glad I was.

In three milliseconds, I had my Chevy in high gear headed for Farm Supplies & Power Equipment Company. Arriving an hour before closing time, we gathered the pieces of iron, bent, paint off, rusted, shovels worn out, and we stuffed the pieces into gunnysacks. What wouldn't go into the sacks, we wired together with baling wire. John Balazs's truck took the shipment directly to the truck terminal rather than wait until the freight line's truck came the next day. We wanted that cultivator on its way, just in case John Walker changed his mind.

At our next sales meeting, John said something like "Let's have a little honor among thieves."

Of course, Gary Schmidt blew a fuse when he saw that cultivator that had once been a gleam in a LaCrosse Works engineer's eye. Fortunately, Gary was resourceful. He steam cleaned the pieces, straightened those that were bent, and replaced the worn-out shovels with brand new ones from his parts bins. A new coat of Persian orange paint made the cultivator look respectable again. Gary delivered the implement and the customer was pleased. As time went by, Gary ordered more #56 cultivators from the factory.

And everybody lived happily ever after!

## 10

# DEAFNESS CAN BE A VIRTUE

Mr. Quail, a man in his 80s, did the selling and Mr. Quail's son-in-law, Sam Deise (pronounced Dice) did the service work at my dealership in Chagrin Falls, a suburb to the southeast of Cleveland. Mr. Quail had spent many years selling International Harvester Company farm equipment. Sam Deise had been the farm manager for the Van Swerigens at their farm southeast of Cleveland. The Vans were two bachelors who owned a dray horse and wagon that they pyramided into the ownership of two railroads, Shaker Heights, and half of downtown Cleveland.

Sam and his father-in-law couldn't work together, but then on the other hand, they could ill afford to work separately. Their cat-and-dog verbal fights were a spectator sport at Quail & Deise. Mr. Quail was conveniently deaf. If a farmer whispered in the back room that he intended to buy a tractor, Mr. Quail could hear that in the front office. However, if a farmer asked for a little more money for his tradein, Mr. Quail would say, "I'm glad that you're happy with my offer. Here's where you sign." Farmers shook their heads, and signed.

The clientele of Quail & Deise varied from near-penniless Geauga farmers to rich Cleveland business and professional people who farmed in the county because they loved the land. The odd thing was that when you saw this assorted group of people gathered around the stove at Quail & Deise, you couldn't tell which group was which. All were dressed the same and all spit on the hot stove.

The groups differed in one way though. If there were past dues, you could bet that it would be the wealthy customers who didn't get their checks in the mail. Mr. Quail was often beside himself when he couldn't collect for machinery that had been delivered. One broker who occupied one whole floor in a downtown bank building in Cleveland resolutely refused to answer the phone or give the slightest inkling of payment plans. Letters to him were completely ignored. Mr. Quail had to borrow money and pay interest in order to accommodate the broker's past due account.

When customers came for parts, Sam Deise had the uneconomic and unforgivable habit of saying, "This will be a charge, won't it?" Put that way, of course it was a charge. One customer pulled me to the side to tell me, "Can't you break Sam of that habit of 'this will be a charge, won't it?' I come in for parts and have the money in my pocket to pay for them. Then I end up charging the parts and find some other way to spend the money. When I can least afford it, here comes Sam's invoice for the parts." I told the customer that I had worked hard at reform, but, to that point, had failed miserably. Sam was philanthropic without the means of philanthropy.

One Saturday morning, one of the men around the stove told us, "I sure hit it right this year." He had watched the weather reports in the newspaper. This was long before TV newscasters or *USA Today* showed the nation's weather. He saw a warming trend moving from the southwest, so he tapped his maple trees weeks earlier than usual. He predicted correctly that maple sap would run early that year. The early maple syrup brought double and triple prices from Cleveland hotels and restaurants.

I generally called on Quail & Deise on Saturday, when all the business crowd from Cleveland had the weekend off and came into the store. For instance, there was Doc Swam who owned a small hospital. Doc bought an All-Crop Harvester that he intended to pull with his Cletrac tractor. Cletrac (contraction of Cleveland Tractor) was a little crawler tractor built by King White about a mile from our home in Cleveland. City farmers knew King White (a brother of the White who built trucks, another who made sewing machines, another who manufactured band instruments), and because of that mutual friendship, they bought tractors that they had no more use for than "teats on a boar," as Grat used to say. Crawler tractors were nuisances that were not permitted on the roads of the area.

When we found that an All-Crop was going to be pulled by a Cletrac, I took the serial number of the tractor and went to the factory. You never knew what kind of power-take-off speed had been built into the tractor. The All-Crop Harvester and other power-driven pull-type machines in the industry were built to run at a speed of 545 revolutions per minute on the drive shaft. That was the American Society of Agricultural Engineers standard.

At the factory, a clerk checked the records to see if what PTO speed had been built into that particular serial number. If it wasn't 545, I brought back the parts necessary to change it to 545 rpm.

Sam told Doc not to touch the combine until he got there, but Doc just couldn't wait. He hooked the combine to the tractor and started it up. Luckily, Sam got there just after that happened. The combine was going at about twice the speed it was built for; it sounded like a 747 taking off. Sam shut things down immediately and checked to see if any damage had been done. He found that the cylinder bar holes that held the bolts that held the cylinder bars in place were becoming cup-shaped. Had Doc run that machine a few more minutes, one of those cylinder bars would have come flying through the top of the combine. We would have had a cylinder bar in space before John Glenn got there. Sam went back to the shop to get a new set of cylinder bars, I went to Cleveland to get the Cletrac parts needed to slow Doc's tractor power-take-off down.

**GRANDMA KULP**

When Harry Merritt bought the Birdsell Clover Huller, he received a considerable amount of inventory, and with the inventory came Harry Kulp. It was Harry's job to dispose of the last of the Birdsells. When Willis Scholl moved into Toledo Branch as sales manager, Harry Kulp took Willis's place on the Adrian, Michigan, block. He had sold all of the remaining Birdsell Hullers.

The name "Grandma" was hung on him by his dealers and fellow blockmen. Harry whined about myriads of details, using a very monotonous tone of voice. Harry was not the type that authors of you-too-can-be-a-leader books point to with admiration. But year after year, Harry beat all of us, or almost all of us, in sales volume.

When dealers saw Harry coming in the front door, they tried to escape through the rear door. Despite all this, Harry was a moneymaker for his dealers. He prodded his dealers into doing all of the right things by just wearing them down.

Dealers knew better than to ever take Harry out on a retail deal, because his incessant droning was the quickest way to kill a sale.

It's hard to believe that anybody could get into trouble by saving the company's money, but Harry managed. His expense books looked like the widow's mite. All other expense books, meager as they actually were, looked like the expense accounts of a senator on a junket to Monte Carlo. Grat and F.A. expected at anytime that some watcher-of-the-purse in Milwaukee would point to Harry's expense books as a standard of excellence. Then the rest of us would have had to swallow part of our travel expenses, and Grat and F.A. knew what kind of revolution that would start.

I can still hear Grat telling Harry, "But don't you *ever* eat a meal on the road? You never charge for one." Each time Harry promised to mend his ways and spend more of the company's money, but each time he backslid three months later. Once again Harry's expense book, that included a $30 per month car allowance, was under $50.

Harry is gone now, but the memory of an unusually dedicated business manager remains.

## JOHN WALKER

Unorthodox, one-of-a-kind John Walker hailed from a farm near Avoca, Iowa. He was our blockman on the Van Wert, Ohio, block.

When John was still in Iowa, he worked for Red Gibson (I'm guessing at that last name) who sold Chevrolets in Avoca. Red also sold Allis-Chalmers farm equipment and John was the Farm Equipment Division of the firm.

One day Red told John, "I've traded for an old International 10-20; traded it in on a pickup. Its motor is pretty well shot, but a guy twenty miles north of here said he would pay $200 for it. If you can deliver it and get the money, you can keep half of the $200. Because the motor is worn out, you can't crank the tractor to get it started. You'll have to belt it up here in the shop to get it started and haul it out to the farm with the motor running, otherwise you'll never get the thing unloaded. Deliver the tractor, get the money, and get out of there fast."

John did as instructed. Near the potential buyer's farm, John backed the truck into the ditch, thereby tipping the truck bed so that he could unload the tractor. He drove the tractor into the farmer's barnyard, then knocked on the door. John told the farmer, "I got the tractor you bought. Could you pay me so that I can get to a funeral in Avoca on time?" The farmer looked the tractor over, then went to the house for his checkbook. He tried to write the check on the rear fender of the tractor, but the 10-20 was shaking so much that he went around to turn off the engine.

"Oh, don't turn it off," John said. "I understand this tractor has just been overhauled. We're running it in. Let it run for another hour or two before you turn it off."

The farmer found another place to write the check. When John was handed the check, he thanked the farmer and left, right now!

Several years later John and Red were driving through the country north of Avoca. Red pulled into the lane of the farmer with the 10-20. John screamed! "Do you want to get me killed?" Red just laughed. When the farmer came out, he took one look at John and said, "I understand it has just been overhauled. Let it run for an hour or two to break it in. That tractor was loose as a goose and you knew it. You didn't gyp me as bad as you thought you did. I spent $52 having it overhauled, used it two years, and sold it for $50 more than I had invested in it."

One fall, after All-Crop Harvester production had ceased for the year, John was down to one machine left in inventory on his whole block. He drove past a farmer's place where he had tried to sell a combine for two years, but without success. There were people in the clover field surrounding a John Deere combine. John took a jar of clover seed from the back window of his car and went inside the gate and sat on a big rock. Finally the farmer came over to tell John that he had decided to buy a John Deere combine, all of which was pretty obvious. John said he had guessed that, and that he had just left (he lied) a farm where he had started an All-Crop Harvester in clover. "Took us about fifteen minutes. Here's a sample I took out of the bin."

"The servicemen are making some final adjustments. We'll be running in a few minutes," the farmer said. John said he would wait, out of the way of the people who had the responsibility of getting the green machine running.

An hour later the farmer came back again, repeating that it would be a few minutes now and they would get the combine running.

An hour later it was lunch time so John went into town to eat, and on the way back, he bought a case of beer. He returned to the rock and set the beer down alongside the rock.

The farmer came over and repeated for a third time that it would be a few minutes now, and they would get the machine running. John said, "As long as I've shot the day,

## Deafness Can Be a Virtue

I'm gonna stick around until it is running. Here, take some beer over to the guys around your machine. They must be dry on a hot day like this."

An hour later the farmer returned and asked John, "When can I get an All-Crop Harvester?"

John replied, "Now wait a minute. You got me all wrong. I'm not out here to queer anybody's deal. I'm down to one combine in inventory and will have no trouble getting full list price with no tradein."

The farmer shot back, "Who asked for a discount? Who said there was a tradein?"

John demurred, "You bought a combine fair and square. Why don't you live with your decision?"

The farmer said emotionally, "I may have bought it, but I ain't paid for that blankety-blank hunk of iron yet. When can I get an All-Crop Harvester?"

John replied, "How about five o'clock tonight?"

"Sold!" the farmer said.

One year, at the Ohio State Fair, John asked Service Manager Paul Grimes, "When are you coming down to my territory?" Paul told him that he would come down if there was something to come down for. John allowed that he would think of something.

John went to Grat and told him, "I have a poor old widow lady with a Model RC tractor that doesn't have starter and lights. (Uncle Sam had forbidden them during World War II, so we later had a program to put them on wartime stripped tractors.) I think it is a crying shame that this company of ours can't put lights and starter on this poor widow's tractor." John explained that a former dealer had sold the tractor, so no dealer was obligated to install the equipment. "Why don't you send Paul down to do it?"

Grat cried crocodile tears with John over this poor old widow lady who had to crank her RC tractor, and promised that Paul would be right down. John came down, and he and John headed out to the poor old widow lady's farm. John told Paul, "Now don't laugh."

"Waddya mean, 'don't laugh?'" Paul asked.

"I told you not to laugh," John replied.

At the farm they found a young man in the barnyard. John asked, "Where's Sally (not her right name)?"

The boy had a speech impediment. He said that Sally was out "ditching," which meant she was laying tile. John asked why he wasn't out in the field helping her. The boy answered, "She would kill me. She's a horse!" John told the boy to go get Sally.

Sally came around the corner of the barn. She was a tall, lanky woman with high laced shoes, arms that dangled to her shoe tops, a long dress, and a wide brim straw hat with myriads of little fuzzy balls dangling around the brim. As she came around the corner of the barn, she picked up a milk can with one hand and set it in a wheelbarrow. Paul told me, "I had to keep my eyes to the ground to keep from laughing. I looked in that milk can and it was full. She picked it up in one hand. She didn't need a starter for her tractor. She could have picked up the tractor in one hand and spun the crank with the other."

After Howard Shireman quit, John inherited part of Howard's block which lay to the north of Van Wert. One day, while checking out a time deal, John noticed that one of his dealers had pulled the old "double-financing" trick on him. The dealer had sold the time paper to both Allis-Chalmers and the bank. The mortgagor whose entry was on the courthouse books first had a first mortgage, the other mortgagor had a second. John wasn't happy about his second place position. The way it was done was illegal. John went to the dealership. The dealer wasn't in, but his son was. "I came to say goodbye," John said.

"Where you going?" the son asked.

"I'm not going anywhere. It's your Dad who's going," John explained.

"Where's he going?"

"Down to Columbus, where they have those big iron swinging doors with the big padlocks on them," John explained.

"Why? What happened? What did he do?"

John explained about the double financing. The son said, "You sit right here. I'll be right back."

It was only a few minutes and he was back. "Everything is all right now. Go look at the courthouse record."

John looked and, waddya know, he now had prior claim. The kid, with the help of some ink eradicator, had reversed the entries. John went to see the banker, "How would you like to buy a first mortgage?"

The banker looked at the deal and said, "I already have a first on that deal." He smiled a twisted smile, like one thief having outwitted another thief.

"Oh, is that so?" John commented. "You just think you have a first."

"Don't I have prior claim?" The banker looked worried. He rushed across the street to the courthouse. A few moments later he returned and told John, "I'll buy the deal. I thought I had a first. Now that I see that I don't, I better have the whole deal. Yes, I'll buy your mortgage." John received a check to pay for the tractor that was involved.

These financial shenanigans weren't up to the level of Texas Savings & Loans capers in the late '80s or the misadventures of Billie Sol Estes, but the sheriff might have been interested in hearing more of the details.

Fellow-bachelor Jimmy Gast was the Columbus Branch blockman just south of John's block. The two were together quite often. Jimmy lived in a hotel in Wapakoneta. At the Ohio State Fair, John told me to sneak out with him when Grat wasn't looking, to take a look at the races. On the way to the racetrack, we went through the Farm Bureau tent. John looked at the coveralls that were displayed there. He told the clerk that he needed coveralls for winter service work, but hadn't brought that much money.

"Would you please send me six pairs of coveralls C.O.D.?"

"Be glad to," the clerks aid. "Where should I send them?"

John gave the clerk Jimmy's name and hotel address. He ordered his size but Jimmy was about twice as big as John. The coveralls arrived at the hotel in Wapakoneta and the hotel clerk paid the C.O.D., charging the coveralls to Jimmy's hotel tab. For weeks Jimmy wondered how he managed to get six pairs of coveralls, only half his size.

John was a good friend of the Goodrich salesman who traveled his territory. The two called on the empire of the Mueller Implement Company in Delphos, a four-story building that housed everything from tires to tractors, to fly nets and whip sockets for the horse and buggy trade.

One day the Goodrich man brought a new sales manager with him. In order to impress the new manager, the Goodrich man asked a farmer who was sitting there (the farmer had bought tires from the Goodrich man thirty days before), "I want to impress my new boss. I'm gonna tell him that I've tried to sell you a new set of tractor tires but have failed. I'll ask him to take a crack at you. You go there in the office with him and give him a hard time, but end up buying the tires all over again. Oh, by the way, he's a little hard-of-hearing, so you'll have to speak up." The farmer agreed to help polish the salesman's apple.

Then the Goodrich man approached his boss. "See that guy over there. I've tried to sell him tractor tires for two years and haven't gotten to first base. Would you mind taking a crack at him to see what you can do?"

"Be glad to," the new sales manager said.

"Oh, yes, there's one more thing that I should tell you. This farmer is a little hard-of-hearing. You'll have to speak up," the salesman told his boss.

Farmer and sales manager entered the office and the door was closed. John and his Goodrich friend listened while the two went at each other in voices loud enough to wake the dead.

In the optometry trade, they call perfect vision "20-20 vision." Those two individuals in the office had 20-20 hearing, yet both were yelling at each other.

P.S. The new sales manager got the order all right, but couldn't get a deposit.

**CIRCUMCISED PLOW**

In John Walker's tough clay territory, most of the plows sold were two-bottom, twelve-inch plows. Over our way, we sold two-fourteens. One day, for reasons still unknown, someone on the Cleveland block wanted a two-twelve plow. I called John Walker to see if he would transfer one to me. He said he would.

When the plow arrived at Lewie Lipps's place of business, Lewie told me, "This is a two-fourteen, just like the plows I have."

I checked the plow bundles, and sure enough, Lewie was right. I called John to tell him that he had shipped us the wrong plow, that he should ship us another plow, but this time "make it a two-twelve."

"I shipped you a two-twelve," John said. "Get your glasses fixed." John could be so compassionate.

Lewie suggested, "Let's just make a two-twelve plow out of it." He proposed to cut two inches off of one of the axles. I commented, "Hey, that'll work. Just nick that axle with a hacksaw two inches over, and circumcise it with a sledgehammer."

"It's pretty tough stuff," Lewie reminded me, as if I didn't know. He hacked away with a hacksaw for an hour. He finally got enough of a nick around the 360 degrees of the axle to hasten the circumcision. He laid the axle on an anvil. A serviceman wielded a sledgehammer and WHACK, the two inches of surplus axle broke off.

Just then the phone rang. It was John Walker. "I just checked my stock. You were right after all. I sent you a two-fourteen axle. Send it back and I'll send you a new one for a two-twelve.

"Too late, John," I told him. "Five minutes too late!"

## HENRY FORD RIDES AGAIN

Henry Ford's Fordson tractor had about run its course in 1927. Then Henry found a good excuse to close the plant.

Dearborn Michigan's Mayor Orville Hubbard told Henry to get his trucks out of the street, trucks that were backed up to the Ford plant's docks. Ford said there was no other way to get stuff in and out of the plant. Orville wasn't impressed. He was reported to have told Henry, "Get those trucks out of the street or I'll get them out for you."

"Are you serious?" Henry asked.

"Yes, I'm serious," the Mayor replied.

So Henry Ford closed the Fordson tractor plant. The last U.S.A. Fordson had been built!

"That wasn't what I had in mind," said Orville.

One day Henry Ford talked to Ray Savery, our dealer in Ann Arbor, Michigan, the dealer who sold Ford his All-Crop Harvesters. Ford asked, "Who is responsible for this machine?"

"I would guess Harry Merritt," Ray replied.

"I'd like to talk with that man," Ford told Ray.

Merritt came to Toledo Branch and Grat saw to it that he got up to Ford Farms to visit with Henry Ford. Ray introduced Merritt to Ford. As they became acquainted, Ford said, "You know, I built tractors too, once upon a time."

"I've heard rumors to that effect," Merritt said and smiled.

"Yes, but it's all over now. I'll never build another tractor in this country," Ford told Merritt. Ford complimented Merritt on the All-Crop Harvester and the Allis tractor line. The two talked shop for an hour.

Several years later, Harry Ferguson came over from Ireland. He showed Henry Ford his hydraulic three-point hitch system. Ford liked what he saw, and forgetting what he had told Harry Merritt about never building a tractor in this country again, the two shook hands, and started to build tractors. Henry told the world about this new tractor on his estate on June 29, 1938.

I found out quickly that Ford was back in the tractor business. Russ Horner, Ford's dealer in Geneva, Ohio, outsold all of my dealers in his two counties. Russ had been around since Year One and knew Ford personally. He had plunked a Fordson on almost every farm in Lake and Ashtabula Counties. The folks in Dearborn knew better than to give Russ Horner a bad time, because he could call the boss and get through.

We never lost a deal to Russ, but he found one hundred the first year that we didn't know existed. When we were on the same deal with Russ, we always sold our Model B and he lost out. That rankled Russ, but he really didn't miss the deals he lost to us. He just kept selling his old Fordson customers who we didn't know were in the market for a tractor.

I kept dangling our Allis-Chalmers contract before Russ, and he was tempted, but I'm glad he never bought the proposition. He could call Dearborn and get a truckload of tractors almost overnight. My dealers often waited two months before their tractors arrived. Russ would have given me fits.

Russ Horner had capitalized on the Fordson in every way possible. For instance, he made spuds for Fordson steel wheels, the kind of spuds you have on your golf shoes, only much bigger. Russ sold these spuds by the barrel to Fordson dealers all of the country. They, in turn, sold them to people who wanted to pull big lawn mowers around to mow big lawns—golf courses and parks, for instance. Spade lugs wouldn't have worked, but Russ Horner's golf spuds were just right.

An effective draft line made the Ford-Ferguson do an efficient job in the field. "Draft line" is the line of pull engineered into both tractor and implement. The convenience of the hydraulic lift could not be denied. Mystique built up around this new Ford tractor. Some felt it was some form of magic.

"There's no magic to it," we told prospects. "Here, look at the pictures in this Ford catalog."

The first Ford-Ferguson catalog was a small one, about the size of a giant postcard. In every picture the farmer was shown with his hand on the hydraulic lever.

"Notice that the farmer must keep his hand on the hydraulic lever. The plow is tipped on its nose and wants to head for China. The tractor operator has to keep raising the plow or get stuck a dozen times across the field. There's nothing magic about tipping a plow on its nose. Sure, the plow will penetrate but it will also wear out plowshares fast." That was our assault on the Ford sales pitch.

I believed the story at the time, but in reality, I knew something that wasn't so. Home Office Serviceman C. V. "Brownie" Brown used to say, "It ain't the liars that cause all of the trouble in the world . . . it's the people who know things that ain't so." The effective draft line on the Ford-Ferguson tractor and plow would have sunk the plow to its beams if the tractor had enough power to pull that kind of load.

It wasn't long before Ford came out with a new catalog, and waddya know, there wasn't a picture in it that showed a farmer with his hand on the hydraulic lever.

Someone in Dearborn evidently heard that the first catalog was being used by competitors to sell against Ford.

One of the early Ford-Ferguson catalogs was a stroke of genius. Not one word was said about the tractor, but picture after picture was shown of equipment that others made that fit the Ford-Ferguson tractor. Russ, with his wheel spud experience to guide him, told me that he foresaw a tremendous industrial market for this new tractor. Russ was right! That's exactly what happened. Russ's contribution to that market was a "hog pole." He placed a telescoping reach from a wagon on the three-point hitch. On the far end was a hook. At butchering time, farmers could dunk the stuck hog in and out of a barrel of scalding water.

After a few years, Henry Ford filed for economic divorce from Harry Ferguson. He showed Harry the door and took all of the Ford-Ferguson distributors (Ford was the only company in the industry that didn't use branch houses) with him except the one in Columbus, Ohio. Ferguson sued and collected $57 million in economic alimony.

When Ferguson and Ford separated, Massey-Harris welcomed Ferguson into its fold. It was Massey-Ferguson-Harris for a while, three good British Empire names. Then Harris was dropped and it was then Massey-Ferguson.

For a good many years, Henry Ford had the industrial tractor business pretty much to himself. It wasn't until the postwar years that International, Deere, Case, Allis-Chalmers and others introduced industrial equipment.

## REEXAMINATION OF THE CHRISTIAN ETHIC

In 1940, Fordson tractors, regardless of their age or condition, had no used machinery resale value. Every farmer had one and didn't want another. Junk dealers bought them for twenty-seven dollars apiece. We allowed fifty bucks for a Fordson tradein. My dealers were out twenty-three dollars and the cost of the trip to the junk yard. It amounted to a five to ten percent discount.

It was an every-farm wrangle. "This Fordson is the only one in the neighborhood that starts, that doesn't use water. As you can see, I've taken very good care of this tractor."

We always came back with, "Yes, it looks like it just came from the factory, but there's no resale for the tractor. Nobody wants it at any price. You're trying to get rid of yours. So is everybody else. Fifty bucks. That's all we can allow. We'll take it to the junk yard." Round and round we went at every farm.

I had five dealers in Ashtabula County. International had nine, Deere two, Oliver one, Ford-Ferguson one, and Minneapolis-Moline one. That lone Minny-Mo dealer was a good hundred miles from the nearest other M-M dealer. He could raise his prices and nobody could check on him unless they drove a hundred miles. We caught him raising the price of his tractor $300, then offering a $250 tradein price for the farmer's Fordson. In other words, the farmer paid this dealer fifty bucks to take his Fordson off his hands.

When we encountered a prospect who was so tempted, we always said, "But how much difference must you pay?"

"But he's giffing me $250 for my guud Fordson and you're tryin' steal it from me fer a measly fifty dollars."

"But how much difference must you pay?" we repeated. "What's it going to cost you in dollars and cents to own that tractor?" We tired to awaken the farmer to the real cost of the transaction.

To their credit, most farmers weren't fooled, but there were a few hard liners who saw only the $250 tradein offer and not the price. It was the old story of the two half-million dollar cats traded for the one million dollar dog, all over again.

I reexamined my Christian ethic. I asked myself, "If a customer insists on being took, is it sinful to rip him off or is it sinful not to give him what he wants?" I still haven't found a satisfactory answer to that moral brain teaser. Billy Graham, can you help?

### GRASS ROOTS SALESMAN

C. W. "Tick" Ticknor was my dealer in Jefferson, the county seat of Ashtabula County, Ohio. Tick's father-in-law ran the store when Tick was out in the country. This elderly gentleman had made his living the hard way, selling appliances door-to-door, but now he was retired from that work. He taught me more about selling than any other single individual.

"Never get discouraged when the prospect says 'no,' " he philosophized. "You're one house closer to making a sale. Every salesman has a law of averages. Whatever your average is, keep making calls and you'll make sales. If your law of averages is one sale for every ten calls, you'll have to work harder than a person who gets one sale for every eight calls, or settle for less business."

He told me that he had once sold vacuum cleaners in Pittsburgh. His wife wanted to go back to Cleveland where her family lived. He told me that he didn't want to throw all of his efforts overboard and leave. He reasoned that somebody might like to have his customer and prospect list. He told me that he ran a blind ad in the paper and waited in a hotel room for the prospects for his business to come in.

A young man came to the hotel room and asked, "Whatcha sellin'?"

"Vacuum cleaners," my friend told him.

"Ha! Just like bungholes. Everybody's got one," the caller commented. (The word was a bit more earthy than "bungholes.")

"Yes, my dear young man, you're right. Everybody's got one. However, do you realize that there are seven people here in the Pittsburgh area that all live in big homes up in the hills, their wives have maids, they drive Cadillacs, their children go to private schools, they belong to all of the right clubs? They could buy and sell you and me a hundred times over. They are specialists. They specialize in the one person in seven who doesn't have a good bunghole. Would you care to venture a guess how many housewives there are in the Pittsburgh area who do not have a good vacuum cleaner?

So much for market saturation!

## WE DON'T NEED THE WELFARE STATE

Our Lorain County market was all screwed up when I came to the Cleveland block; and Lorain County was the highest farm income county I had. A previous dealer had cut prices, had sold a lot of machinery that he didn't service, shortchanged people, and just generally fouled things up. Inevitably, he folded.

How to recover? Houghton Brothers had a little establishment just north of Oberlin. They dealt in used machinery. Stan was a very capable and able-bodied man, but Charley was a cripple. He had had polio when he was three years old. From the waist down, he was helpless, but from the waist up, he was all man.

I called on my Oberlin prospects as regularly as I called on my dealers. Interest was there, but I couldn't get the Houghtons to sign their name on a Dealer Sales & Service Agreement. After a year of weekly calls, dumbbell that I was, I finally asked, "You're interested or you would have kicked me out a long time ago. What's holding this thing up?"

The stumbling block was my repeated mention of a "carload of Model B's." Even though all of my dealers sold at least one carload of Model B's each year, to the Houghtons "a carload of Model B's" sounded like I expected them to buy out General Motors. What I innocently considered routine, they considered impossible! I didn't sense the impediment. They were too proud to tell me.

When the barrier was discovered that night in Oberlin, I heaved a sigh of relief. I told them, "OK, so I'll sign an agreement that promises to transfer as many of those tractors on the carload as you want transferred." That did it. I had a dealer in Oberlin. When the carload of Model B tractors arrived, they told me, "You're not going to transfer a one. We have almost all of them sold." They wanted to order another carload.

There's a lesson here for all sales people. If there is interest but the customer won't sign the order, ask what is holding things up. Had I asked that question eleven months earlier, I would have had a new dealer eleven months earlier.

Stan told me that Charley had made his own living, despite his handicap, ever since he was seven years old. Stan said that Charley used to pump an Irish Mail around the sidewalks of Oberlin selling baking powder. He would pull up to the steps of a house and rap on the steps with a cane. If the housewife came out, fine. If not, he went to the next house. He sold baking powder one week and delivered it the next week. When he finished canvassing Oberlin, he went to the interurban. The conductor placed Charley and his Irish Mail on board and he canvassed the homes of Wakeman and Elyria.

It has been a long time since the Irish Mail was made. It's too bad that it lost out. In my youth, most boys owned a coaster wagon, a scooter, an Irish Mail, and maybe a bicycle. We sat on the seat of this four-wheel vehicle, then placed our feet on the front axle to steer it. We gave a bar in front of us a push-pull action to provide power to the wheels. Since Charley's legs were useless, he did his steering with a rope fastened to the axle next to each front wheel. He steered with one hand on the rope, propelled himself with the other hand on the push-pull bar.

Stan said, "When we had a team to break in on the farm, we placed Charley in the middle of the hayrack and put the reins in his hands. He couldn't go anywhere. When we had plowing to do, we cranked up the old Fordson and placed Charley on the seat. If the tractor stalled mid-field, Charley crawled off and pawed his way to the front of the tractor, where, in a sitting position he cranked the Fordson. Then he remounted."

At age eighteen, Charley took the contract for building the water reservoir in Oberlin. He had a team of horses and a one-yard wagon. At the cut, workers shoveled the wagon full of dirt and then Charley drove to the fill. There he crawled off of the seat of the wagon and crawled around to the back. Sitting on the ground behind the wagon, he turned the 2x4s that were the bottom of the wagon, so that they were 4x2s and the dirt in the wagon sifted to the fill. That was standard procedure in those days. The 2x4s were tapered at the back end to make it easier to get a solid grip on the 2x4s.

When I first met the Houghtons, Charley had a Model A Ford that he drove with hand levers. He had an overhead door in his bedroom; drove his car right up alongside his bed and tumbled out of the car into bed. In the morning, he drove his Model A to as near the front door of the store as he could. Using his cane and crutches, he wiggled his way inside the door and plunked himself down into a swivel chair that was surrounded by three tables and desks. On these tables were all of the requisites of doing business—parts cards, price books, catalogs, order blanks, cash register, the whole bit.

When a farmer came for parts, Charley looked up the parts numbers, placed those part numbers on a grocery store pad, added the bin numbers, then handed the slip to the farmer who went on to pick his own parts from the bins. The first self-service parts department in the country!

On Sunday afternoon, Charley drove his Model A to call on farmers. After he drove into the farmyard, he honked twice. If the farmer came out, fine; if not, Charley drove on to the next farm. That's the way he did the selling for the firm.

Stan Houghton had tried to sell a tractor to a farmer near Elyria for a year without success. Finally the farmer and his wife told Stan that if he would come back at ten o'clock in the morning, they would have their mind made up one way or the other. When Stan came at ten, there stood a brand spanking new John Deere tractor in the yard.

Shaken by the sight of this green paint, Stan went into the house to find out what had happened.

The farmer and his wife were in tears. They sobbed, "After you left last evening, the John Deere dealer from (blank) came in and he talked so fast. He said some nasty things about you and your tractor and before we knew it, we had signed an order. This morning he delivered the tractor at seven-thirty."

"Did you pay for it?" Stan asked.

"Yes." They told him. Almost hysterically they continued, "But we don't want that tractor. We want your tractor. Do you suppose he would take it back and give us our money back?"

"No, knowing him, I wouldn't guess that that would happen," Stan explained.

Crying bitter tears, they said, "Would you take it in on trade? We'll trade even up." Note: The list price on the Deere was about $65 higher than ours.

Stan said, "I've done a lot of crazy things in my life, but nothing as crazy as that. I have no calls for a new John Deere tractor."

The sobbing and crying continued. "Please! Please, Mr. Houghton. Take that tractor and bring us one of yours."

Stan began to soften. Most tough men can't stand tears. Further, some people are drawn toward wacky adventure from time to time, taking leave of their senses in the process. "Well, this just has to be the most stupid thing I've ever done. OK, I'll bring my tractor over and pick this one up."

This particular model John Deere tractor was the first one that Deere produced that had a cushion seat. The seat went from fender to fender. The seat back prevented entry from the rear. Frontside, on one side there were foot pedals and on the other side, the flywheel for the two-lunger. There just was no good way to get on this tractor. To mount the tractor, one had to step on the axle, then on top of the tire, then on the seat, then wipe the seat off and sit down. Stan noted this as he loaded and unloaded the tractor. He set the tractor on his show floor and set a stepladder beside it. Then he advertised.

Curious farmers came to see the tractor. "What's wrong with it?" they asked.

"Nothing that I know of. It's brand new. A customer near Elyria bought it but before he used it he decided to trade for our tractor. Go ahead. Climb up there and get the feel of it."

The prospect would look at the tractor and then the stepladder. "By George, that is the only way to get on that thing, isn't it?"

Houghton Brothers sold nine, yes NINE, Allis-Chalmers tractors off of that one John Deere tractor before some farmer came in who bled green and wanted to be buried in Moline. That tenth customer bought the green paint. He paid $65 more for the green tractor than he would have paid if he had bought a Persian orange tractor, but for some people loyalty doesn't wear a price tag.

As you might well imagine, Charley did not attend sales meetings. In 1959, however, there was a sales meeting I wanted him to attend. Stan agreed to bring his brother to Toledo for the meeting and Charley reluctantly agreed to come. On the morning of the meeting, I stood in front of the meeting place shaking hands like a politician in front of the courthouse the week before election. Stan came up, but without Charley. I was about to light into him. "But you promised to bring your brother," I complained.

Stan hung his head and tears came to his eyes. "Charley died last night," Stan sobbed.

What a way to start an enthusiastic sales meeting! After the shock wore off a little, I opened the meeting and told the assembled dealers that Charley Houghton was dead. Everyone either knew the man or knew of him. We asked everyone to rise for a moment of silent respect.

Somehow the spirit of Charley Houghton caught hold of that group of dealers that day, and it may very well have been the most successful sales meeting we ever held.

I'll never forget those evenings when we sat beside the stove at Houghton Brothers, listening to Charley expound. He had no use for giveaways, handouts, subsidies or assorted freebies. Charley Houghton often said, "In this country, anybody can make it if he wants to make it bad enough." Charley Houghton was certainly living proof of that statement!

R.I.P. Charley Houghton!

## WE BLEW IT!

The Charter Engine Company produced the nation's first tractor in 1889. The C. W. Best Company of San Leandro, California, built a crawler tractor in 1896. Huber of Marion, Ohio, introduced their tractor in 1897. In 1901, C. W. Hart and C. W. Parr joined to produce the Hart-Parr. Somewhere back in those ancient days, the Heider tractor made its appearance. Ah yes, the Heider!

Stan Houghton, my dealer in Oberlin, Ohio, took me to a prospect who had ten acres of apple trees, a Heider, and a sprayer made out of the frame of a deceased and skeletonized Heider on which was mounted the spray tank. The Heider used a great deal of its own power just to propel itself through the apple orchard. Then, the jerry-rigged sprayer required power not unlike the power needed to tug the base out from under the Statue of Liberty. As you can guess, this farmer had difficulty placing dormant spray on his apple trees when the ground was wet.

We suggested to our prospect that he buy a Model B tractor and an inexpensive pull-sprayer on rubber tires, for something less than $750 total. Instead, the customer wanted a crawler tractor to pull his homemade sprayer. He was not about to scrap that homemade sprayer he had put together any more than he was willing to sacrifice an arm or a leg.

When dormant spray had to go on, dormant spray had to go on, and excuses like "The wheels won't take me through that mud" were not acceptable. Who were we to argue with the customer? Give him what he wants. If he wants a $1,950 tractor instead of a $525 tractor, who were we to argue? He wants a crawler tractor so that he will never miss with his dormant spray. Never before had there been a $1,950 crawler tractor sold on the Cleveland block. Visions of sugar plums floated in our heads. A $1,950 sale instead of $525. Wow!

Stan offered a tradein price of $95 for the aged Heider. The order was all written up and signed. Then, as we were about to leave, Stan said, "Whoops, we forgot the power-take-off. You'll need a PTO to drive your sprayer." When Stan looked up the price of the PTO, it was $95, the exact figure he had allowed for the old Heider. Oh, no!

Naturally, the farmer flipped his lid. "Ninety-five dollars for those few pounds of iron and you're only allowing me $95 for my good Heider?"

The farmer stalked off and we never saw him again. NO SALE!

We blew it!

First of all, I should have caught the missing PTO as we wrote up the order and should have included it in the price of the tractor. As long as I was half asleep, Stan should have done a little fast arithmetic in his mind when he thought of the missing PTO. When he saw the $95 figure in the price book, he should have said to himself, "I'll just give it to him," and then he should have told the customer, "No, I was wrong. It comes as standard equipment with the tractor." Even if he had said, "That will be an extra twenty-five bucks," he would have saved the deal.

Stan and I received one more degree from the School of Hard Knocks where the class yell is "ouch" and the school colors are black and blue. Of such bloopers is experience built.

**RACE TRACK MONEY**

One of the steel mills in Lorain, Ohio, paid their employees in cash, in the largest possible denomination bills. If an employee's pay was $54, he got a 50-dollar bill and two 2-dollar bills.

A rural tank truck driver bought a Model B tractor from Houghton Brothers and paid for it with this racetrack money, 2-dollar bills. Almost every payday, steel mill employees got at least one 2-dollar bill in their pay envelope. Quite naturally, some of these steel mill folks paid their oil bills with 2-dollar bills. The tank truck driver saved all of the 2-dollar bills he received until he had 250 of them, enough to buy a Model B tractor.

This wasn't the only out-of-the-ordinary deal that we encountered. Near Detroit, a farmer paid for his Model B tractor with the proceeds from his pumpkin crop. Each year he planted pumpkins. He then looked for the most promising pumpkins, then slit the stems and inserted siphon hoses. The other end of the hose went into a bucket of water sitting on a potato crate. It was a most unusual form of irrigation!

When the pumpkins grew to half size, the farmer carved names in the sides of his promising pumpkins . . . names like J. C. Penney, Sears Roebuck, J. L. Hudson Company, Texaco, and dozens more. When the pumpkins grew to maturity, the firm names were imbedded in scar tissue in the sides of the pumpkins. Then our customer took his pumpkins to the various establishments where he sought out the person who did the store and show window decorating.

He told us, "When they see those pumpkins with their name on the side in scar tissue, they can't get their checkbook out fast enough. Even though I don't take orders ahead of time, even though I go in cold, I sell 95 percent of the pumpkins I raise at five bucks apiece." This man bought a Model B Tractor with the proceeds from 100 pumpkins.

**PEARL HARBOR**

PEARL HARBOR ATTACKED. THIS IS NO DRILL.

That was the message that came over the wire from Hawaii to Washington, D. C. It was Sunday, December 7, 1941.

Within minutes, the wire services had the news, and stations interrupted their radio programs to give the news to the nation.

Norma and I and our two sons were on our way to visit the Spelzhausens on the other side of Cleveland that Sunday afternoon when we heard the news on the car radio. When we arrived at our destination, we gave the news to Spelz, a classmate of mine in college. Spelz said, "Give our guys a couple of weeks and they'll clean up on those Japs." That was the attitude of most of the nation, but of course we know now that it took a lot longer than "a couple of weeks."

War was declared the next day and everything was frozen into a wartime state of affairs. Since Japan had cut off our source of rubber, and we had not yet developed synthetic rubber, tires were rationed. No new automobiles were built except for a few that went to the military.

Our guardian angel stood over us again in that week before Pearl Harbor. That week I had taken delivery of a new Chevrolet from my dealer, Barney Rothgery, in Grafton. Then on Wednesday of that week, the man at the filling station where I bought my gas and had my car serviced, sold me on the idea of buying premium tires that would last the 50,000 miles that I drove each year. That car and those tires lasted the 95,000 miles I drove during the war. Each of the tires had boots and the tread was all but gone, but they still offered transportation.

The company landed two contracts to build prime movers, a vehicle that would carry a crew of twelve men, 105 rounds of ammunition, and pull a gun at thirty-five miles per hour. More dollars worth of orders for parts and subassemblies were placed in the Cleveland area than anywhere else in the country. Marshall Noel, the man who headed up our Construction Machinery Division, asked me to expedite parts for the prime movers, so I said goodbye to my dealers and for the next two years, chased parts. But that's another story for another day.

## DISAPPOINTMENT IN MENTOR

After Norma and I had paid $50 per month rent for a while, like most young couples, we did the Sunday afternoon "Open House in Beautiful Green Meadows" routine.

We came upon a two-year-old six-room brick house in Mentor that fitted our needs and pocketbook. The asking price was $9,000. We bid $8,100. Another potential buyer raised the ante to $8,500, but he couldn't come up with the money. We bought it for $8,250, but made the mistake of not putting earnest money down. When we came to sign the final papers, we found that the owner had sold the home out from under us. Another couple bought the house, a cash deal, for $8,500.

Norma and I took turns crying over spilled milk. We cried Sunday, Monday, Tuesday, Wedn..., but Wednesday's tears were interrupted by a call from Toledo Branch. Willis Scholl told me over the phone, "Grat has been transferred to Home Office. He's the new Northwest Territory Manager. I'm the new branch manager in Toledo and I want you to be my assistant. Do you want the job?" It was a little hard to believe. I had been the youngest blockman the company ever had. Now I was to be the youngest branch sales manager in the company.

Norma and I took turns thanking our guardian angel who had saved us from the trials and tribulations of selling an "owned three-days" home.

1. It seemed like a Fordson tractor was on every American farm between 1917 and 1927. The Fordson replaced some of the horses on the farm, but not all. Photo courtesy of Ralph W. Sanders for DuPont Co.

2. "Kerosene Annie," the last of the Rumely Oil-Pulls.

3. When Harry Merritt bought the Rumely operation in LaPorte, Indiana, there were a few of Doc Rumely's threshers left over. We quickly painted "Allis-Chalmers" on the windstackers and sold them. I wrote up the last order in 1936.

4. At state fairs in 1933, Barney Oldfield set an all-time tractor speed record on a rubber-tired Allis-Chalmers tractor. It was Sales Promotion Manager Ellzey Brown's way of bringing air-tired tractors to the public's attention.

5. Walt Buescher was born in this home in Bremen, Indiana, on July 11, 1914. This photo, taken in 1983, shows that the combination wood shed and outhouse and the old pump are gone.

6. Since teaching eight grades of kids in a one-room school was not a full-time job, my father was also choirmaster and organist at St. Paul's Lutheran Church in Bremen, Indiana, and church and school janitor. (Author, second from left, front row.)

7. International Harvester's Farmall said in its name that it could do it all, that it could replace the last horse on the farm. This tractor could be used to cultivate the corn as well as pull the plow. Photo courtesy of Ralph W. Sanders for DuPont Co.

8. When the 7,100 customers who had bought tractors in the fall of 1963 came to town, we put on a show for them in the building that was soon to be used to assemble tractors. Albert Schroeder, of Waukesha, Wisconsin, was the first man to buy a rubber-tired tractor in October of 1932.

9. General Sales Manager W. L. "Shorty" Voegeli. Photo courtesy of the Milwaukee County Historical Society, Milwaukee, Wisconsin.

10. Branch Manager Willis Scholl at his desk in Toledo Branch, 1945. Later Scholl was Eastern Regional Manager, General Sales Manager, and finally President of the Allis-Chalmers company.

11. General Sales Manager W. A. "Bill" Roberts, General Manager Harry Merritt, and Sales Promotion Manager Ellzey Brown, the three men who introduced air-tired equipment to the American farm. Photo courtesy of the Milwaukee County Historical Society, Milwaukee, Wisconsin.

12, 13. In 1940, Jim Hardgrove proved to Ohio farmers at the Ohio State Fair that the new Model B tractor was highly maneuverable and quite capable of replacing the last horse on the farm. Without saying a word, a fiddler, caller, eight young people and eight Model B tractors said all that needed to be said.

14, 15. At our first national sales meeting in French Lick, Indiana, in 1959, fifty-nine new machines were introduced in this show tent.

16. Harry Ferguson came from Ireland with his patented hydraulic three-point hitch and joined with Ford who went back into the tractor business producing the Ford-Ferguson tractor. The Ferguson hitch set a standard for the industry. Photo courtesy of Ralph W. Sanders for DuPont Co.

17. At our first national sales meeting at French Lick, Indiana, Vice President Wes Davis congratulates J. P. Mehlhaff, 82, the oldest dealer in the organization, a man who had been selling equipment since he was sixteen years old. Vice Presidents Boyd Oberlink and Bill Klein look on.

18. Agribusiness trade shows were a male domain until 1970 when these three young women brought wall-to-wall people to our trade show exhibits. D. C. Berg, Barbara Waters, and Ginny Haberman took turns doing twenty-minute stints, from 8:30 a.m. to 4:30 p.m.

19. Each Crop Clinic closed with a question and answer period. I fielded the questions, then passed them on to a panel made up of representatives of every company on the day's program.

20. After Harry Merritt's first rubber-tired tractor in 1932, he asked engineers C. E. Frudden and Walter Strehlow to design this Allis-Chalmers WC tractor that would use rubber to best advantage. Photo courtesy of Ralph W. Sanders for DuPont Co.

21. Marketing Man of the Year, 1974.

# PART FOUR
# BACK TO TOLEDO

## 11

# A NEW SWIVEL CHAIR

I sat down in that assistant branch manager's swivel chair as gingerly as a hound dog sits on a cactus. There came the realization that my decisions could effect the lives of hundreds for good or bad. If a lowly sales manager has feelings like that, what do you suppose it's like if you have to make a decision whether to introduce a new product or not, whether to build a new factory or not? Executives can live through the sin of underexpansion several times, and receive absolution, but overexpansion gets them at the first whomp. The higher a person goes up the corporate ladder, the more people are effected by decisions that are made.

H. A. "Grat" Gratner, formerly branch manager of Toledo Branch, was now Northwest regional manager and Willis Scholl was branch manager at Toledo. Willis gave me full rein, for which I was very grateful. Not all branch managers operated that way. He didn't try to dictate change in my style of operation, confided in me in all matters except those that were ordered confidential by Home Office. We talked things over before we moved in a new direction. From time to time, we disagreed on management tactics, but most of the time Willis's decision proved to be the way to go. I felt like the district attorney in Matlock's television cases.

Branch sales managers received $350 per month salary and a quarter of one percent of all settlements over the $840,000 mark for the branch each year. I made money those first two years. Then my salary was raised to $375 per month but a lid of $10,000 per year was placed on total income. During my remaining eight years as sales manager at Toledo, we easily hit the ceiling every year.

**WARTIME PRIORITIES**

During World War II, whole goods sales were no problem. The machinery that was made was allocated to dealers on the basis of the 1940-1941 sales. Keeping dealers in parts, and keeping the farm machines running, were the wartime priorities of everybody's farm equipment branches. The United States was not only feeding itself, but much of the rest of the free world as well.

The whole industry was congratulated by the people and government because of the patriotic manner in which it tackled the job. All manufacturers worked to keep prices under the legal ceilings. They did their best to get their allotments distributed and worked to eliminate black markets. They also tried to get machinery to the most productive farm producers. During the Viet Nam war, potential draftees ran off to Canada or Sweden. During World War II, they moved to a farm because farmers were way down the list of potential draftees. Their parents didn't have the money to buy machinery, but had enough influence with local boards to get the necessary permits. Among real farmers who were desperate for machinery, this sort of thing was as popular as poison ivy in a nudists' camp. The whole ration system was an open invitation to black markets and under-the-table settlements, of course, but to the credit of the industry, those shenanigans were kept to a minimum. People who had sons in the service did the best to blow the whistle on such covert operations.

Overall the War Production Board attempted to hold farm equipment production at 83 percent of prewar levels—83 percent of the prewar tonnage of iron. No single machine was to receive exactly 83 percent since Uncle Sam spelled out item-for-item what steel would be available for what piece of farm equipment. The percentages varied from zero percent of 1940 production to 353 percent. One of the low percentages was horse-drawn cultivators at 35 percent. Hay presses, on the other hand, were 353 percent while tractors varied by size from 59 to 81 percent. Combine percentages were 56-92 percent. Implements, more often than not, had 100+ percentages.

## JOE TUCKER'S HARVEST BRIGADE

At the outset of World War II, all long-line farm equipment manufacturers were told that they could build two models of tractors and one model of combines. We had no difficulty with that regulation because we really had only two models of tractors and one combine. Our Model U and Model A tractors were outdated; no tears were shed when we parted with them. The forty-inch cut All-Crop Harvester, like the Edsel car, had gone nowhere, so here was a good excuse to dump it.

At Massey-Harris the decision was not that easy. Massey had the Clipper, a pull-type combine that ran a poor second to our All-Crop Harvester, but it was second, and ahead of Deere and International. Massey also had a new self-propelled combine that Tom Carroll had engineered, but it was an unknown quantity. What to do? Play it safe or take a chance? Massey took a chance and chose their self-propelled combine. They dropped the second-place, pull-type Clipper.

Joe Tucker was Massey's VP, and a very good sales promotion manager he was too. Have you heard of the hordes of itinerant combine operators that start at the Texas-Oklahoma border and come up through the Wheat Belt as the harvest moves north? They're called custom-cutters. In my day, they charged something like $3.50 per acre to custom-cut wheat for farmers. Before the days of the self-propelled combine, the migrants harvested wheat with all methods from binders and threshers to prairie combines pulled by dozens of horses.

Joe Tucker dubbed this movement of custom-cutters, "The Harvest Brigade." He painted word pictures of the Harvest Brigade feeding all of the hungry people in the free world. Joe's promotion brought the War Production Board down in tears. They could just visualize Vladimir Tzelencho, a six-year old starving child in the Ukraine, being saved by Joe Tucker's Harvest Brigade. Media folks picked up Joe's line and gave it a real good free-ink ride. The rest of us sat there in dumbfounded amazement, gnawing at our nails.

Joe said, "Picture this: 500 operators cutting 2,000 acres each, one million acres in all, fifteen million bushels, 1,000 tractors released, a half-million gallons of fuel saved, a half-million bushels of grain saved by more efficient opening of fields." (That last one was a dig at us because when the All-Crop Harvester opened a field, the tractor driver had to run over some standing grain to thresh the wheat nearest the fence. It was a problem that all pull-type combines had, including Massey's Clipper.) No politician or bureaucrat could oppose Joe Tucker's holy crusade? He was thought of as a man who could walk on water, heal leprosy, and balance the federal budget. Having had a bit of success myself in the field of sales promotion, I look back and take my hat off to Joe Tucker.

While the rest of us cuddled our steel allotments and low priorities, the War Production Board, Congress, the D.A.R., newsboys, and courthouse-step habitués all insisted that Massey should be given more steel to build an extra 500 combines. The rest of us in the industry, individually and collectively, ground our teeth because any of us could have saved the hungry children of the world with our combine, but we gave Joe Tucker grudging admiration.

Joe Tucker should have been canonized by his company. Sad to say, he wasn't. After an in-house squabble, he left Massey and hired on at New Holland where he ended his farm equipment career. Miracle man Sam White of Oliver was to have the same experience of in-house rejection years later. One of the Cleveland Whites bought Minneapolis-Moline, Oliver, and Cockshutt, a Canadian farm equipment company. Instead of consolidating the operation, White ran these three divisions of the company separately. When Sam White (no relation) was appointed president of Oliver, he just about doubled sales in a year. His sincere personal approach at management won him great admiration and respect among his dealers, his employees, and competitors too. One year he and I were on the same program at the Saskatchewan dealers' association convention, so I experienced his personal magnetism firsthand. No sooner had Sam taken Oliver to the heights, an in-house disagreement took place and Sam took off. Almost overnight, Oliver's sales volume slipped to where it had been before Sam White appeared on the scene. The CEO of the parent corporation, White, incidentally was Mr. Black.

Success seems to breed resentment.

## AMERICA REAWAKENS TO REALITY

Right after World War II, there was tremendous pent-up demand for our equipment, but an eleven-month strike intervened. We had been allies of Josef Stalin's U.S.S.R. during the war. The brave Soviet stand at Stalingrad earned our nation's respect. Then, when our nation began to recognize Stalin as no less of a tyrant then Adolf Hitler, the U.S.S.R. and Communists in general fell out of favor here. When it was discovered that the people who led the Allis strike had communist connections and had perjured themselves in that regard, eight were sent to prison and the strike ended.

Dealer Zygmundt "Zig" Zima of Geneva, Ohio, and several thousand other Allis-Chalmers dealers heaved a sigh of relief. Zig was a veteran who we signed as a dealer shortly after he came back from serving in World War II. It was a miracle that he was able to hang on for eleven months without machinery to sell. All of us in the field wakened as if from a bad dream. We had gone without a cent of commissions for eleven months. No one in the field deserted ship. Loyally, we hung on. Picture a Kentucky Derby with all of the horses leaping from the starting gate, but one horse lags behind to give the others an eleven-furlong head start. That was us! The demand for machinery was filled by our competitors. It was the beginning of the end for Allis-Chalmers. I'm convinced of that. We never completely recovered from that strike.

## ROUND BALES OF HAY

Everybody knew that hay bales had to be square. J. I. Case had come with a pull-type, wire-tie square baler, that called for two men to ride along to wire-tie the bales. George Delp of New Holland had brought the first one-man, pull-type, twine-tie square baler to market. Ummo Luebben disagreed. Since 1937, Ummo had dreams of round hay bales. He said unto himself, "Everything that is made in lengths goes to market in a roll, except hay. Cord string, binder twine, wire, carpeting, wallpaper, newsprint, linoleum, they're all rolled. But we jam windrows of hay into a square box and knock off half of the leaves. That ain't right."

Ummo built himself a baler that baled round bales of hay. Lininger Implement Company of Omaha, Nebraska was one of Ummo's dealers. Lininger advertised with confident modesty, "See this machine on exhibition and be convinced that you have seen a perfect baler . . . that does perfect work." The ad said that this perfect baling machine preserved the sweetness and nutrition of the green plant, that it saved all of the leaves, that the bale was waterproof, that the baler had a capacity of thirty to seventy tons of baled hay per day. Bill Roberts bought Luebben's baler and moved the operation to our LaPorte Works. Wartime restraints prevented its introduction during the early 1940s. Several prototypes were built during the war. But when the baler was introduced right after World War II, we had no trouble selling all we could build.

During all of our experimental work with the baler, we had no accidents. No sooner had the baler hit the market when one farmer stuck his arm into the press rolls, and severely injured that arm. When the last of the hay didn't catch the twine in the twine arm to start the wrapping process, our engineers knew that they should stay clear of the press rolls. They would toss a handful of hay or straw at the twine to restart the baling operation. But farmers didn't know that. This farmer had stuck the twine into the rolls with his fingers and *zip*, there went his arm too.

When this first accident happened, Willis Scholl called all of our blockmen into the branch. We gave them a set of shields to put on each baler that had been sold and each baler that was still in inventory. Now hands could no longer be stuck in where they did not belong. We gave blockmen affidavits that were to be signed by baler owners testifying that they had been instructed NEVER to try to insert the twine into the press rolls with their fingers. There were to be signatures of two witnesses that operators had been told. The problem was solved, or so we thought. Now farmers stood on something and, reaching over the safety guards, stuck their arms into the rolls. One even walked up the hay gathering table and stuck his leg in.

We eventually won all of the lawsuits, but lost arms and legs make for lousy public relations and lawsuits aren't cheap. That was one problem that the baler developed. There was another. We didn't keep the pressure on our competitors hard enough to pull them into the round baler business. We heard that both International and Deere had round balers in their experimental departments. Finally, there should have been yearly improvements in the baler, but those were not forthcoming. Some customers asked, "Can't you make bales that need no twine at all?" Since I'm not an engineer, I don't know, but the question is a logical one.

We built 3,000 Roto-Balers in 1947, 10,000 per year in 1948, 1949 and 1950. After that it was all downhill. After our production and sales dwindled to nothing, the round bale concept lay dormant for about fifteen years. Then a manufacturer by the name of Vermeer of Pella, Iowa, introduced a round baler that turned out big, one-ton round bales.

We missed the big bale development. In 1955, a Virginia farmer told me, "You made it the wrong size. A 75-pound bale is too heavy for a man but not heavy enough for a machine." He suggested either a bale the size of a big lump of coal or a big one-ton bale. When I mentioned this in Milwaukee, Louie Adams's comment was, "You can never tell what crazy ideas farmers can come up with."

The brass ring was there all right, but we missed it!

## BARNUM WOULD HAVE LOVED THE ROUND BALE

The Roto-Baler was a fun thing to sell. It was so different! It saved leaves, it saved on twine, and the bales were weather resistant, like a thatched roof.

Lloyd Coulter demonstrated weather resistance in a dramatic way at his dealership in Lapeer, Michigan. On top of a set of wobbly 2x2 legs, Lloyd built a chicken wire coop, in which he placed a round bale of hay. The putting-in and locking-up ceremony was witnessed by the banker (who placed the key to the cage in his bank vault), by the editor of the *Lapeer County Press*, by the county agent and by other assorted interested citizens, scientists, farmers, hangers-on, and delivery boys. There was a picture and write-up about the locking-up process on the front page of the paper, and Lloyd mentioned it in his ad.

In the spring, the cage was opened by the banker who had hibernated the key over the winter in his bank vault. The opening-up rite and bale inspection were duly noted by the press and interested witnesses. The county extension agent passed on the quality of the hay that had been in the weather all winter long. He declared it to be as good as hay kept in a barn all winter. Once more, Lloyd Coulter got himself a couple of columns of front page free ink. Once again, Lloyd Coulter had something real to talk about in his weekly ad in the *Lapeer County Press*, which covered Lapeer County like the dew. Lloyd Coulter was a promoter! His promotion sold balers!

The New Holland square baler, the A-C round baler, and the Vermeer big-bale baler changed the handling of hay and straw completely. The reason for big red barns on the farm, used to store loose hay in earlier days, were starting to disappear. This hay/straw mechanization, along with others described in this book, moved the nation and the world ever closer to ample, better, and less expensive food on the nation's tables.

## THE TOLL OF INNOVATION

Having just considered the round bale and its reincarnation, this might be a good place to look back to see the role that innovation has played in the nation's economy.

When I retired from the farm equipment industry in 1975, Deere & Company was Number One in the business, but few looked on Deere as an innovator. I kidded my John Deere friends with, "The last new thing that you guys have come up with that's new is that plow that Blacksmith Jack Deere made over a hundred years ago." Chalk up the Farmall and plateless planter to International Harvester Company. Oliver was the first company in the industry to introduce a six-cylinder tractor, the first diesel-powered tractor, and they had the first self-propelled combine that threshed corn. Minneapolis-Moline had the first tractor cab. New Holland gave us the first one-man baler. Allis had this list: the first rubber-tired tractor, the first tractor designed for rubber, the first one-man combine, the round baler, no-tillage. Ford developed the three-point hitch.

Deere, the non-innovator is still in business, and at the time of this writing, is still #1. Innovator International Harvester was swallowed by Case. Innovators Oliver and Minny-Mo are gone. New Holland became part of Ford Motors, and Fiat then bought a big chunk of Ford-New Holland. Allis-Chalmers's farm equipment operation was bought out by Germany's Deutz. That circumstantial evidence doesn't say much for innovation, does it? Most certainly, innovation was not the cause of the demise of these companies, but in each case, it could have been a contributing factor. Research and product introduction costs money, lots of money. In everbody's business, there are some who lay back and let the competitor spend the money on research. If the innovation clicks, there's a quick clone.

Wouldn't you agree though that it would be a sad, sad world without innovators? Can you envision a world without plywood, Styrofoam, antibiotics, penicillin, Dr. Salk's vaccine, radio, TV, direct distance dialing, camcorders, VCRs, fast food restaurants, nylon, automatic transmissions, steel tops on automobiles, bar codes, Velcro, zippers, computers, fluorescent lighting, caps that adults can't get off of medicine bottles, electric vacuum cleaners and dishwashers, heat pumps, and copying machines? We even have a used car on the moon. We have fenders that rust out in two years and beer cans that last 1,000 years.

**A $400 ROCK**

At approximately the same time that the Roto-Baler was introduced, we also added a forage harvester, a blower, and a rake to the line. The baler, forage harvester, blower, and rake were built at our LaPorte, Indiana plant. As was usual for Allis-Chalmers, the forage harvester was different. Our cylinder's knives that chopped the crop, were J-shaped while competitors had straight knives. A-C knives, designed by Milwaukee's C. E. Frudden, not only cut but, by centrifugal action, threw the cut crop back into the wagon. The A-C forage harvester had a knife sharpener that no one else had. "Open the lid over the cylinder, drop the stone on the blades and start rotating the cylinder. Adjust the stone down just a hair, and pull the stone back and forth across the rotating knives. As sparks fly, repeat the process until the knives are sharp." Those were the instructions we gave to our customers. Competitors' owners had to remove their knives and take them to the blacksmith shop to have them sharpened. You know that those knives really got dull before they were sharpened.

There was a safety device, a couple of press rolls ahead of the cylinder, that kept stones out of the cylinder. One customer brought Dealer Bill Taylor a $400 stone. He said, "This stone didn't go into my machine because of that stone-stopper feature. On my previous machine, a stone went into the cylinder and it cost me $400 to get going again. That's why I call this my $400 stone."

The cylinder area of the machine was engineered so solidly that we could set our knives ten thousandths of an inch from the shear bar. Competitive instruction books said fifty thousandths. That meant clean cuts. The J-shaped knives threw the cut crop into a trailing forage wagon. In that lay a limiting factor. Not all farmers wanted to tow a forage wagon. Some wanted to use a truck, running alongside the chopper and not behind it. To them, and there were a lot of them, we had to say, "Sorry, can't do it."

When Allis came with the baler and forage harvester, not one extra person was added to our sales forces. When we got around to selling hay machinery, we found that the New Holland, Gehl, and Fox salesmen had already been there. These companies that were hay/forage machinery specialists (and that's all they did) spent twelve months out of the year engineering, producing, and selling their machinery. When our sales people paused from selling tractors and combines in order to sell hay/forage machinery, we not only didn't get tractor and combine sales, we didn't get many hay/forage machine sales either because the shortliners had the business.

The industry's changeover to forage harvesters made ensilage more readily available, a godsend to farmers with animals. In labor-intensive days, farmers had ensiled only corn. Now hay went into silos too. Pit silos could be used so that silage could be stored horizontally instead of vertically. A. O. Smith's Harvestore silo, patterned after the lowly vacuum bottle, became a new tool for farmers with livestock and dairy herds. Lucky for Harvestore, those blue silos became a status symbol for people who liked to keep up with the Joneses.

## DON'T CONFUSE ME WITH FACTS

"You cain't win 'em all," the man said and he was right.

Our mounted corn-picker differed from those of our competitors in that there were shields over the snapping rolls. Instead of the ear's tip or butt being snapped off of the stalk against a couple of rotating steel snapping rolls, thereby shelling some corn, on our machine the ear was snapped off at the adjustable, smooth shields immediately over our snapping rolls. There was much less loss of corn at this smooth surface, when compared to losses at rotating corrugated rollers. But, and it was a big but, we didn't get the husks off of the ear nearly as well as competitive corn pickers did.

We continued to have sales resistance over the husks that our corn harvester left on ears of corn. No one denied that we saved more corn in any given field, but the husks that we left on ears of corn were our nemesis. I heard from a professor at Michigan State that Ohio State had done some work on the subject of husks. When I inquired, I was told that corn dries better when there are a few husks left on the ear to serve as wicks. I was impressed, but farmers weren't. They wanted clean corn, period.

We said that corn does not dry through the kernel's shell, it dries through the tip of the kernel into the cob and out of the cob at its butt. We said that a few husks left at this point would serve as a wick to dry the corn quicker. That logic fell on deaf ears.

In the field, I kept saying, "Look at those yellow streaks down your corn field. That's lost corn. That's money!" Farmers came back with, "Yes, but look what a clean load of corn I have in the wagon." With blood pressure raised just a little, I would shoot back with, "Corn only goes three places—into a hog or sheller or grinder. I don't know of a hog or sheller or grinder that knows the difference. Farmers knew the difference and they bought somewhere else. You don't have to have the best product or service to get the most business, you have to make people *believe* that you have the best product or service. Right after World War II, were Japanese products really as junky as American consumers thought? Several decades later, were they really as good as American consumers thought?

Our corn picker, with shields over the rolls, went nowhere, until . . .

But that's another story for another time.

## HENRY FORD'S NEW TRACTOR

Henry Ford's new tractor caught the farmers' fancy. To farmers, who had spent a lifetime raising and lowering levers by hand, Henry's automatic hydraulic system on his reincarnated Fordson was something akin to having a butler or winning the Irish Sweepstakes. Ford's three-point hitch didn't make sense to any of us competitors, but doggoned if Henry didn't make it a world standard. Author Louis Bromfield gave the Ford-Ferguson tractor a good ride in the *Reader's Digest* with an article entitled "Can the Farm

Catch Up With the Machine Age?" Then International Harvester Company's McCaffrey unwittingly helped advertise his competitor's tractor with his white paper letter that he sent to *Reader's Digest*.

In April of 1945, at Toledo Branch we received a mimeographed bulletin from our home office entitled, "Can Ford Put It Over Again?" The author was Hosea Pratt. There was no clue as to who Hosea Pratt was. Certainly he wasn't one of us. He sounded like a veteran farm journalist. Hosea surely talked plain. Here are some of the more interesting quotes.

"Henry Ford, it is said, is unpopular among automobile and tractor men. Perhaps the reason is Henry's efficiency as a competitor. Perhaps also there is a feeling that Henry's methods in public relations, which are just beginning to be understood by professional press agents, lack certain elements of what is known as good cricket."

> Certainly he doesn't want another scare like the one General Bill Knudsen gave him by blanketing Fords with Chevrolets in the middle '30s. And just to make sure it won't happen again, this time with tractors, Henry has brought from Ireland an inventor named Harry Ferguson. Harry and Henry are presently engaged in bringing out what is known as the 'Ferguson Hitch,' an automobile device which controls the depth of which a plow or similar digging implement sinks into the earth behind a tractor.
>
> At the present writing it looks as if Henry and his Ferguson Hitch are getting set to give International, John Deere and other tractor tycoons the same sort of going over he gave the auto boys of the late teens and early twenties before the resourceful Knudsen turned the tables, and Henry [Ford] white.

What International needs is a top executive, either owner or hireling, with personal color. General Motors dug up one in General Knudsen and with him and his Chevrolet, they made Henry sweat. If Deere, Allis-Chalmers, International or any of the other old line farm implement men had an ounce of poetic imagination, they would have set up such a straw man long ago.

In politics, they call this "negative campaigning."

# 12

# SOME OF THE GUYS

**PIGGY WILLSON**

At each home office sales meeting, each of our product sales managers gave us the latest scoop on their department's products. Even though Piggy Willson was not employed by the company, he was always on the program. Allis bought Piggy's disc plows and marketed them in areas where "stump-jumper" plows were used. If that term is new to you, there were parts of the country, particularly in the South, where the land was bare but stumps still existed, some of them buried. Hit an obstruction like that with a moldboard plow and you were yanked to attention. Hit a buried stump with a disc plow and you rode over the impediment.

Piggy was the highlight of each meeting since he never talked about the stump-jumping disc plows that he made in Athens, Tennessee. Instead of talking nuts & bolts, Piggy told good Southern stories. Piggy's perpetual half-laugh was contagious. I don't know that I ever heard what Piggy's rightful name was. He probably wouldn't have recognized it himself. He had gotten the tag of Piggy because of his porcine stature.

One of Piggy's favorite stories told of the day that he crested the hill on a dirt road leading into a little crossroads town in Georgia. Just as he came to the top of the hill, a rooster ran out in front of Piggy's Model A Ford. Piggy dodged but the rooster dodged at the same time, and now he lay there trying to shake off his death throes.

Piggy told us, "I continued on without stopping. At the crossroads I gassed up at the filling station. After I had paid my bill, the man at the filling station asked if I knew that I had killed a rooster 'up yonder.' Yes, I knew."

Said the dispenser of automotive fuel, "Waal, Ah wouldn't a mentioned it, Mister, but that rooster belongs to tha Widder Smith, tha one most cantankerous female that tha Lord ever created. Ah would be mahty obliged, Mister, iffen ya would go up yonder and tell tha Widder that ya killed her rooster and offer ta pay fer it. Ah'll give ya tha money, 'cuz it will be worth it not ta have tha Widder complainin' about some furriner killin' her rooster fer the next year anna half."

Piggy explained that he was remiss in not stopping, that he would go up and do his civic and Christian duty. He would tell the Widow Smith and pay with his own funds. Piggy parked his Model A Ford in front of the widow's house, went up, and knocked on the door.

"Are you Mrs. Smith?" Piggy asked, as if he didn't know.

"Yaas. Wad y'all want?" the widow asked.

"Well, I was acomin' into town and when I topped the hill, that there rooster (he pointed) ran out in front of me and I run over him. I want to pay for the rooster and apologize for killing that bird of yours."

"Wad y'all kill 'em with, Mister?" the widow wanted to know.

"My car there. It's parked right out there in front of your house."

"Y'all mean that there Model A Ford?"

"Yes, ma'am, that's the car," Piggy explained.

"Mister, y'all doan owe me nuthin'. Iffen that rooster a mine couldn't get away from that there car of your'n, he couldn't a caught no hens no-how anyway. Thanks for stoppin' jist the same, Mister."

Then Piggy told of the time that he overnighted in a hill cabin in Tennessee's Smoky Mountains. Weather had settled in on him and Piggy preferred an overnight stay in the cabin to driving down the dirt road in the dark, a winding road that led down the mountainside, and all this during a driving rainstorm.

"We set in the living room of the cabin next to the fire," Piggy said. "After a little conversation the old lady asked her husband if it wasn't time to turn the chickens. I had never heard that expression before, so I wondered about it. Her husband said it wasn't time yet. We set and rocked another spell and then she asked again about turning the chickens."

Piggy told us that now his curiosity had gotten the better of him. He couldn't refrain from asking, "I've never heard that expression before. What do you mean by 'turnin' the chickens?'"

"Aw, tain't nuthin', Mister. Ya see tha chickens roost on tha meal barrel, and we turn 'em before we go ta bed."

Then Piggy told of the time that he ran for political office. He saw his friend on the street and commented, "Fred, I didn't see you over to the courthouse when I made my speech last night."

"No, Piggy I warn't there. My wife, she heerd ya and my mother-in-law, she heerd ya, but I didn't get there."

"Well, that's all right. I'll be talking over to the school Tuesday night. Y'all come then, y'hear."

"Ah'll be thar, Piggy."

But he wasn't. When Piggy saw Fred again, he said, "I didn't see ya over to tha school when I made my speech Tuesday night, Fred."

"Naw, I didn't make it. My wife, she heerd ya, and my mother-in-law, she heerd ya, but I couldn't make it."

"Well, it warn't all that much."

"Yeah, that's what I heerd."

## THE JUNK DEALER

Mr. Mueller died, so the Mueller empire of Delphos, Ohio, was no more. We had dealers on both sides, so we didn't worry, but the Chamber of Commerce of Delphos insisted that we install a new dealer in town. Delphos merchants were losing too much business to neighboring towns as A-C customers bought parts there. Since this was a new and flattering pitch, we complied. We signed Gene Sheeter, the Chrysler-Plymouth dealer in Delphos, and the town's junk dealer. What farmer doesn't have some junk around to trade in?

When John Walker returned to his block from World War II, at first he was skeptical about Gene Sheeter, but both soon learned that they were kindred spirits. Gene told John how he intended to remodel the building that now housed the farm equipment business. The parts department wall would be moved over there. The office would be moved up-front. After Gene outlined his architectural dreams several times without implementing any of them, John said, "Now tell me again. Tell me all of that over again. Tell me exactly what you're gonna do."

Gene went through the plans once more and then left to attend to his auto business. John picked up a sledgehammer and started knocking plaster off of one of the walls that Gene said would be moved. Dust flew and plaster and laths fell to the floor.

Terrorized, Gene came on the run. "What in the blazes are you doing, Walker? You crazy nut, you!"

"Moving the wall that you said you were going to move," John answered.

"I didn't say I was gonna do it today, for God's sake," Gene screamed.

"Can you think of a better time?" John shot back.

"No, I guess not," Gene said, resigned to the fact that this new blockman of his wouldn't take a lot of bull. If he had successfully dodged shells at Anzio and scrounged C-rations in North Africa, it wasn't likely that he would take a lot of guff from Gene Sheeter. As a Traffic MP, he had barked back at all kinds.

Gene's plans included an office up in the front window.

John asked, "Why?"

"My wife wants it up there," Gene told John. Gene's wife was the office force. Gene was homelier than a mud fence with turtles on it, but his wife was almost half his age and was BEE-YOU-TEE-FULL!

John said, "How you ever managed to land such a doll I'll never know, you homely old wart, but you've got her and I expect you intend to keep her. So I'm asking you, do you want to keep her or do you want to put her on display for all of the young and handsome hot pants farm boys to gawk at through the front window?

"She goes in back!" Gene said and that was that!

## YOU CAN ALWAYS TELL A GOOD CIGAR

Serviceman Paul Grimes and I ate at Fanny's in Flint, Michigan one evening. We philosophized, "Why do you suppose it is that men complain about paying a dime for a cigar that lasts an hour and yet they don't complain about paying a quarter for a shot of whiskey that goes gulp and it's all gone?"

When we paid our dinner checks, we instinctively bought one of those real fancy two-bit cigars in a glass tube. I asked Paul, "What are we going to do tonight?"

"How about going out to visit with Walt and Sylvia?" Paul suggested. Walt Burow was our blockman who lived just south of Flint in Fenton, Michigan. Walt was a prima donna who adjusted his tie in reflections of the show window before calling on a dealer. He shined his shoes before entering by rubbing the tips on the back of his pants legs.

I told Paul, "If we're going out there, wait just a minute." We had just lit up our twenty-five cent cigars. Now I bought two two-for-a-nickel King Edwards, replaced the two-fer label with the fancy cigar labels, then sealed up the glass tubes again.

When we got to the Burow household, I handed Walt the cigars saying, "Don't tell me we never gave you anything."

I wish you would have seen the ceremony that Walt staged for us. "Oh, thank you! Thaaaank youuuuuu!" He took the tape off of one of the glass tubes ever so carefully. Even more g-e-n-t-l-y he slid the cigar out into his hand. He didn't want to disturb the tender, golden leaf in any way. He got out his cigarette lighter and with all of the appropriate gestures (holding the flame one and one eighth inch from the tip), he lit the cigar. Then Walt settled back in his chair, blew a puff of smoke at the chandelier and said, "You can always tell fine tobacco!"

Paul and I had to keep our heads down because we couldn't keep a straight face. I never told Walt about the trick we played on him, and there's one more thing I haven't done. Since then, I have never ever claimed that I could tell one of anything from another. I've never claimed that I could tell cheap beer from Budweiser or Pabst. I've never claimed that I could tell a $1.25 wine from a $125 wine. I've never claimed that I can tell Folgers from Maxwell House. My comment has always been, "That's good!" Whether it's twenty-five cents good or five dollar good makes no difference.

## STIM

Wilbur Stimmel, our blockman at Port Huron, Michigan, was known to all as Stim. He was the most beloved of blockmen. His dealers were his greatest fans, and he had a host of partisans in Toledo Branch too. Stim wasn't a paperwork man, his paper came into the branch with round beer bottle marks and cigarette burns, but it was legible. Stim was a salesman's salesman.

He drove a Hudson (or was it an Essex?) over the gravel roads of the Thumb of Michigan. There was but one paved road in all of his territory, a road that ran right up the middle of Stim's block from Imlay City to Bad Axe.

Stim never permitted his Hudson to be contaminated with soap, water, or a broom. Grime on the outside and debris on the inside kept piling up until it was time to trade. In front, the ashtray began to overflow early on, and layer upon layer of cigar ashes, pipe ashes and cigarette butts built up on the floor. In the back seat there was an ever thicker layer upon layer of order blanks, catalogs and old newspapers, all trampled into illegibility. By tradein time, these compounded strata of debris in the rear came up to seat level.

Stim was not a British immigrant, but he always drove on the left side of the road. Coming and going, he drove to the left. I asked why and his illogical answer was, "smoother over here." When a car approached us, Stim ignored it until the last few seconds. I could see the horror in the other driver's eyes. At the last moment, Stim veered to the right to allow the other car to pass, and then he moved over to the left side of the road again.

"Some day you're going to have one big bloody accident, old chap," I told him.

"Never had an accident yet," he reassured me.

Stim spoke too soon!

Accidents were piling up in the wings, waiting to come on-stage with frightening regularity. Stim invited accidents. Driving along, he would stick his head under the dashboard to fix the wire to the car radio, and fly blind. If he had a back seat passenger, he turned around to face that person when he talked to him. When he knocked the ashes from his pipe, he concentrated on the pipe and not the road ahead.

When our drinking dealer in Bad Axe, Allie Bowron, retired, we had a retirement party. Stim, Allie, his son who would take over the business, and I, made all of the bars in the eastern half of Huron County. As he drove, Stim kept his window open. Gusts of Arctic air that had only recently air-conditioned polar bears, came in that open window.

Allie yelped, "Shut the window. I'm freezing." The Thumb of Michigan is no Garden of Eden in the wintertime.

"I don't want the windows frosted up," Stim explained.

Allie, then half froze and half drunk, lit a match and set fire to the debris in Stim's back seat area.

We'll skip the expletive because you know what Stim yelled. He screeched to a halt and got out of the car. Desperately, he pulled the burning debris out of the car, burning his hand just a little in the process.

"I was just trying to get warm," Allie explained with unassailable logic. "With that window of yours open, I about froze to death." Allie had made his point effectively.

Stim rolled up his window and turned on the Hudson's heater which surrendered about as much heat as a match does at Point Barrow. We visited several more bars to accumulate a little more antifreeze, and when the evening ended, all agreed that we had properly retired Allie Bowron.

Stim bought an Army Surplus one-room building to serve as a cottage at the lake in Lapeer County. Dick Mulnyx, Cope and their wives were visiting Stim and his wife one Sunday afternoon. The group went fishing. Stim, his wife, and Cope's wife were in one boat, and the other three were in the other boat.

Clumsily, Stim stepped in the bait pail, tripped over the tackle box, lost his balance, and "yeeooow," he fell into the water, pulling the boat over with him. Stim's wife couldn't swim, but she tried to swim to shore. Stim had to grab her and pull her back to the overturned boat. Cope's wife couldn't swim either, but Cope had coached her to hang onto the boat if she was ever confronted with this problem. Help soon arrived and all six returned to shore, three of them dripping wet. The neighbor lady came over and told Stim, "See! I told you that your horoscope said that you shouldn't be on the water today."

Stim's comments were unprintable.

The following weekend Stim and Walt Burow were headed for Toledo and the introduction of the new forage harvester, blower, and rake. They were in Stim's Hudson on this rainy night, confronted by all of the traffic returning from the lakes up north. Stim's foot missed the brake and hit the accelerator. He plowed into the car ahead, breaking Walt Burow's little finger. After Walt was bandaged up at the emergency room of the hospital, they parked Stim's dinged-up Hudson in Walt's driveway in Fenton and drove to Toledo in Walt's car.

These were the days before fancy forage wagons. We had a hayrack with one-foot sideboards. Bob Howard, our service manager from Home Office, drove the tractor that pulled and powered the forage harvester. Blockman Allen Shank was kneeling on the hayrack, and Stim, like George Washington in that boat, stood up. Bob should have known better, but he let out the clutch too quickly and Stim started going overboard. He let out another "yeeoooow," as he did a back flip out of the wagon. Al tried to grab Stim but succeeded only in falling off the back of the wagon with him. Al's back was sprained and Stim broke his arm. Our "never had an accident yet" blockman had been in the emergency room of a hospital twice in less than twenty-four hours.

Stim returned to Flint, recovered his mutilated car, and took the car to a repair shop in Port Huron. He had to pay the bill himself because he had canceled his car insurance two weeks before with the statement, "I've paid those blankety-blank thieves enough." Now he bought new car insurance.

Catastrophe struck again as Stim came home late at night after working two county fairs in one day. He fell asleep at the wheel and crashed his Hudson into a culvert. Now the new insurance company canceled his policy.

At the Michigan State Fair, Stim told me, "You know when a man gets a little older, he doesn't pay enough attention to his appearance. Look at these pants . . . no crease. And my shoes aren't shined." No sooner had he made this statement about sartorial decorum when calamity struck again. Stim walked into the "back room" of our display tent and stepped into an open bucket of black tire paint. The paint flipped up, dousing Stim with black tire paint up to his shirt pocket. This time he heaped loud verbal abuse on people who leave open buckets of tire paint sitting around. His language made a Texas mule skinner's language sound sacred and liturgical by comparison. Years later, a farmer near Bryan, Ohio, asked me, "Who was that guy that swore so loud at your tent at the Michigan State Fair?"

Stim tried to get some of the tire paint off by tapping a tractor's gasoline filter bowl for a little gasoline that he placed on his handkerchief. He then rubbed his arms with this gas-soaked handkerchief, burning his arms. I took him to the emergency medical service room at the fairgrounds.

As anyone who travels Michigan can tell you, Michigan closes down during deer hunting season. Stim and his fellow deer hunters headed north. One night, while several of the men played poker in the cabin, Cope's son said he had to go into town to get some cigarettes. He knew where Stim's car was parked in the dark. More correctly, he knew where the car *had been* parked. Stim had moved his car.

With youthful abandon, Buddy Coplin shifted his pickup into reverse and zoomed backward 0-60 in six seconds. In the process, he creased the Stimmel Hudson's front fender, front door, back door, and back fender. Buddy came into the cabin quite shaken. "Stim, I hit your car."

"Think nothing of it," Stim said. "I've got a body man hired by the week."

After deer hunting season, business-as-usual took Stim to an evening customer meeting at Ruth Farmers Elevator. Stim told me afterward, "When I got there, it was still light. Chuck (Chuck Higgins, the manager of the operation) and I stood there talking, and I saw that open manhole. However, when I came out of the meeting at about eleven o'clock, I forgot all about that open manhole. I stepped right into it."

Two planks lay loosely over the manhole. As Stim's leg went down between those two planks, the planks tore the hide off both sides of his leg from the knee to the groin. Stim was on crutches for a month.

After all this, Stim's guardian angel returned from her coffee break, and years of no excitement followed. Things were disgustingly uneventful up on Stim's block.

## OF THINGS TO COME

At the Ohio State Fair, I was unsuspectingly trapped in the corner of our tent by an inventor. There were no means of escape. I was trapped and had to listen. Inventors always wanted you to listen but then they complained that you stole their invention. My inventor friend told me, "I've invented a combine that doesn't have a cutter bar, cylinder, straw rack or cleaning shoe."

"How does it work?" I wondered, amazed at this incredible marvel of engineering.

"That's just it, it doesn't work," the inventor told me, shaking his head. Such disarming truth, coming from an inventor, is a rarity. Naturally, I asked him how it was supposed to work. "Well, instead of a cutter bar, I have a stripper," the inventor told me. Instead of cutting the crop off at the ground, then threshing stalk, chaff, and grain, he had some kind of device that only stripped the head off the grain. The stalk was left in the field, the combine had less volume to thresh, and consequently, moved faster. "Instead of a cylinder, I use belts rubbin' together that work kinda like rubbin' your hands together to get grain out of a head of wheat. As to the back end, the best way I can explain that is to tell you that looks like a giant Hart-Scour-Kleen." Farmers added Hart-Scour-Kleens to their combines because these cylindrical, centrifugal force devices further cleaned grass and legume seed. Seed, with some impurities like little sticks and weed seeds, went in one end. Centrifugal action drove the seed through the cylindrical sieve, and the unwanted "dockage" flowed out the end and was discarded. The elevator, as you can guess, paid more for a clean crop than they did for "dirty" grain or seed.

My inventor friend had obviously worked with our LaPorte Works engineers because later we saw pictures of an All-Crop Harvester that had a cylindrical rear end instead of rectangular.

Inventors were intrigued by rotary threshing from the 1920s. In 1923, H. L. Strong of the Strong Trading Company of Wichita, Kansas, patented a "New Centrifugal Thresher." Off again, on again, all combine engineers had tried their hand at rotary combines. New Holland was the first to pop with a rotary combine in 1979. IH followed a year later. A-C and White a year after that.

The strong point for rotary combines is the cleaner sample in the bin and the vastly increased capacity of the machines. Our self-propelled combine expert, Bill Barber put it this way: "We've got to learn to build them bigger on the inside, not the outside." The industry, all except Deere, moved to rotary design. That was not surprising since Deere hung with two-cylinder tractors a good twenty years after everybody else quit. The capability is now with us to deliver cleaner grain and beans to the world, but we're still living with 1908 grain standards that accept 2.49 percent foreign matter in shipped grain and soybeans. As long as farmers can't get paid for #1 grain and beans, they're not going to use their combines at their full capability.

Japan's #2 soybean importer, at an American Soybean Association field day, once told me, "We can't blame you. If we order #2s (with 2.49 percent foreign matter), we can't blame you for delivering #2s. I understand the economy of adding worthless foreign material, up to the 2.49 percent limit."

## HOW MANY IS TOO MANY?

For branch management there was the eternal problem of, "How many dealers should we have?" There's no good answer. We had six dealers around Detroit who seldom ran into each other because they served different segments of the market. Four dealers in the western part of Allen County, Ohio, seldom locked horns with each other for the same reason. Chauncey Craig had a grain elevator that could take grain in on trade. Gene Sheeter had a junk yard and what farmer doesn't have junk? Tamey Stemen served the earthy trade (there was a jug under a loose board in the floor) of which there was an abundance. Ed Spees wouldn't walk on the same side of the street with a saloon, so he got the reputable trade, of which there was an abundance too. Each had a niche.

When John Walker was branch manager in Minneapolis, he said he had a dealer at Aberdeen, South Dakota, who had four dealers around him. The Aberdeen dealer came into the branch and fired his contract on John's desk. "If you don't get rid of those pirates that are always nipping at my deals, you can stuff this up your you-know-what."

Then, John said, attrition eliminated those four dealers that the Aberdeen dealer spoke about. Now he was back in the branch and, once again he fired his contract down on John's desk. "If you don't put some new dealers around me soon, you can take this contract and stuff it. When I had those other dealers around me, we all used to warm up deals, and one of the five of us would get the deal. Now I'm the only guy out there warming things up. The further I get from Aberdeen, the cooler it gets. I need some new dealers around me. I'll take back everything I said about dealers close to me."

# 13

# LIVE AND LEARN

W. Ellzey Brown was the Tractor Division's first sales promotion manager. He put A-C's rubber-tired tractors on the map by hiring Barney Oldfield and Ab Jenkins to race rubber-tired tractors at State Fairs in the '30s. That was discussed in detail in Chapter One. Ellzey built a fast track for those who followed.

Tony McGraw succeeded Ellzey Brown. Tony was all salesman and promoter, but for reasons that were never made clear, he didn't get the budgets necessary to carry out his promotional ideas. He left in disgust and signed on with Ford. In the field, we all hated to see Tony go.

When Tony McGraw left A-C, General Manager Bill Roberts realized that a mistake had been made. Roberts had great respect for Tony, but now Tony was gone. In an unprecedented letter, Roberts wrote all branches extolling Tony's virtues, telling us how much he would be missed.

After Tony moved over to Ford, he sent me a handwritten note dated April 21, 1947. He said that there were opportunities at Ford that paid better than branch sales managers were getting at A-C. Much as I respected Tony, I was happy where I was and told him, "Sorry, but thank you anyway." I was pretty sure that the guys at Ford had less leeway than I had.

## Live and Learn

Charley Karr replaced Tony McGraw. Willis Scholl and I met Charley Karr for the first time at Toledo Branch one evening just after quitting time. Willys-Overland, next door to our branch in Toledo, had had a demonstration of its Jeep. They hoped to prove that the wartime Jeep could now become a peacetime tractor and farm conveyance. Charley had thoughts of joining that promotion. Dreamers dream dreams! During the days of the Model T Ford car, every blacksmith shop in the country sold gadgets to turn it into a tractor. In Germany, the Unimog was to be a tractor/auto/truck, but customers walked out without buying. Jeep's dream of moving to the farm didn't materialize either.

Willis Scholl and I were the only ones still at the branch when Charley came in to see us. He kept saying, "Bill wants me to come back." It was Bill this and Bill that. Charley was at his name-dropping best. He said, he had once worked for Allis-Chalmers and now if we were to believe him, Bill Roberts was begging him to come back. Charley laid it on as thick as a Dagwood sandwich that evening.

Willis told me after Charley left, "Did you ever hear such a blow-hard in all your life?" I admitted that Charley's bull had set a new record for me too.

A week later, Willis came into my office with a home office bulletin. "Read this," he said. Bill Roberts announced that Charley Karr was our new advertising manager.

Charley Karr now got the budgets that Tony McGraw wanted but couldn't get. Charley Karr did the very things that Tony McGraw said should be done.

To Charley's credit, he put a topnotch advertising department together. Rube Smith was his assistant and Bob

Crosby was a mainstay in the department. Jack Wade took pictures. When Jack retired, Don Ackerman, Herbie "One Shot" Zeck and Daryl Pries took over the photo department. Herb would say, "Why take a second picture when I know the first one is perfect?" Ann Rosnik filed our photos. Frank Barth helped with meeting planning. Jim Foley, Harold Hopkinson, and Carl Schuster worked up on Charley's fifth floor too. Carl took care of 4-H and FFA relations.

Charley Karr was something else. He once told me, "Propose anything. Write down the Declaration of Independence. They won't buy it but it will get the discussion started." There's a lot of truth to that statement.

One particularly good idea Charley had was the "school calendar." We had beautiful four-color calendars depicting the American scene; small ones for the home and large ones for schools and places of business. Dealers gave the large calendars to schools in their farm areas. Charley discovered, however, that during summer vacation, school janitors washed or painted the walls and destroyed all the calendars hanging there. School teachers and students were without a calendar from September to December. Charley Karr's school calendar started with the month of September and ended with June. A flyleaf on the calendar listed the 16-mm films we had that schools could borrow. We had hard-sell films and soft-sell films. At Toledo Branch, we kept one of our ladies busy about half time reading film requests, filling those requests, and cleaning and checking returned films.

There was a twenty-minute film entitled *Highway To Alaska* and another called *Pan-American Highway*. Both of these films were narrated by Paul Harvey, back in the days when you could buy Paul Harvey's services for one hundred bucks per day. Each year, there was a new film on the subject of soil conservation.

# Live and Learn

Charley Karr gave us our first direct mail program. He offered an impressive array of giveaway novelties that dealers could use in their sales work. Toy tractors were a favorite.

Charley Karr's appearances at home office sales meetings were always well-rehearsed. One morning I woke up at 3:00 a.m. in the Deshler-Wallick Hotel in Columbus. I went to the bathroom and on the way noticed Charley Karr rehearsing his speech as I looked in a window across the court. Who else but Charley Karr would rehearse a speech at three o'clock in the morning? He shouldn't have bothered. He was no William Jennings Bryan, rehearsed or unrehearsed.

Even though he ate only an apple for lunch, Charley's waistline did not shrink. He nipped at the bottle now and then, a little more now than then. When he had one too many, he bragged to us how cheap he was buying the watches he was giving to us in our incentive programs.

After one riotous night, Charley made it to the platform and gave his speech the next morning to the complete astonishment of all who had attended the party the night before. The shape he was in late last night, I never believed that he would be able to make it to the platform this morning. Astonishing! That's the only name for it . . . astonishing!

Wes Davis tells that Charley went to Salt Lake City to buy space in the Mormon magazine. Wes was called to take Charley to see Mormon President Albert Smith. In Smith's office, Charley asked, "What would you do if I smoked a cigarette in here?" Smith answered gently, "When a gentleman smokes in this office, we usher him out."

Charley Karr walked where angels feared to tread!

P.S. Charley got his space in the Mormon magazine. Without smoking.

## WARRANTY CLAIMS AND FIX KITS

Since machines are made by humans and humans aren't perfect, no machine is perfect. That's why we have warranties. Ours was one year; the rest of the industry had a six months warranty. No big deal though. If the defect in parts or workmanship doesn't show up in six months, it's not likely to show up at all.

My most telling lesson in warranty management came when I was interim branch manager in Des Moines. An angry farmer came into the office with this complaint: "Jim (the previous branch manager who had been fired) gave my neighbor $660 worth of free parts and that so-and-so didn't have a cent coming. He rams his machinery. He doesn't use grease and oil. If you're going to build those kinds of costs into your machinery, I don't want any more of it." You can't argue with that logic.

Unfortunately, the American economy rewards the careless, and sends the careful the bill. When Sears gives money back to someone who abused the product before returning it, you and I pay the bill the next time we're in the store. We had dealers who screened warranty claims before they hit the branch. Those guys we NEVER turned down. On the other hand, we had dealers who told every parts customer, "Let's send it in, let's see what they say." Those we shut off from time to time to get them to quit sucking eggs.

No farm equipment manufacturer can take the time or spend the money to be sure that the new machine that is being introduced has been tested in every part of North America under every conceivable ground and weather condition. No farmer would be willing to pay the extra price of such exhaustive testing. The new machine would be obsolete before the testing finished. The equipment industry does the best it can before product introduction, knowing full well that there probably will be some "fix kits."

## PRETTY SOFT!

Bill Jeffrey, our parts manager, repeatedly passed Willis Scholl's office and mine mumbling. "Pretty soft. Ride around the country on an expense account. Pretty soft."

Willis told me, "I'm going to cure Jeff of that 'pretty soft' business if it's the last thing I do."

World War II had just ended. Since Willis's uncle was a Plymouth dealer, he got a new car before the rest of us did, but the heater was back-ordered. Willis invited Jeff to go with us to a series of January block sales meetings. The two of them rode in Willis's unheated Plymouth. Willis got Jeff up at 6:00 or 6:30 each morning. They called on dealers all day long. Late in the afternoon, they arrived at the location of the evening meeting, where Jeff was to be the featured speaker.

A good parts manager Jeff was, but a good public speaker he was not. He was as incoherent as the Federal Register. I didn't tape any of Jeff's speeches, mainly because the tape recorder hadn't been invented yet, but they went something like this:

"In behalf of the parts department . . . well, you know . . . the back-orders that we get . . . some of you don't have your stock orders in yet . . . in behalf of the parts department

. . . if you're asking about an order you've got to give us the order number . . . I know you don't like back-orders either . . . then there's that lift arm, part number 503643, we got some in now . . . in behalf of the parts department . . . well, you know when your stock orders are due . . . every dad-blamed stock order we get from the factory has some back-orders on it, but it ain't my fault . . . some of you have asked about that ratchet, I think it is number 602314, well that ratchet . . . in behalf of the parts department."

About the twenty-seventh time that Jeff said, "in behalf of the parts department," Willis would cut in with, "Thank you, Jeff, for that clear explanation of how things are in the parts department." Then Willis would proceed to tell how things really were in the parts department.

Jeff's show was better than a $38 show on Broadway. I thought that Allie Bowron, Herb Fisher, and Clint Tenniswood would split a gut laughing. Even though dealers didn't know what Jeff was talking about, he was a legend, and he got more than one standing ovation for his oration.

While the block meetings generally ended by 9:30, there were always some hangers-on who wanted to stay and ask questions, so it would be eleven o'clock before Willis and Jeff got into the zero-degrees Plymouth Frigidaire to drive back to the hotel. The bed was over on the next territory.

"Care for a cup of coffee or a beer before you go to bed?" Willis would ask.

"No, thank you, Willis," Jeff would say as he hurried toward his room.

It took two weeks to cure Jeff, and Willis said it nearly killed him in the process, but never once after that did Jeff ever say anything about, "Pretty soft. Riding around on an expense account. Pretty soft."

## THE NEW BROOM THAT DIDN'T SWEEP CLEAN

"Willis, it's for you." We were together in the territory when the phone rang. Somehow Willis Scholl had a premonition what the phone call was about. He responded to the call with an unaccustomed expletive. And, "I don't want to go to Milwaukee."

But he accepted the promotion. Willis Scholl was now our eastern regional manager. He was to move to Milwaukee. Bill Roberts appointed J. C. Brown (not the right name) branch manager at Toledo. I suspect that the job would have routinely come to me, but Bill Roberts wanted to give a lifelong friend of his three years of higher income to provide him with a larger pension. J.C. had been assistant branch manager at Memphis Branch.

J.C. was a very proper Southern gentleman (with Yankee roots) who, somewhere along the line, had lost the use of one lung. Roberts thought it was safe to bring J.C. into Toledo, since Willis Scholl would be the regional manager who would oversee Brown's work. I'm sure Roberts felt, "Nothing can go wrong." Instead the phrase came out, "Nothing can go wrong go wrong go wrong go wrong go wrong go wrong go wrong."

Bill Roberts was mistaken. A good many things went wrong. What was intended as a favor turned out to be anything but a favor for the company, for Toledo Branch, its dealers, its blockmen and for J. C. Brown himself. The

Brown years weren't my most pleasant years either, and that's stating it mildly.

From Day One at Toledo Branch, ours had been a very democratic organization. Grat used to go to the fruit stand across the way and buy a watermelon. We would all stand on the dock, spitting out watermelon seeds. Grat shot the breeze with everyone in the office. We all stopped at his house for a beer from time to time. Willis Scholl carried on that tradition. He would sit on our desks, shooting the bull and trading banter. Willis Scholl's democratic management style was just like Grat's. J.C. had a diametrically opposite management plan, a sort of "lord and peasant" management plan. He spoke only to heads of departments. He isolated himself in his office. When he went back to the can, he held his head down so that he wouldn't have to speak to any of the peasants.

No amount of pleading on my part changed his philosophy. J.C. always treated me with utmost courtesy. I was part of "management" and therefore "in the club," in the "old boys' network." Norma and I visited in the Brown home often, and they came over to see us. Mrs. Brown was a delightful hostess. I had no personal complaints, but I was all but certain that Jim's aloofness in the branch would lead to trouble.

Since he had that one-lung physical disability, J.C. never went to the field. I was gone from Monday noon to Friday noon almost every week, doing all of the field work, all of the field contact with blockmen and dealers. I wasn't all that much in touch with the way things were going in the office.

During wartime, when we needed a new employee, Willis Scholl sent me to the neighboring small towns to check with school teachers and civic leaders to see if a 4-F (excused from the draft) farm boy could be found who would come to work for us. J.C. called the unemployment office. "That's what we're paying taxes for," he told me. Anyone who had to have the government get a job for them during the war wasn't very employable. That's the way I felt, and it turned out just that way.

J.C. hired three female office workers by contacting the unemployment department. One was to be my secretary. Once in a while she got one letter out per day, provided she typed it over three or four times. After that I typed my own letters. In college, I had gotten rich typing term papers for two pages for a nickel. I could type about as fast as I could dictate.

One day, J.C. came into my office and his face was as white as the driven snow at Yutursk. He handed me a calling card. "Our office people have joined a union," he said. "That guy that just left was the union official for this area." I was surprised, yet I was not surprised.

J.C. had asked for it and now he had it. A labor union! The three he had hired from the unemployment department had called the union official in. They wanted to secure their place on the payroll after servicemen came back from the wars, and management could hire whom they wanted again. The rest of the folks in the office joined in to secure their place in the office too. J.C. was too much of a question mark to them to take chances.

Not only did we have a revolt in the office, we had it in the field too. J.C. also had a dealer revolution to contend with. A dozen or so of our good dealers banded together to tell us that they would not sign their Sales & Service Agreements for the forthcoming year. They wanted free choice. They did not want mandatory allotments crammed down their throat, now that the war was over. We were just beginning to shift from sellers' market to buyers' market, and to many in company management, that came as an unwelcome shock.

I pleaded to be allowed to go to the territory to talk with these dealers, fully confident that I could resolve the situation. Our regional manager finally granted me permission to try. I headed for my old Cleveland block first and took on Sam Deise of Quail & Deise. Sam, as I knew he would, blew off a head of steam. Then we discussed what was at stake. Sam and Mr. Quail signed their contract. I took that signed contract to another dealer, and he signed his contract too. The revolution was broken, but mandatory allotments were broken too. We shipped to dealers only whole goods and parts that the dealer ordered. The disruption had lasted ten days. The labor union thing lasted a lot longer than that.

The moment that Home Office heard that J. C. Brown had, by his management style, invited a labor union to invade the Toledo operation, J.C. was shunted into early retirement and Sherm Anderson, sales manager at LaPorte Branch, came in as the new Toledo branch manager.

This whole thing had festered under my nose. I should have known, even if I was out in the territory most of the time. At the time, I figured the company made the right move by bringing Sherm Anderson in as branch manager. In retrospect, no outsider had the chance that I had of talking the five old-timers out of their camaraderie with the three from the unemployment office.

I had been appointed blockman and branch sales manager before I thought I was ready. Now I was overlooked when I was ready. In corporate life, you win some and you lose some. As it turned out, it was just as well. Had I been appointed branch manager at this point, I would not have had the chance to go to Home Office as described in the next chapter. I would have missed an assignment that I thoroughly enjoyed, and which gave me national recognition.

## WHO PINCHED YOU?

It was completely out of character for J.C. to suggest a thing like this, but there was a little fun in the old boy after all. Before the labor union thing, that is.

We were to hold our annual dealer sales meeting at the Hillcrest Hotel in Toledo. J.C. told me to seat Blockman Harry "Grandma" Kulp in a marked chair. Harry was our most sedate, most serious, most sober, most august, most decorous blockman, and he generally gave us more sales volume than any other blockman. J.C. gave me two bucks with which to tip the waitress who would serve Harry. When she set Harry's plate down, she was instructed to scream and jump back.

When the waitress screamed, J.C. got up from the head table and asked, "What's going on back there?"

"He pinched me," the waitress screamed.

"Who pinched you?" J.C. asked.

"HE pinched me," the waitress said, holding a plate in one hand while pointing at Harry with the other.

"I did not. I did not. NO! I didn't pinch her." Harry's denial of sexual harassment was so vehement that the waitress could hardly keep a straight face. She kissed Harry on the head and placed her arms around him to the enjoyment of the gathered Toledo Branch organization. The two received a hearty round of applause.

"I wondered why you told me to sit in that particular chair," Harry told me afterward.

## YOU AND ME OUGHTA TALK

When Blockman Al Shank moved on to Harrisburg to be sales manager there, he moved just before our quaint ritual of annual dealer contracting. Lucky me, I got the job of writing the dealer contracts on what had been Al Shank's block. When I came to Merritt Gehrisch at Arlington, Ohio, I asked which banker I should visit to get the bank report. He told me, "I have a checking account across the street, but don't sell any paper there. The banker wants recourse and I'm not about to give him recourse as long as four or five other banks are after my business."

I asked, "Do you mind then if I have a little fun with your banker?"

"Be my guest," Merritt said.

After the banker filled out the report, I used my stock opener, "Making any money on this account?"

"No, it's just a little checking account."

I acted shocked. "You mean you're not taking any of Merritt's paper?"

"No."

"Why?"

"He won't sign his paper." Said as an economic indictment.

"His paper? You mean, if he signed it, he would get the profit?"

"Nooooo."

"Then it's not his paper, it's your paper, isn't it?"

"He brings it in."

"What difference does it make how or where it came from? Through the front door, back door or skylight. If you buy it, it's yours, isn't it?"

"He ought to be willing to sign his paper."

"If he signed his paper so that you would have guaranteed profit, would you guarantee him a profit on every deal?"

"Nooooo."

"Then why should he guarantee you a profit. You must be new at the banking business."

"Nooooo. I've been here thirty-eight years."

"And haven't learned how to judge a credit risk? You ought to be ashamed of yourself, asking that young man to double-guess you and assure you of profit. Goodbye!" I walked out of the bank.

Sixty days later, Merritt was in the branch. He said, "Guess who came to see me."

"Your banker?"

"Yep. When I came in from the field last night, he was sitting behind the stove. He said to me, 'Merritt, I think you and me oughta talk.'"

## THE CHANGING WORLD

When World War II started, we placed our dealers on allotments based on two years of prewar sales. If Dealer A sold 3.87 percent of our cultivators in those two years, he got 3.87 percent of all of the cultivators we received during the war years. All other allotments were figured in the same manner.

As time passed, problems arose. In some parts of the country, before the war, farmers had not bought cultivators when they bought their tractors. Now they wanted a cultivator. In Toledo Branch territory, however, prewar tractors and cultivators went together like coffee and doughnuts. LaCrosse Works began using more of their steel allotments to build cultivators. LaCrosse built more cultivators than Milwaukee built tractors. The War Production Board (WPB) ordered it! Now I ask you, how do you sell 1.25 cultivators per tractor? That's what we received. In other parts of the country this 1.25-1 ratio was just what the doctor ordered, but for us it spelled chaos. No amount of pleading with Home Office did any good. We offered to trade cultivator allotments for something we could use but all we heard was, "NO! Uncle Sam says this is the way it should be done and that's the way it will be done, period. Do you understand?" When something is sanctified by government, however wrong it is, it takes on the sanctity of the Magna Charta and the Gospel according to St. John.

Another such case: all we got from LaCrosse was 6-foot mowers for the Model B. Ours was 5-foot mower country. We offered to trade but Home Office said "no." Consequently our dealers had to saw a foot off the end of a mower and throw it into the scrap pile. Uncle Sam conserved steel!

Enter Yoder & Frey. These two enterprising gentlemen at Archbold, Ohio, started a used machinery monthly auction that both alleviated and compounded our problems.

Surplus cultivators (and a few surplus other things too) found their way to Yoder & Frey's monthly auction sales. Buyers came to this sale from almost everywhere east of the Mississippi River. When dealers found things going on the auction block that they had tried unsuccessfully to get from us, we heard from those dealers, loud and clear we heard from them.

When serial-numbered machines landed at Archbold, invariably the serial numbers had been ground off. The origin could not be traced. Rather than transfer a machine to a neighboring dealer at no profit, dealers took the machines to Archbold where they demanded Office of Price Administration (OPA) ceiling prices. Prices frozen by government are always an immediate invitation for black market operations.

Over and over again, we heard, "Gary Schmidt is peddling his stuff at Archbold." So we began to ship Gary's machinery through the branch. At the branch we center-punched equipment in various places and kept track, by serial numbers, where the center punches were. One of our men attended each Archbold sale, but never found any of Gary's equipment on the lot. Not once could the man find any center-punched tractors. Dealers refused to believe our story.

One time we thought we caught Gary red-handed. A blockman came into the branch with Polaroid pictures of Gary's truck being loaded with Roto-Balers on his whole goods lot in Continental, Ohio. Another series of pictures showed the same truck going through the gates at Archbold. I rushed down to Continental and found every serial number baler there that was supposed to be there. We never did unravel that mystery.

The Yoder & Frey sales were more popular than anyone had dreamed. The success of these sales led to establishment of other auctions around the country. They were a first class headache for us during wartime and immediately afterward.

When the buyers' market returned, the sales yards served a good purpose. They acted as a clearing house for large regions of the country. Prices paid at the auction sales became a sort of Blue Book price for used equipment. Trade magazines published the prices then and they still do. A free market economy always finds a way to match buyer and supplier.

The British economist, Adam Smith, spoke of the "invisible hand" of the marketplace. Yoder & Frey's sale was a terrific example of the invisible hand at work. Painful as it was at times, it was still better than a more controlled economy.

### TOLEDO BRANCH'S LABOR UNION

The National Labor Relations Board held a hearing, and Eastern Regional Manager Frank Mussell testified. For two days Frank twisted his handkerchief and sweated as lawyers quizzed him about his alleged, stated, uncouth, antagonistic attitude regarding unions. NLRB ordered an election, and the union won, 5-3. If Frank Mussel's tough attitude hadn't been so tough, one more might have voted "no union." A tie would have ended things. Now NLRB told us to bargain. A man by the most unusual name of John Smith was the union's organizer and bargaining agent. John had spent a lifetime in the Piedmont section of the country, organizing tobacco plants.

### NEXT CLAUSE, PLEASE!

After the union won the election at Toledo Branch, labor negotiations began. I was the longhand shorthand reporter at those sessions. I abbreviated as fast as I could in my illegible-except-unto-thyself longhand, then rushed to the office to transcribe before the notes grew cold and became completely unintelligible. Sherm Anderson was there, of course, because he was boss.

Home Office sent down two of their legal eagles, one by the name of Bill McGowan and the other was John Waddleton. All-alone John Smith represented the union. Four to one. That should have been a premonition, but John did his best to protect the rights of the downtrodden and distressed. His union's home office had abandoned him, because they knew that the chances that Allis-Chalmers was going to give John a more favorable contract than they gave to the national UAW-CIO were about as great as the chances of making birth control retroactive.

John Smith was a likable sort of a guy. He was really in semi-retirement. He had a handful of small contracts in Toledo—one, a wholesale drug firm with about twenty employees, another, an automobile dealership with about the same number of people.

Realizing the futility of it all, John opened with, "Come on, fellas. Let's give 'em a coupla bucks and let's get out of here. I don't expect you to match my other unions in one jump, but let's give 'em a few bucks. Let's cut out all of this formal crap. Give 'em a few bucks and I'll sign whatever else you want me to sign."

Bill McGowan and John Waddleton feigned shock. They took on the demeanor of a Supreme Court judge, the inner turmoil of a picket in front of the White House. "Oh, no, John. The NLRB has ordered us to bargain and bargain we must. What is your proposal?"

"I ain't got none, fellas. Let's just give 'em a few bucks."

Bill McGowan, handing John a piece of paper, said, "Well, in that case then, here is our proposal. Clause #1."

John looked it over and said, "Looks OK to me...let's get to the wage clause. All of this is just standard junk."

Bill McGowan insisted on discussing Clause #2, Clause #3, Clause #4, ad nauseam. John grunted a little when he read one clause that stated "no closed shop." He commented, "I expected that. Labor unions don't know what a closed shop is. Now take lawyers. That's a closed shop. People can't defend themselves. They got to hire an expensive lawyer. A lawyer on both sides, and who sits in front of the courtroom? Another lawyer . . . a judge who can't make a living in private practice so they make him a judge. If the case is appealed, who is it appealed to? Another lawyer. Now, gentlemen, that's a closed shop." John's reasoning was unassailable.

Finally Bill McGowan came to Clause #10, the wage clause. It read, "Wages remain the same." John exploded! He got up and pounded the table in righteous wrath. Blue smoke was intermingled with four-letter words. He screamed, "Waddya you guys want? A strike right off the bat? You know very well that I gotta get those members of mine a few extra bucks. You know that. Don't give me any of your wages-remain-the-same crap."

Bill McGowan waited until the walls of Hotel Secor (that's where the sessions were held) stopped shaking, then said, "OK, so let's see your proposal on wages, John."

"I tole you guys, I ain't got no proposal. You know as well as I do that I gotta get them people a few bucks raise. Now let's give 'em a few bucks and let's cut out all of this wages-remain-the-same baloney."

Bill McGowan asked to see John's figures for his other unions. John had spent a lifetime in the American Federation of Labor, but he wasn't familiar with CIO bargaining practices. Incredible as it may seem, he did not know that CIO wage contracts of the day consisted of four columns.

1. Wages
2. Improvement factor
3. Cost of living adjustment (COLA)
4. Total of the three, which is what the worker was paid.

Numbers two and three were politicians' ways of making labor happy, by getting around wartime frozen wage legislation. When John asked us to increase our salaries to those of his other unions, he looked only at our Column #1, not Column #4. All this Bill McGowan and John Waddleton did not know and didn't even suspect. Obviously, Sherm and I didn't know it either.

When Bill asked for John's figures, he proudly plunked them down. "There," he said. "Now as I told you, I don't expect you to jump to the top in one jump. Just give 'em a few bucks."

When Bill and John looked at the union's figures for Smith's other unions, they were stupefied. Allis-Chalmers, with present wage rates, was higher in every category (except one person in one of John's unions) than all of John's other unions. McGowan and Waddleton didn't know what John was trying to pull. They called a recess.

We sat in the lobby and collectively addressed the question, "What's he trying to pull on us?" Bill McGowan called his boss, Buck Story, in Milwaukee. Buck answered, "You're in Toledo and I'm in Milwaukee, you figure it out."

Bill and John tossed out all sorts of wild guesses, but none seemed to make sense. Bill said, "Let's go back in and let the chips fall where they may." We reconvened.

When we sat down again, Bill placed our figures alongside John's and asked him to make comparisons. Bill looked at Column #4 and John Smith at Column #1.

"Hey, you're looking at the wrong column," John said.

"No, I'm not," Bill replied. And then came the dawn! John Smith, a labor union organizer and negotiator all of his life, didn't know the UAW-CIO pattern of wage calculation even though it had been mentioned in local papers at least 17,878 times. When it was shown that we were higher in every category than every one of John's other units, except the one category in one union, John threw up his hands and moaned, "I know when I'm licked. What's the next clause?"

John Waddleton asked, "John, would it help you if we cut our wage rates to match your other unions?"

John's reply was unprintable.

Clauses #14, #15, and #16 spoke of union elections to be held on company premises, on company time, under the supervision of an NLRB agent. Once again, John wailed, "You're usurping union prerogatives!" Our guys kidded him by asking him if he intended to hold clandestine elections in the upper loft of some warehouse on the East Side at 11:30 p.m." John kept insisting that it was none of our blankety-blank business where or when he held his elections. On those three clauses there was an impasse. The NLRB, to our great surprise, said they were bargainable issues and ordered more negotiations.

John's labor union was not ready to bargain on these issues, lest they lose some hard-fought victories of the past. Bargaining over Clauses #14, #15 and #16 could have set a dangerous precedent for the union, and that the union was not ready to do. We didn't hear from either John or the union again.

When neither showed up in the next thirty days, I suggested to Sherm Anderson that we should fire the two employees that we knew had started the whole thing. More cautious minds prevailed. Two from the unemployment department eventually quit and were never heard from after that. They knew the union's rug had been pulled out from under them, and that their days were numbered. The third left town with her chiropodist husband after one of his patients charged him with a sex offense.

During the negotiations Sherm Anderson and I got to know Bill McGowan and John Waddleton quite well. Bill said that when he got out of law school and signed on with a law firm for the first time, it was up in the iron mine/lumber camp area of the Upper Peninsula of Michigan. His boss was a crusty old counselor who fit the area. He told Bill, "In this firm we have one rule that we obey implicitly. Do not have intercourse with the help . . . (pause to puff on a cigar) . . . on company premises . . . (another pause, another puff) . . . on company time."

## AND NOW, THIRDLY . . .

Since our bosses were away on a factory tour, George (I've forgotten his last name) and I had to take over our company's dealers' luncheon at the Michigan Farm Equipment Dealers' Convention. Tradition had it that the company sprung for a lunch for our dealers at this convention in Grand Rapids each year. George was sales manager at LaPorte Branch, and LaPorte was a few thousand dollars ahead of us in sales volume. I knew that George would tell one and all about, "those small eastern branches . . . Blah, blah, blah."

En route to Grand Rapids, I stopped to get a cup of coffee at a Walgreen's drug store in Three Rivers. The druggist was unpacking some Christmas merchandise. When he came to false teeth, he held up a set for all to admire. These false teeth were gags, a windup set of uppers and lowers made of plastic. When wound up and then released, they would start to chatter. Like a man auctioning off livestock or a sales manager pounding his chest and lipping off about sales expertise.

"How much for the teeth?"

"A buck."

"You're sold your first set of false teeth," I told the druggist. I knew exactly what I would do with them.

At the luncheon, George, as anyone could have prophesied, bragged about LaPorte Branch and castigated "those small Eastern branches." When it came my turn to speak, I told the audience: "You have heard what George had to say. George is an honorable man, but as far as my rebuttal is concerned, this will suffice." The wound-up teeth were released and the teeth chattered beautifully. The gag got a good laugh from the crowd.

When the teeth ran down, I began my speech. There was firstly, then secondly, and when I came to thirdly, I pounded the rostrum with a good rap of my fist. The teeth started to chatter again. If you think the crowd laughed the first time, you should have heard them the second time.

The technical term for this sort of thing is "backfire."

## 14

# DON'T TRY TO STOP THE TIDE

Before Rudolf Diesel drowned in the English Channel after falling from the deck of a channel steamer in 1913, he gave the world the diesel engine. Following Diesel's visits to America from his native Germany in 1904 and 1912, the diesel engine was accepted in the United States. By 1944, diesel engines built in the U.S.A. added up to over thirty million horsepower. The diesel engine burned less expensive fuel and converted a higher percentage of fuel burned into mechanical energy. Diesel engines seemed to last longer and required less maintenance.

It was inevitable that one day some farm equipment manufacturer would place a diesel engine in his tractor. As it turned out, Oliver Corporation was that somebody. Oliver built tractors in the old Hart-Parr plant in Charles City, Iowa. They introduced the first six-cylinder engine to the industry, back in the days when Deere hadn't gotten beyond two. Now Oliver's top man, King McCord, did it again. He introduced a diesel-engine tractor, and that tractor's sales began to zoom.

We didn't have a diesel engine for our tractors, so I had to find some reason why diesels were impractical for farm tractors. It's always foolish to try to fight progress, but salesmen never learn. I came up with figures that proved, beyond the shadow of a doubt, that a farmer could not afford a diesel-engine tractor. Farmers paid as much attention to my figures as a Baptist preacher pays attention to Jack Daniels's advertising. Some farmers bought Oliver's diesel tractors because the hired help couldn't siphon off fuel for their cars from the tractor's fuel supply.

Oliver had a head start, but their lead didn't last long. Soon every tractor manufacturer offered a diesel-engine tractor. Eventually, all large tractors had diesel engines, with no gasoline models offered. Allis bought the Buda Company for its diesel engine. Vice President Boyd Oberlink told me about the Buda acquisition, "It was like marrying a virgin bride only to find out that she has venereal disease." The Buda engine needed updating badly.

## THE AMERICAN TRACTOR COMPANY

While farm equipment was still scarce in postwar USA, a ten-page, two-color ad appeared in our farm equipment trade papers. The American Tractor Company of Churubusco, Indiana, offered a fine line of crawler tractors. I pinched myself. Churubusco was a small town near my small hometown in northern Indiana. How could I have lived all of these years beside greatness without discovering it? Why had I not heard? Why had I not learned to fear and respect this formidable competitor? I felt stupid!

When I asked around in order to fill in the blanks in my cranial memory bank, I was told that Marc Rojtman was the man who really was the American Tractor Company. I was told that he and his father had built equipment in Germany for the German army, and after the war, the younger Rojtman had emigrated to America. He had bought some war surplus tractor parts, designed a tractor, and was now offering it for sale, if there was enough front money. The American Tractor Company was a tin shed in Churubusco, Indiana. I was told that Rojtman had spent 90 percent of his earthly goods to finance that ad and that the ad had done what advertising is supposed to do, which is to bring prospects in by the hundreds. The American Tractor Company prospered. The price of American Tractor Company stock soared way past book value.

Jerome Increase Case fathered a full line of farm equipment. Jerome Increase Case has to be considered one of the greatest men the industry ever produced, if not the greatest. But Jerome Increase Case was long gone and his offspring hadn't fared so well. Rojtman's stock was worth $6 and sold for $32. Case's stock was worth $32 and was selling for $6. If those figures are off a little, they're not off much. Case was interested in Rojtman and Rojtman was interested in Case. An even-up trade of shares of stock was arranged, and Rojtman became the chief executive officer of Case Company.

The Case Company came out of its siesta roaring. Rojtman introduced a whole new line of equipment, including a fluid drive tractor. He called all Case dealers together for a giant revival meeting in Phoenix. There the fluid drive tractor that had been flown to Phoenix from Racine, when hooked up end-to-end, pulled every competitive tractor out of the ring. Mouths gaped. The gathered throng applauded. Unbelievable! An economic Houdini!

Dealers sat in the stands with order blanks on clipboards, and began to write furiously. Rojtman had no trouble getting orders for *this* tractor. In fact, Rojtman, in this postwar sellers' market setting, had no trouble getting orders of any kind.

And then, little by little, the industry awakened. Why would anyone fly a tractor to Phoenix if there was time to ship it by rail or truck? Was this tractor rushed out of the lab with wet paint and without an hour of test work? Where were the plants in which Rojtman would build all of the equipment that he had orders for? What was the magic of that fluid drive tractor, that David of tractors that slew the whole lot of competitive Goliaths?

It didn't take long for competitive dealers to discover the way the magician pulled his trick. A fluid drive adjusts to load. If low-low is required, the drive shifts to low-low automatically. Rojtman had hooked rear-to-rear with tractors that were in road gear. Given something near equal conditions, any pulling force in low gear will outpull a pulling force in high gear.

When Case dealers took delivery of their new magic tractors, competitors challenged them to a pull on the town square. From in front of the courthouse, the dime store, God and everybody, Case tractors were pulled backward to the Case dealership. The Case fluid drive tractor disappeared as rapidly as it had appeared.

When we heard of the Case wizardry at A-C, we asked ourselves, "What does Marc Rojtman know that we don't know?" Our Springfield, Illinois, crawler tractor plant had patented a fluid drive crawler tractor, but didn't offer it for sale because it overheated and you had to own an oil well to keep it in fuel. We had copyrighted the name "Hydromatic." When Oldsmobile came with the nation's first automatic transmission, they ran into our copyright and asked if they could buy it. We said we didn't think we would ever use it. "Change one letter. Call yours 'Hydramatic,' and go ahead."

While A-C people had the conversations with Oldsmobile employees, they got to know some General Motors people. Some of the GM executives had farms. One of their engineers or one of ours, I don't know which, suggested, "Why don't we try fluid drive in a farm tractor?" On one of the General Motors executive's farms, we tried the idea and found it sadly wanting of practicality.

After the Phoenix extravaganza, media people had a bonanza. Column after column was written about Marc Rojtman, the miracle man of Racine, the paragon of perspicacity, this combination Horatio Alger and Thomas Edison, this twentieth century Moses who was leading his people across the Red Sea of agribusiness. New York City bankers flocked to Racine to offer money. As I recall, Rojtman did business with fifty-two banks.

Then things began to unravel. Bankers evidently missed the financial report that spoke of $170 million in sales and $40 million in red ink. The bubble began to leak. When it burst, Rojtman departed to lands unknown, and Bill Grede, one of Milwaukee's most conservative businessmen, came in to salvage what he could of the Case Company. Media hype continued until the week before the crash. Talk about egg on the face. It was like the *Chicago Tribune* headline, "DEWEY WINS." Bankers scrambled to rescue their funds from the economic rubble. The Kern County Land Company bought 57 percent of Case's stock, and Tenneco bought the Kern County Land Company. Later Tenneco acquired the other 43 percent.

Rojtman left one valuable legacy. He knew nothing about agriculture, but he did know industrial equipment. Whereas Ford had the industrial tractor business all to itself for so many years, Rojtman aimed the Case Company at

Ford. Ford's Merritt Hill came to Case to be chief executive officer after Grede left. For the first time, Ford had real competition in wheel tractors, backhoes, blades and other industrial equipment. Case even had a small crawler which Ford had resolutely refused to build.

Case's industrial equipment business did well but Case's farm equipment languished. Only a few models of tractors remained; no harvesting machines, no implements. When independent Case dealers quit, they were replaced by company stores. As every industry person knows, company stores are a desperation move. Case called it the "wave of the future." Finally, in 1985, when Tenneco's Case Company bought International Harvester, a Case executive admitted that the buy out was mainly to get a nationwide lineup of good farm equipment dealers. But we're getting ahead of the story. Let's go back to 1945-55.

## THE MIDDLE LINK IN THE CHAIN

I've always said, "It's 70 percent dealer and 30 percent product." Every economy is built of two halves—the production half and the marketing half, and neither can exist long without the other. We made the stuff. Dealers sold it. We could not have done without them. Farmers could not have done without them either. Dealers were the indispensable middle link in the chain. Here's a quick look at a couple of good dealers, one in Ohio, one in Michigan:

Some people in this great world of ours find the truth a bit too drab, so they dress up the truth a bit to make the story more interesting. Pokey Green, our dealer in Grass Lake, Michigan, was one such person. If we had five more horsepower than the competition, Pokey made it ten. If we could thresh two more acres a day than the competition, Pokey made it four. No matter how superlative the truth was, Pokey embellished it.

When Toledo Branch had a drive on to hire salesmen in dealerships, Pokey hired a man, and sent him to our salesman training school. On my next trip to Grass Lake, I asked about the new salesman.

"Where's Joe?"

"Joe? Joe who?" Pokey wondered.

"Joe. Your new salesman," I said.

"Oh, that Joe. I had to let him go." Pokey said this with a touch of sadness in his voice. His demeanor was that of a pallbearer.

"Why? What did he do or didn't he do?"

Pokey leaned over so that no one would overhear, "Don't spread this around, but I caught Joe lying to me. If there is one kind that I can't stand, it's a liar. You just can't work with someone who lies to you."

Ben Hartzel, our dealer in Republic, Ohio, said he didn't want to work so hard anymore. He told his three key men that he would give them half of the profit if he could go hunting and fishing more often. They were to split the half into thirds. Ben figured he could get by with a little less income.

You know what? The next year Ben made more off his half than he had made off his whole the year before. There's a bit more incentive if you're working for yourself.

## ROD EVERY

Rod Every was our blockman at Defiance, Ohio. Branch Manager Sherm Anderson came from LaPorte Branch, and he lured Rod to Toledo.

Rod Every wore a Western hat, drove an old Buick, and his twisted smile always revealed a gold tooth up front. Rod had money, plenty of money, mainly because he didn't spend any. I was in his home just once. The Every life style was Spartan. I've seen better home furnishings at a rained-out white elephant sale. Mrs. Every had once been office manager for the famous Lunt-Fontaine theatrical team.

Rod had been in extension work in Wisconsin. He said he checked his sources and found that the most fertile land in the country was on the eastern shore of Chesapeake Bay. He told us he went there and bought a farm, fortunately located between two old-line Eastern families' farms. Eventually those two families got into a bidding war over Rod's farm and Rod came out with enough money to retire. It was a sort of blueblood version of Hatfields and McCoys. Blockman Ken Johnson thought Rod's talk of owning a farm in Delmarva was a lot of bull, so on vacation, Ken drove down the peninsula and checked at the courthouse. Sure enough, Rod owned the land free and clear. Ken stood there and shook his head in disbelief.

Rod's block was top block in sales volume while he was in Toledo Branch. He even beat out Harry Kulp. Branch Manager Sherm Anderson got along with Rod very well, but there was no love lost between our other blockmen and Rod. One time we had a steak and beans contest. We divided the blockmen into two teams. The team with the most sales volume ate steak, the losers ate beans. Rod ended up on the losing team. His team mates had let him down. Rod refused to lower himself to eat beans. Beans were below his station in life. He left them in front of him untouched while Stim cut off chunks of his steak and waved the steak under Rod's nose. Rod refused to believe that his great and good friend, Sherm Anderson, would visit such indignity upon him. He was sure that there was steak in the wings for the losers. There wasn't.

When Rod first came to Toledo Branch, he had to have a house to live in. In wartime, housing was hard to come by. Rod went to a banker in Defiance and told him, "I have $50,000 to place in your bank if you can find me a house to rent in forty-eight hours." He had a house in twenty-four hours. Rod had more guts than a two-bit fiddle. More ego than twelve incumbent congressmen.

Without disagreement or explanation, Rod left for parts unknown. I guessed there were new worlds to conquer. Years later I ran into him at a dealership in Sun Prairie, Wisconsin. He told me that he had moved back to where his roots were in Wisconsin. Rod chuckled when he described the bidding war that took place between his two Eastern establishment neighbors over the purchase of his farm on the Eastern shore. The sale provided enough cash to allow Rod to retire without working.

God bless capital gains!

## SSSSH, DON'T TELL A SOUL

Branch Manager Sherm Anderson enjoyed telling about his former job that he had with a competitor of ours. Sherm told me:

"My boss called me into his office to tell me that he was giving me a five dollar per month raise. He told me not to tell anyone. I replied, 'I sure won't. I'm as ashamed of it as you are.' "

## BLOCK SALES MEETINGS

As a sales manager, I had unorthodox work habits. At first I promised myself that I would provide services for our blockmen that I had not received from my branch sales managers. Before the year was out, I found that blockmen were only to eager to have me do their work for them. So I cut that out and then adopted unorthodox unworking hours, unlike those of any other sales manager in the company.

I would go to a block, arriving at noon. The blockman and I then ate lunch with a dealer who had business that called for attention. In the afternoon we called on another dealer or two. In the evening, we held a block sales meeting with all of the dealers on the block represented. I could figure on getting to the hotel on the next block somewhere around midnight. In the morning, I slept in, meeting the next blockman and a dealer for lunch. My working hours were approximately noon to midnight. Kemmon Williams, of Holiday Inn fame, tells young audiences, "Work half days, and it doesn't make any difference which twelve hours you work."

By using this scheduling, I was able to see dealers with special problems quite regularly. Once a month, we met with all dealers to review the seasonal machinery coming up for the next selling season. We talked tractors in January, general business in February, implements in March, and so on through the year.

One day Sherm Anderson said to me, "I like to listen to you and so do the dealers, but if you carry the whole load, we're not training our blockmen to get on their feet and make presentations. From this point on, the blockman handles the block business and product presentation and you will close the meeting as the featured speaker of the evening."

That plan sounded good to me. We invited the blockmen in to Toledo to announce the program to them. There were public speaking hints, and then we put the new order in place. It was a pleasant surprise to see a couple of our men come up with ideas better than I had ever come up with. Two of our blockmen regularly struck out. Even though one man had all the ego in the world, he would actually get sick at the prospect of facing an audience. The other wasn't afraid to face an audience but he ran out of things to say after five minutes. I took over on those two territories.

## STUPIDITY COMPOUNDED

When Don Horton, our very successful dealer at Plymouth, Michigan, died a young man, his silent partner took over. Not a great deal of management skill was required since Don had a sizable wartime allotment and farmers took machinery away from dealers as fast as it came in. Silent Partner surrounded himself with good help. He came to work late, left early for lunch, came back late from lunch, went home early in the middle of the afternoon. Silent Partner's three employees did almost all of the work.

Then Silent Partner decided to sell each of the three young men a quarter of the corporation. He took a note from each man for that man's portion of the corporation's stock. The three men, who now held 75 percent ownership of the business, tired of the boss's absenteeism so they called a stockholders' meeting and, by a vote of three to one, fired Silent Partner. Now Silent Partner was outside, looking in.

He called the branch and I was sent to see what could be done to solve the dilemma. I met with Silent Partner on a park bench. He told me in a chastened way, "What are you going to do about this?"

"Nothing. Our Sales & Service Agreement is with the corporation. Your three men hold 75 percent of the stock in the corporation so they're the people we have to do business with."

Silent Partner said tearfully, "But I haven't been paid for the stock yet."

"Did you sell it to them on time?"

"Yes."

"Are the notes due?"

"No."

"Then things stand as I described. If they default on their notes, then ownership will revert to you and if that happens, we'll do business with you, or whoever holds 51 percent of the stock of the corporation." Legally there wasn't anything else to do.

I said, "Pardon me for laughing. I know you don't think it's funny, but how in the world could any one as intelligent and experienced as you are, paint yourself into such a corner?"

"It wasn't easy," he said with a pained smile. Then he added, "Don and I did business with you for over ten years and now you won't come to my rescue. It isn't fair."

I suggested, "Why don't you buy the business back?" knowing full well that the business was not for sale.

I told Silent Partner, "I might be more sympathetic if I didn't realize that Don did all of the work to build the big allotment that the firm has, and the three young men working there now have done all of the work since Don died. Mr. Silent Partner, you haven't really done a thing to make the business thrive except to provide some of the original investment. I don't blame the three young men for firing you."

Then Silent Partner tried a squeeze play. The store building wasn't part of the corporation. That was owned by a separate corporation. Silent Partner, in a landlord role, doubled the rent for the dealership corporation. The boys paid double rent for a few months and then built an identical building next door. They moved into the new building and now Silent Partner didn't have a business or a tenant. And it wasn't likely that the three majority stockholders would declare a dividend soon.

No job! No tenant! No dividends! Woe is me!

**DON'T WANT TO BE OUT**

The names are changed in this one. I called on Frank Swenson in Fictitious, Ohio, but Frank was out and Jeanette was in. She said that Frank would be back soon, so I sat down and read a year-old copy of *Farm Implement News*. The phone rang. Someone had asked if a certain part was in stock. Jeanette said, "Just a minute. I'll go see." She came back to the phone and told the caller, "Yes, we have one in stock, but we can't sell that because we don't like to be out."

That was a marketing technique that I had never heard of before. My marketing education had been neglected, for later it became evident that other firms also had a "don't want to be out" policy. When we planned our retirement move from Milwaukee to Pigeon Forge, Tennessee, I went into the local Sears store at Brookfield Square. Pointing at a filing cabinet, I said to the clerk, "I would like that filing cabinet, please. It matches the other three I bought here."

"I can't sell you that one because it is our last one and we don't like to be out." Those weren't his exact words, but that is what he meant. So Sears Roebuck had adopted Jeanette Swenson's don't-like-to-be-out policy. And I'll bet a dollar to a tube of lipstick that Sears didn't pay Jeanette any royalty for using her marketing idea either.

**GOODBYE AGAIN**

For eight happy years, I had been sales manager at Toledo Branch. The two years under J.C. weren't very happy. Now, in 1955, Home Office decided that there would be "fruit basket upset," a term that kids use when everything gets shifted around. Sherm Anderson moved to Portland, Oregon, to be branch manager there. I moved to Home Office to be the company's first sales training manager.

Mobility is the name of the game in corporate life. With each move, there are tearful farewells and new friends to become acquainted with. Goodbye friend, hello stranger!

# PART FIVE
# MILWAUKEE

## 15

# CENTRALIZATION IN, CENTRALIZATION OUT

It's the corporate version of "musical chairs." It's centralization-in, centralization-out, moving from one to the other with disturbing regularity. Like the Britisher who descended from upstairs on the London bus, because, "Old chap, there was no bloody driver up there," there's a period of driving from the central office. Then corporate heads discover that everybody knows more about the business than anybody, and they relinquish central control in favor of distributed management. There are things to be said both for and against each system. It's an expensive game, but expense be hanged if new management wants to prove the old adage, "A new broom sweeps clean."

When I arrived at our Milwaukee home office in August of 1954, centralization was in. Bill Klein, longtime branch manager at Minneapolis, was called in to be a sort of amalgamated sales mogul of what used to be called the "Tractor Division." In 1954, the new Tractor Division consisted of the Farm Equipment Division, the Construction Machinery Division, and the Engine & Material Handling Division, three widely varied businesses, in three widely varied markets, that had in common only that most of the products were powered by an internal combustion engine, and all of the products were sold through independent dealers. Bill's job was almost impossible. I reported directly to Bill Klein and not to any of the people in the three divisions. I was to be sales training manager for all three divisions, in title that is. The Farm Equipment Division had no formal training program and neither did Engine & Material Handling, but Construction Machinery had a full-blown training center, with a full-time staff at the factory in Springfield, Illinois. They were not about to take orders from me. The most I did at Springfield was sit and listen. Anything more than that would have been the blind leading the sighted.

Bill Klein had a good thing going for him when he was branch manager of Minneapolis Branch. Every year it was a real horse race between Bill and George Karcher, in Memphis, to see which branch would be Number One in sales volume. Both branches had multi-state territories. While in Minneapolis, Bill had time to play golf and attend to many Shrine activities. In Milwaukee, in his new assignment, he didn't have time to sharpen a pencil or sneeze. Bill's secretary, Stephania "Stephie" Todorovich played traffic cop, giving each of the people lined up at the door five minutes of green light. At age nineteen, Stephie did a masterful job of sorting us out.

Construction Machinery and Engine & Material Handling people unwillingly moved into our Farm Equipment Division branch houses. Invariably our branch manager became branch manager of all three divisions. The one exception was in Dallas where a Construction Machinery man became branch manager. Each branch manager of these new and enlarged operations had three or more sales managers.

In this new centralized setup, branch managers fell heir to a windfall. They received commissions on sales of all three divisions. As happens with most income windfalls, people get the idea the extra money is earned. But history teaches that windfalls seldom last, and that mankind is well advised to bank the windfall against the day when the windfall ends. When centralization inevitably went out a few years later, some of our branch managers howled like a neutered coyote, as their income plunged.

Since we had a pretty good sales training program going at Toledo Branch, and Willis Scholl knew that because he had been there and had been a part of it, I got the newly-created job of sales training manager. I've never felt that this was part of some grand management plan. If the truth were known, I suspect it was one of those "give him a title and see what he does with it" sort of thing. There was no job description.

Since Bill Klein had weightier things to do than to sit down with me to blueprint a sales training program, in those first months some of my more important work was working crossword puzzles. If some branch manager had a sales training program of his own, I went to see what I could learn. The first program I attended was at Wichita Branch, followed by one in Memphis Branch.

When I did get a few minutes with Bill Klein, I was always impressed with a plaque he had on his wall. "The sales department may not be the whole company, but the whole company had better be the sales department." I've quoted that adage hundreds of times, in speeches around the country. How many businesses have you quit patronizing because of a negligent order clerk, a stupid anti-customer policy, or a fouled up accounting department? Everyone in a corporation either makes or loses sales for that business.

## BILL ROBERTS LATE?

Some people are always late. No matter when the event starts, they're ten minutes late. And then there are people who are ALWAYS on time; in fact, they're always ahead of time. Bill Roberts was one of those people. When he called a meeting, if we weren't there fifteen minutes ahead of time, we were considered late.

No sooner had I arrived in Milwaukee when Bill Klein told me, "You're going to Kansas City with Mr. Roberts." The Future Farmers of America convention was being held in Kansas City, and Mr. Roberts was president of the FFA Foundation. He wanted a couple extra handshakers with him; reinforcements, you might say.

It was customary for the president of the FFA Foundation to address the Chamber of Commerce luncheon at the Muelbach Hotel each year at FFA convention time. At the table, I sat next to another Mr. Roberts, an executive of the *Kansas City Star*, and no relation to our man Roberts. Just as the luncheon was about to begin, Ernie Mehl, the sports editor of the *Star*, came in to announce that "it's official." Connie Mack's Philadelphia Athletics were moving to Kansas City. Rumors to that effect had floated around for weeks. Now it was officially confirmed.

Bill Roberts tore up his prepared speech. Instead, he told the history of the Kansas City Blues from the day they started to play ball in KC. He quoted statistics: years the Blues won the Little World Series, scores of the games, winning pitchers, batting averages, the works. He pulled it all out of his memory. Then he told about Connie Mack, starting at the time that Mack was in knee pants. He quoted about ten minutes of A's history.

Roy Roberts leaned over to me and asked, "Where in the world did that son of a gun bone up on all that this morning?" I told Roberts that he didn't need to bone up, he remembered it from when it happened. Roy Roberts told me, "I've got to get my sports editors with him this afternoon."

Rube Smith arranged the dinner that Bill Roberts would host at the Muelbach. Rube told our guests that Mr. Roberts was a stickler for punctuality. "Please be on time." Everyone *was* on time, except Bill Roberts. No host!

No host at six o'clock.
No host at 6:03.
No host at 6:04.
No host at 6:05.

Rube Smith chewed his nails. "Where in the world do you suppose he is?" Guests looked at their watches.

No host at 6:06.

Then at 6:07 Bill Roberts came sailing by us with his shirt tail sticking straight out behind. Mrs. Roberts tried to keep up. As he sailed past Rube and me, he said, "Those guys didn't know a thing about baseball." Bill Roberts had gotten so wrapped up in baseball with the *Kansas City Star*'s sports department people that he had forgotten to look at his watch.

Roberts had a deep-seated compassion for the farmer, particularly the small farmer. When Doc Sorenson worked at our home office, Mr. Roberts ("Mr. Roberts" is what we

## Centralization In, Centralization Out 267

in the field called him) called him into his office to overhear a phone conversation. Roberts called Branch Manager Thomas to tell him something like this, "I have just learned of a small farmer in Kansas who lost everything in a fire. I understand he owes us some money. I want you to deliver this man a brand new WC tractor and tell him it is with our compliments, a gift to get him started again. Tell the farmer that he dealt with a corporation that has compassion for its customers. Tell him to dig in and start over."

Turning to Doc, Mr. Roberts said, "I wanted you to know the facts, but don't consider this a precedent in every case. This was a very special situation."

This incident is similar to one told about Jerome I. Case. Case heard that a farmer in Minnesota was unhappy with his Case thresher. He went to investigate the matter himself. What he saw disgusted him so much that he set fire to the thresher and burned it up. He then sent a new one from the factory in Racine. No charge.

As has been said, Bill Roberts loved baseball. He knew a contractor in Boston by the name of Perrini who owned the Boston Braves, a team that certainly was no Massachusetts Miracle. Bill Roberts and others lured Perrini to Milwaukee. The county built a stadium that had a grove of trees just beyond the wall in center field, a grove that everyone called "Perrini's Woods." Roberts went to as many Braves games as possible.

One night he left a game a little early, but before he got out of the stadium, some new exciting action erupted in the field. He stopped, turned around, and watched from the aisle, blocking the view of people behind him. There were the usual loud admonitions of "sit down." An usher asked him to sit down too but Roberts kept watching. The usher then had a policeman lead Roberts out of the stadium. When Braves' management heard about this altercation, they called to apologize. Mr. Roberts said no apology was needed since the usher did what he was supposed to do. Roberts found that the usher worked for Allis-Chalmers, so he called the employee to his office. When the worker saw whom he confronted, he was sure he was going to get the hook. Instead Mr. Roberts complimented him for doing his job.

Ever so often Roberts wrote a bulletin to the field sales people. I remember one about expense books. He expressed amazement about plebeian tastes that once knew hog hocks, that were now opting for T-bone steaks, and Coca Cola tastes that had graduated to imported champagne.

Mr. Roberts told us several times about a letter he had received from a cemetery monument dealer in Ohio. "We have a most unusual request from a family that is buying a monument from our firm. Since the departed always used Allis-Chalmers equipment, would it be possible for your staff artist to make us a simplified sketch of a WD-45 tractor pulling three plows? We think that you will agree that this will be a very unusual bit of advertising for you."

## GLEANER COMBINES

No sooner had we arrived in Kansas City for the Future Farmers of American convention when Mr. Roberts asked Branch Manager Ed Dillon, to take us out to the Gleaner combine plant in Independence. I couldn't figure why he wanted to visit a competitive combine plant. A flat tire on the way out to Independence turned us around and the trip to the Gleaner plant was scrubbed. It wasn't long before I

## Centralization In, Centralization Out

found out what Bill Roberts wanted at that Gleaner combine plant.

A short time after the 1955 FFA convention, Roberts bought the Gleaner operation. The story goes that he came to the factory in Independence at 8:00 a.m. to meet with George Reuland, president of Gleaner. By 9:00 a.m. the sale was closed. At l0:00 a.m. a Ford representative came to buy the plant (Gleaner used Ford engines for power) but it was too late. George Reuland had sold the family jewels. The Ford people had to go back to Dearborn and explain. The Gleaner purchase was the last big move that Bill Roberts made for the company.

Those of us who grew up with the All-Crop Harvester couldn't believe this Gleaner thing. It was a self-propelled combine, not a pull-type. It was an expensive combine, not an inexpensive one. It was an unpainted monstrosity, not a beautiful Persian orange combine. My comeuppance came at Wichita Branch at a sales training school. I casually mentioned the Gleaner acquisition and that brought a standing ovation. Right then and there I changed my tune. If our people in Kansas had such great respect for a combine that had been their competitor, it just had to be something special.

The day we introduced the Gleaner combine to our Southwest territory people, in a hanger at an airport in Oklahoma City, the phone rang and Bill Klein answered. He came back ashen and said, "Mr. Roberts just died of a heart attack." We sat in disbelief, as the meeting was recessed for an hour. All Milwaukee, and many from all around the country, came to mourn.

Mr. Roberts's last major decision pumped new blood into the corporation. Roberts's decision to buy Gleaner was a godsend. Several years in succession, the Gleaner plant's profits were equal to 95 percent of the net profit of the entire corporation.

## THREE STAR DEALERS

One of the last things that Mr. Roberts did before he died was to institute the Three Star Dealer program. In the mid-fifties he said, "If a dealer sells twelve tractors and twelve harvesting machines, he will be called a One Star Dealer and the branch manager will buy dinner for the dealer and his wife. If a dealer sells twenty-five tractors and twenty-five combines, we will call him a Two Star Dealer, and the regional manager will buy dinner for all of the employees of the dealership and their spouses. If a dealer sells fifty tractors and fifty harvesting machines, we'll throw a party for all customers." Those words "all customers" were soon to cause consternation. Mr. Roberts hadn't spelled out who he meant by "all customers" before he died. I doubt if Roberts thought there would be over two or three Star Dealers.

In mid-August, an Ohio dealer hit fifty-fifty. Bill Klein told me to go to Columbus Branch to find out what the dealer thought he won. At Columbus, I found that Branch Manager F. A. Spilker and the dealer had things all set. They had rented the fairgrounds, had given a caterer a guarantee for 3,500 meals, and they had hired the Hoosier Hot Shots and other artists from radio station WLW in Cincinnati to come to entertain. When I passed this word on to Bill Klein, he blasted the east windows out of his office with his bombast.

## Centralization In, Centralization Out 271

"That crazy nut Spilker. Why, I've worked all my life in Minnesota to get audiences together, and I've never been able to pull a thousand. Now that screwball thinks he can pull 3,500." Bill Klein sent Regional Manager John Walker down to stop F.A. but stopping F. A. Spilker was like trying to stop the tide at the Bay of Fundy.

President Willis Scholl called me to his office. "Mr. Roberts said 'customers,' not the whole town."

"Yes, Willis, you're right. But how to you define 'customers?' Is it this dealer's customers who bought the fifty tractors and fifty harvesting machines? Is it this dealer's customers of last year and the year before? Is it this dealer's used machinery customers? Is it this dealer's parts customers? Is it our customers? (We had had two previous dealers in that town.) Is it the dealer's customers for short-line equipment. Is it . . ."

"OK, OK, we're stuck. Nobody has kept track of customer names so we wouldn't dare invite one and possibly miss another very important customer," Willis told me. "We've got to invite them all." What Willis said "yes" to turned out to be one of the greatest sales promotion ideas since Columbus took what he thought was a short cut to a Chinese restaurant. In each Three Star Dealer community, we told everyone in the area, "This man of ours is the top . . . better deal with him." And it didn't cost us a fortune either.

Bill Klein cooled down and began to catch the spirit of the thing. The day of the party, Bill flew down to Ohio in the company plane. There he was met by the mayor of the town and other dignitaries. Bill was in his element.

Thirty-eight hundred meals were served. At the next one, 2,700. From then on, it was 1,500-1,900. The first two

Three Star Parties were in F. A. Spilker's Ohio territory. We had all but canonized F.A. But the next year, the first dealer got into trouble with the law and the second one ran away with his partner's wife. F.A. returned to earth again.

There were six Three Star Dealer parties in Missouri. In Liberal, the whole town closed down to celebrate with the Curlesses. There was a sign over the main street, "Congrats Hap, Bub and Mary." The caterer dug a barbecue pit in the center of the football field to barbecue hindquarters of beef. He offered farm women two bits for any pie they would bring in. That wasn't so dumb. He knew every time he paid out a quarter, he sold two more full meals. His pie offer brought enough pies to cover tables a half block long.

In Chatham, Ontario, frugal Bill Leeson said he had sold his fifty tractors and fifty harvesters at full list price. When I asked him how he did it, he said, "I tell them that if the company ever caught me cutting prices they would cancel my contract just like that."

"And you get by with that malarkey?" I wondered aloud.

"Have so far," he said with a smile on his face.

The only Three Star Dealer party in the West was at Modesto, California, where Jack Moore hit the jackpot. When I arrived for the Modesto planning meeting, I asked Jack about Plan B, the rain plan.

"Rain? In California?" Everybody laughed. "At this time of the year? Rain? Come now!"

I woke up at 4:30 a.m. and California was getting the most beautiful downpour you ever saw. I called Jack to ask him what that was that was falling out of the sky. He mumbled something that didn't sound courteous and slammed the receiver.

By 5:00 a.m., the rain stopped and by noon the ballpark seats were dry. That's where we held JM Equipment's party.

## THE 23RD AND LAST THREE-STAR DEALER PARTY

Mr. Goad said he didn't think he could pull 1,000, but my man, Herb McCormack, gave the caterer a guarantee of 1,200. Our train was late coming into Springfield, Tennessee, a town in the hills just north of Nashville. After checking the details with the dealer, we went over to the shelter house in the city park to see if the caterer was ready to go. He was. He had six serving tables, each with a washtub of barbecue.

Horror of horrors, however, there were 1,000 people waiting to get in an hour ahead of time. We were in trouble with that 1,200 guarantee. The caterer assured me: "Don't worry, son, don't ya worry one little bit." But I was worried. When I saw that I couldn't shake the caterer, I gave orders to open the doors and let the people in. "When we run out, we run out," I told myself.

People came, and came, and came, and came. Every time I looked up, here was a station wagon with two more washtubs of barbecue. At 2:30 p.m. I asked the caterer, "how many did you serve?"

I about fell over. He said, "4,800."

"How in the world could you serve 4,800 on a 1,200 guarantee?"

"Waal," my friend said, "you said you were gonna run two full-page ads in the paper . . . you were gonna tell the folks that it was gonna be my barbecue and the folks in these pahts knows 'bout my barbecue . . . an Minnie Pearl and tha Grand Ole' Opry folks was comin' . . . and it was gonna be FREE. Ah knows these hill people. They comin'. Ah woulda been crazy not to be reddy for y'all. Man, Ah never made so much money in all mah born days. A dollah and a quatah a plate . . . wooweee!"

Ever since that day in Springfield, I've never had any doubts about the biblical report of the feeding of the 5,000.

## MINNIE PEARL

The Three Star Dealer Program ended with a bang. Not only did we serve 4,800 people, we had Minnie Pearl on the program. During her performance, she jumped off of the stage and kissed a fellow in the front row. She said, "As I live and breathe, ladies and gentlemen, this is Bob Barrow (I've forgotten the right name). He's the man who put me in ray-de-oo."

That evening our Nashville Branch Manager John Conwell said we had a dinner date with the branch's banker. Waddya know, our host was Bob Barrow. I asked, "Are you part of Minnie Pearl's act? Did you put her in radio?"

Bob laughed. He told us, "Minnie Pearl's daddy is a banker in Centerville. She graduated from one of those fancy Eastern girls' schools. I don't know what she majored in, Greek literature maybe. Well, there wasn't much call in Centerville for Greek literature during the Depression so she put an act together. One night we had a regional bankers' meeting in Centerville and Minnie Pearl entertained. She had us all rolling in the aisles. When I got back to Nashville, I told a friend of mine at WSM about her. He had a new program that he called 'Grand Ole Opry.' After that, I forgot all about the incident.

"A year or so later, we were back in Centerville for a bankers' meeting, and Minnie Pearl entertained again. For the second time she had that audience of bankers busting up with laughter. When I got back to Nashville, I asked my friend at WSM why he didn't audition her. He told me, 'I did, she wasn't any good.' I told him that bankers are not known for their sense of humor, but I had seen two rooms full of them bust a gut laughing at her humor. I suggested that he have her back. You know the rest of the story.

"Oh, by the way," Bob said, "Minnie Pearl is the smartest financial brain in Nashville. We all ask her advice on investments."

## BILL ROBERTS FOIBLES

L. W. "Wes" Davis was branch manager at our Pocatello, Idaho, branch. Before that he had been a blockman and before that an International Harvester company store manager in Kansas. He got fired from that job for stocking tractor tires in days when IH still believed in steel wheels. Wes went on to be Pacific Coast regional manager and then he came to Home Office to be our division's manager. A number of the items in this book came as a result of conversations with Wes at his beautiful home in Sun City West, Arizona.

Wes told of the time that Billings Branch Manager Earl Begley hauled Bill Roberts and Wes around the territory. Earl had a flashy, yellow two-door Oldsmobile. Roberts took off on Earl about that two-door car. "It's an insult to ask a guest to crawl into the back seat of a two-door car on all fours. A customer or prospect should be welcomed into the back seat through a private door." When blockmen heard about that blast, at the time of the next trade, they all bought four-door automobiles. I still do.

Roberts wanted to see some of Montana's cattle country. It's the sort of thing that writers write about and painters paint, but from a farm machinery standpoint, there's little business to be had. Roberts asked Earl Begley who the blockman was in that territory. Earl mentioned the name and said, 'He's honest and he's a hard worker.'

Roberts shot back, "My mother was honest and a hard worker too but she would have made a lousy blockman." Even though Roberts was hard on good ole Earl, Begley respected Roberts as did the rest of us. Earl was a true Westerner who always had five panatellas in his breast pocket and who always ordered branch water with his whiskey. He had a little ranch in Billings just below the Rimrock.

When Roberts asked Earl to take him out into the territory, he really wasn't looking for business. He had shirt-tail relatives who had homesteaded in the area, and he wondered if one could be located out there in Big Sky country where the buffalo roam and the deer and antelope play. Roberts watched the mailboxes as they passed to see if he could spot a familiar name. Finally, we stopped at a small cancellation post office. Roberts asked about some people he suspected lived in that region. He was told, 'Alma's out in back.' Alma was Bill Roberts's cousin. The two sat on some mail sacks for two hours bringing each other up-to-date.

## BILL KLEIN

My boss, Bill Klein, was the world's greatest hand shaker. He was equally at home with a penniless farmer as he was with the governor of Minnesota. He had an infectious giggle that stood him in good stead. If something he said didn't draw a laugh, he would giggle and the audience joined in.

He was a great public speaker, and he generally set himself up in a spot on the program where he would shine, in a spot where there was no competition. At one eastern regional sales meeting, Bill was to be the banquet speaker. The afternoon program ran late, as usual, so John Walker, the regional manager at the time, didn't get in his closing remarks. Bill placed John on the banquet program, just before the main speech of the evening.

It was Gettysburg all over again. You'll recall that Lincoln was only a fill in speaker with a few remarks, while Edward Everett was the main speaker with the one hour speech. Everybody knows what Lincoln said but nobody remembers what what's-his-name said.

John's short remarks went something like this, "When you guys get home and you're out there in the weeds taking inventory, listing that rusty disc harrow there in the weeds behind the chicken coop, the shadow that comes over your shoulder will not be the shadow of the apple tree behind you. It will be the shadow of the Widow Smith and Sylvester Kronovich. The Widow Smith's late husband bought some Allis-Chalmers stock as an investment and she has to live off of the dividends. Sylvester Kronovich lives in Pittsburgh. He worked for the company for thirty-eight years and he too bought A-C stock for his retirement years. The Widow Smith and Sylvester Kronovich are looking over your shoulder to see if you have guts enough to list that rusty, weed-covered disc harrow as 'new and unused merchandise.' "

John's few remarks brought the house down. Then Bill Klein got up to speak. He had been topped and he knew it. He poked at John and good-naturedly insulted him. "You so-and-so . . . you stole my thunder . . . how am I going to top that? . . . John, you . . . you . . . you . . . " He stalled and stuttered and cajoled and stalled some more. He was trying to wait until the Walker magic worked its way out of the system. I don't think a person present that evening remembers what Bill Klein said, but we all remember what John Walker said. Yes, it was Gettysburg all over again.

## SALES TRAINING

I'm sorry to have to report that the sales training that I was supposed to initiate fell somewhat short of world renown. W. L. "Shorty" Voegeli came up with an idea of Horace Mann-type training. He suggested we send three instructors to Florida to train twelve dealers, a week at a time. As the season advanced, we moved to Milan, Tennessee, where we leased a facility on the grounds of a deactivated wartime government facility. Then, the script read, we would move to Milwaukee where we would train in the new training center. There was also to be a sales training school in Victoria, Texas, that would move to Sioux City with the season.

Shorty insisted that the twelve to be trained should be dealers and not hired help. He predicted that if we loaded the hired help to the brim with A-C zeal and ambition, their collective bosses would say, "simmer down, Buster, simmer down." If we started at the top and caused the dealer to be Persian orange born again, he would in turn want his hired help to come to a later school. The logic was sound!

## Centralization In, Centralization Out

The Florida and Milan operations went quite well, but when it was time to move to Milwaukee, almost all of the crops were in, and nobody came to the schools we had scheduled in Beer Town. The training center had been built on a farm south of Milwaukee. We sales people had the front half of the farm, and the company's engineers had the back half. I don't know who ordered the training center built, and I'd rather not find out. The building was an abortion if there ever was one. I'm guessing that our architects drew the plans and management gave a quick OK without a careful examination. Some architects are architects only because that's what it says on the door.

The building consisted of a small office up front alongside of the furnace room, and a unisex rest room. There was one training room about 35x35 that had a door that incredibly was too small to allow a Gleaner combine to come in. When we trained people about Gleaner combines, we put on our coats and went outside. The room was heated by a $10,000 Johnson Controls unit that included a sophisticated ventilator that pumped tractor fumes outside quickly. Alongside the 35x35 room there was another room the same size, but this room was unheated. The entire building didn't have one square foot of storage space. The architects had forgotten to include closets. Shorty Voegeli told me to buy a heater for the second room. The price of the heater for the second room was $9,615 less than the one in the main room.

When I was checking on a locale for our field sales training schools, I checked annual rainfall reports. I was told that Topeka and Oklahoma City had thirty inches a year and Milwaukee thirty-two inches, which seemed incredible to me. Then the man at the Weather Bureau explained, "You forget how Oklahoma gets its rain. They get fifteen inches during the State Fair and fifteen inches the week the wheat is ready to cut. Then they don't get anymore." Put that way, I understood.

## GIVE ME A TIMETABLE

When I checked out the Florida location for a training school, I flew into Atlanta's airport that, at that time, had a huge Quonset hut as a terminal. On the plane from Chicago, I read a *Saturday Evening Post* story by one of the Alsops, that, half seriously and half in jest, told about how he treated insolent hotel clerks and surly waitresses.

In Atlanta, I walked up to the Delta counter just as the clerk placed a THIS POSITION CLOSED sign in front of me. I asked who flew into north Florida, where and when. The man said, "This position is closed."

"It wasn't when I got here," I told him. "If you don't want to tell me, then give me a timetable and I'll look it up myself."

Once again, "This position is closed."

Then I remembered the Alsop article. I had a thin briefcase which I raised over my head and I brought it down on the counter so that it sounded like Fort Sumpter was being shelled again, like Sherman was back in town. At the top of my lungs, I shouted, "GET ME A TIMETABLE." The clerk stood there aghast, mouth wide open, eyes bulging. That Quonset had a great inside echo that carried my blast into the uttermost reaches of the building. TIMETABLE . . . timetable . . . timetable. . . .

From this door rushed a man with a timetable. From that door came a woman with a table. From here, from there, I had four timetables in thirty seconds flat. I felt gloriously victorious until I turned around. Every eye in that terminal was on me. I could tell what each person was thinking. "Where's the white wagon and the straitjacket?" I grabbed a discarded copy of the *Atlanta Constitution* and hid behind it.

## 16

# THE INDESTRUCTIBLE GLEANER

The DC-3 that I rode into Charlotte bounced around precariously as we landed. When I checked into a hotel room and turned the radio on, I heard that there had been a tornado some thirty miles south of Charlotte. I was in Charlotte to accompany branch sales people to a series of block sales meetings.

At the first of these meetings, the night after I arrived, a dealer said that he had lost his place of business to the wind. And he said, "I lost the first and only Gleaner combine I've sold. The man who bought it wants to talk to someone from the factory." When we arrived at the man's farm the next day, we found that the Gleaner's destruction was not total.

The Gleaner-Baldwin combine had been designed by Curt Baldwin. He was a custom cutter who, with his brothers, moved up the Wheat Belt each year as the harvest moved north. Thousands of custom cutters each year hire out to wheat farmers to cut their grain. Custom cutting isn't unknown to the rest of the country, but it is most common in the Wheat Belt.

The combine-thresher design Baldwin came up with, as you can guess without being told, was one that would fit the needs of custom cutters. There was a short wheelbase,

## The Indestructible Gleaner

so that the combine would fit on a custom cutter's truck. The wheel tread was narrow enough to fit the truck too. The combine's grain header lifted high enough to clear the cab of the truck, making detachment of the header for transit unnecessary.

Since custom cutters didn't know where their next parts supply source would be, Baldwin designed his combine so that it wouldn't need parts. Belt pulleys were cast iron, not stampings. The frame under the machine was like a bridge, and I mean that literally. There were many common bearings, some oversize, but if the operator had eight spare bearings in his pickup, he had all of the bearings that would be needed at the time of bearing failure. The machine's exterior was galvanized steel. Baldwin reasoned that most of his combines would sit outdoors. Texas and Oklahoma dust storms have a way of peeling paint off of machinery. So much for the construction of the combine. Now, back to North Carolina.

When we got to the North Carolina farmer's farm, I saw the Gleaner that had gone through the tornado. It lay at an angle in a draining ditch. One wheel and the header were in a wood lot across the road. The combine had rolled the length of two football fields, end-over-end like a tumble weed. The customer who had lost half of his house and all of his outbuildings, said "I've got to get that machine running. It's my only out. I've got to do custom work to pay for the losses that weren't covered by insurance." The customer pulled on a belt, and miraculously, the machine turned over.

To make a long story short, the dealer and the branch each donated a week's service work, and Bill Barber made a deal on some of the larger assemblies. The combine was pounded out and reassembled. It worked all season needing only $1.25 worth of parts in a year of custom work. No other machine we made or anybody else made could have matched that record.

## COACH McCANCE AND OTHERS

In my role as sales trainer, I attended a school that Memphis Branch Sales Manager Coach McCance conducted in Memphis. Coach McCance, a former Tulane football player, was a friend of man, a man with constant bounding enthusiasm. His audience listened with rapt attention as Coach came up with sayings like, "handier than a hip pocket in a pair of overalls" and "some people wouldn't pay fifty cents to watch the Mississippi River run backward."

In Wichita one dealer said he had saved a deal with quick thinking. A customer asked how much it would cost to overhaul an Allis tractor. The dealer said it wouldn't happen very soon but it could cost anywhere from two to four hundred dollars, depending on what was wrong.

"The John Deere dealer says he can overhaul his tractor for eighty-five dollars," the prospect said.

"Well, he's sure got me beat, but there is one thing I would worry about with that tractor," the dealer said.

"What's that?" the farmer wanted to know.

"Paying $3,500 for a tractor with an $85 engine." The deal was saved.

You can win that kind but you can lose them too. In Montana, the Caterpillar dealer got hold of a customer who had signed for one of our two-cycle General Motors diesel engine crawler tractors.

"Are you aware of the fact that the A-C tractor has a two-cycle engine?" the Cat dealer asked.

Yes, the rancher was aware of it.

"What are you gonna do if you're on the back of the ranch and one of those cycles goes out on you? We have a four-cycle engine. If our tractor conks out, it can get back to the barn on three cycles."

That one we lost.

**CREDIT CORPS**

Elmer Kullman, our Minister of Credit with Portfolio, and others, started the Allis-Chalmers Credit Corps, an in-house financial operation like General Motors's GMAC. Even though we had once chased customers' notes and mortgages away with all sorts of disincentives, now we sought that paper. Elmer dressed like a fashion plate, always had a cigarette holder complete with cigarette in his hand, and Elmer BX (that's before Xerox) wrote letters with fourteen copies. Some of those copies went to people only a spitting distance away from Elmer's office. Elmer's secretary had a secretary.

One of our Credit Corp's customers was a rancher by the name of Billie Sol Estes, whose ranch was near Pecos, Texas. Billie Sol bought about three million dollars worth of our machinery and signed notes made payable to the Credit Corp. Always Billie Sol was late with his payments. Southwest Regional Manager G. R. Campbell was in the next office from mine. I would hear him ask Ralph Bruse, branch manager at Amarillo, "When are we gonna get our money from Billie Sol?"

Then I heard nothing for a while, but didn't miss it because it was none of my business. One morning, coming to work, the car radio reported, "Billie Sol Estes indicted."

"Billie Sol Estes? Billie Sol? I've heard that name before," I told myself. "Ah yes, that's G.R.'s friend in Pecos, Texas." When I got to the office I asked G.R. if we had gotten our money. He smiled.

"Yeah, we got it. Several months ago I told Ralph to go to Pecos and either get the money or the machinery. Ralph called on an attorney to draw up papers. The attorney said, 'You can't do that.' "

"Can't do what?" Ralph wanted to know.

"You can't repossess machinery from Billie Sol Estes. Why, Billie Sol Estes is the most upstanding businessman in this community. He's a fine Christian gentleman," the lawyer insisted.

"I don't care what he is," G.R. said. "He doesn't pay his bills."

The lawyer said to come back at two. When G.R. got there, the lawyer handed him a certified check for $240,000, the final payment for the machinery.

## JOHN DEERE, THE SHORT LINE

Flying from Portland to Pocatello, a man sat down alongside me who turned out to be a Deere dealer in the wheat country of eastern Washington. When he found out who I was, he said, "You lucky guys. You've got a full line of equipment, and I've got a short line."

John Deere a short line? That was a new one on me.

The Deere dealer continued, "You have wheel tractors, we have wheel tractors. You have combines, we have combines. But you have crawler tractors and a full line of heavy duty Western tools. What have we got? Zilch.

## KNOW A BOOTLEGGER?

Bob Engle, a transplanted Michigan blockman, became Louie Adams's assistant in the harvester sales department. Bob's first trip out, armed with a Home Office expense book, was to Oklahoma City. Branch Manager Doc Sorenson met the plane one hot day in August.

Said Bob, "Boy, it's hot . . . I'll buy a drink." Home Office big shot, learning fast.

"You're in Oklahoma," Doc said.

"So?"

"Oklahoma is dry."

"You mean you can't buy a drink in this state?"

"At a bootlegger's," Doc explained.

"Know a bootlegger?"

"Sure."

"I'll still buy a drink."

Doc said, "Wait here, I'll make a phone call."

As Bob related the story, he said, "Doc took me to a nice residential district, drove in a driveway and rang the doorbell. A lady welcomed us in, took our orders, filled our orders and took my money." Then I offered to buy a second drink. We were about half way through that second drink when I suddenly realized that this was Doc's own house. He had tipped off his wife and was selling me his booze at bootlegger prices. When I tumbled, Doc laughed and laughed, and he never did offer to give me my money back."

## THRESHING CORN INSTEAD OF PICKING IT

The year after our Gleaner acquisition, Oliver came with a whole-corn combine. They ran everything, stalk and all, through their machine. Oliver engineers realized immediately that it was only the ear that needed to be threshed, and not the whole plant. Every competitor realized that same thing at the same time. Unanimously, the industry moved its corn picker heads to its combines to thresh corn.

Do you recall the Allis corn picker that we wrote about earlier? The one that left the husks, but didn't shell the corn? The corn picker that had shields over the snapping rolls to keep from shelling corn? The picker that farmers wouldn't buy in great numbers? As the saying goes, "it's an ill wind that blows no good."

We placed our corn picker header, shields and all, on our Gleaner combine. Due to those shields over the snapping rolls, our snapping rolls did not shell corn and lose it before the corn got into the cylinder and grain bin. All of our competitors had no such protection over their snapping rolls, and they lost corn. They left yellow streaks down every harvested corn row. Lost corn was tolerated when farmers wanted clean (no husks) corn in the wagon behind a corn picker. Now that the corn was being threshed, husks and cobs went out of the back end of the combine as corn kernels ran into the bin.

That competitive situation lasted one year. The following year everybody had shields of one kind or another over their snapping rolls. He who laughs last, laughs best.

**FRENCH LICK**

In postwar 1946, we had the goodies that farmers wanted lying in our engineering departments in blueprint and prototype form, but there was no money with which to produce them. The eleven-month strike and antitrust suit drained the treasury. We went without big machinery that farmers wanted. Fourteen years later, in 1960, we finally introduced the big stuff that farmers were buying. We came with bigger tractors and a combine with a 4-row corn head. Bill Roberts had considered our dealer contract sacred. Now that Roberts was gone, the Dealers' Sales & Service Agreement was updated and made more competitive. Shorty Voegeli told me that this time he wanted me to write it in English instead of legalese. To the consternation of our in-house barristers, out went the heretofores, hereinafters, wherewithals, and parties of the first part. We had a new dealer contract to unveil and there were fifty-nine new models of machinery to introduce.

Shorty Voegeli told me, "This time we have to have a national sales meeting. Do you think they'll come?"

"We'll never know until we try," I replied.

"Start looking," Shorty told me.

Milwaukee didn't have anything usable. Chicago was booked and was too expensive even if they hadn't been booked. The field house at the Indiana State Fairgrounds had just had an LP gas explosion. Illinois State Fairgrounds looked a little shabby to me. Someone suggested I check out the new indoor fairgrounds in Louisville.

When I saw that facility, an auditorium seating 24,000, acres and acres of exhibit space on each side of the auditorium, l0,000 parking spaces, a freeway on two sides and an airport on the third, I drooled. The facility was tremendous, but not for us in 1960. Had we placed our new "big" machinery in this facility, it would have looked like a flea crawling up an elephant's hind leg with rape in its eye. Had we seated all of our dealers in that auditorium, there would have been 20,000 yawning, empty seats behind them. That's poor sales psychology!

I said, "There'll come a day" and "come a day" there was. Several years later Louisville called me to tell me that they were going to start a midwinter farm machinery show in their facility. Pausing a second and a half, I said, "Sign us up." We were the only major at that first year's show, but today it's the biggest show in the country.

Leaving Louisville, I remembered Tom Taggart's historic hotel in French Lick, Indiana. Tom was a Democrat boss back in the days when Indiana retired its governors to Atlanta and Leavenworth. Taggart had a big mineral springs hotel in Indiana's southern hills. A railroad siding reached to the front door of the hotel. In the glory days when the Morgans and the Vanderbilts had their own private railway cars, they parked them at the door of Tom Taggart's hotel, then went in for baths.

The French Lick Sheraton was just what Shorty Voegeli ordered. We would have a captive audience. Where else can you go in French Lick? In Louisville, some of them would have gotten lost among the mint juleps. We set a tent on the hotel parking lot where we staged our introductory show. Next door, on the practice fairway of the hotel's golf course, we set a two-block long tent where all the new machinery was on display. The hotel's auditorium and dining room were only 200 feet away.

We could sleep, eat, show, display, and inform with only ten-minute intervals in between.

Hotel Manager John Nolan asked me, "how many do you expect?"

"I haven't the foggiest," I explained. "We've never done this before and don't know if they'll come."

"In your wildest dreams, how many do you think you'll have at the biggest meeting?" John asked. We were to have five back-to-back meetings.

Six hundred was my guess, which I'm sure John cut to four or five hundred in his mind. I asked about competition, and he said one weekend there was a school superintendents' convention. "They won't have over a hundred or a hundred and fifty."

Dealers within a day's drive of French Lick were expected to drive. Beyond that, we chartered planes on a back-to-back basis. By "back-to-back" I mean that we flew in from Portland and back again, then deadheaded (empty) to Oakland. In and back to Oakland, then deadhead to Los Angeles. By going "around the clock" in this manner, we kept deadheading to a bare minimum. Airliners use about as many gallons of fuel when they fly empty as when they fly full. "Back-to-back" charters saved us a pile of dough. We flew our passengers to Louisville, then bused them to French Lick, some seventy miles to the northwest.

President Willis Scholl wouldn't let us announce the program until two weeks before it took place. He figured dealers would quit selling until after they saw what was new. I chartered airliners, ordered hundreds of hotel rooms and thousands of meals without a single reservation in hand. I shouldn't have worried. The announcement was immediately followed by thousands of reservations. We pulled

4,200 people. Even though the sixty-year-old hotel had never had 900 people in it before, we stashed 1,158 into it one night. We had every cot that Sheraton owned in Louisville, Indianapolis, and Chicago parked somewhere in that hotel.

Full houses always bring on griping, but they always leave the feeling, "boy, did they have a mob . . . wow, was that a success!" French Lick was just what we needed. When the new big 4-row corn head on the Gleaner came through the show tent, it almost ran over the toes of the people in the front row. Dealers looked up and said to themselves, "sure is a big one."

In 1959, Dealer Red Rolfsmeier of Seward, Nebraska, had taken me to the introduction of the new "wide track from Pontiac" at the Chicago Theater in Chicago. He wanted me to see how the big boys did it.

At French Lick I tried to put a little pizzazz into our show. We opened with the cast coming into the tent in two surreys pulled by four horses. They sang words that we wrote to the tune of "Surrey with Fringe on Top." Serviceman Ellis Wertz complained to General Manager Wes Davis that he had done everything under the sun for the company, but he was not about to sing for his supper. During the second show of the week, I noticed that show biz was contagious. Ellis was singing, or at least, he was mouthing the words.

Spot and flood lights had been rented to highlight the presenters and the stage area of the tent. Several of our presenters complained to Wes Davis that I was blinding them. Wes said gruffly, "Tell Walt to turn them off . . . him and his nutty ideas." Industrial Equipment Sales Manager J. D. Morris wanted the lights left on. He had mastered the art of looking underneath the light. When the rest of the presenters saw what the spotlight did for J.D., each of them, in turn, sheepishly told me, "turn it on me too." During J.D.'s portion of the show, Bob Blinn shined J.D.'s shoes with a backhoe.

The Allis economic thermometer: Late 30s, up, up, up. Wartime, mark time. Postwar, strike and antitrust; down, down, down. Post-French Lick, a spurt upward. Just maybe we would catch a second breath and become a real challenger again.

The year 1960 was a big one for us, and for John Deere too. For thirty years they had sold a 2-cylinder tractor, the only one in the business. In 1960, they moved to four cylinders and displayed their new line at a big show in Dallas. They did it all in one day. Planes came from everywhere and parked during the day at the Dallas airport. There were no back-to-back savings. With back-to-back, we used only one or two airplanes.

Deere used dozens, and that cost money. Even though they had something like a 6,000-person audience, they had tens of thousands of yawning, empty seats behind them. In sales promotion, empty seats are a no-no. The auditorium was so big that Deere's biggest machinery looked tiny. Speakers had to be enlarged on large impersonal screens.

According to the trade press, Deere paid exactly twice as much per capita for their show as we did. That made this meeting planner feel pretty good.

French Lick was famous for its Pluto Water ("if nature won't, Pluto will"). The bottler told me that Pluto Water was potent in its own right, but he added a dash of salt to make sure. There was a small bottle of Pluto Water in every medicine chest of the hotel. Our guys who had never heard of Pluto Water thought it was mix. The hotel plumbing got a workout the nights we were there.

# 17

# CARROT ON A STICK

Bill Roberts knew what incentive programs would do. For three years in a row, in the early '50s, he had a special train that took sales contest winners to all of our factories. The first year, every executive from Home Office was on that train along with winning dealers, blockmen, and branch managers. Winners slept on the train. There was a marvelous togetherness of field and Home Office people.

The second year, some of the executives were "unavoidably detained" and couldn't make the trip. Or so they said. Repeating winners were disappointed. They couldn't talk to all of our Home Office big shots. The third year, only Charley Karr was on the train. He was the one running the show, so he had to be there. Repeating dealers said, "Send the losers on this trip. We know the routine so well that we know where every drinking fountain and rest room is located." There was no fourth factory tour.

I moved to Milwaukee in 1955. Bill Klein was the man I reported to, but Bill's schedule was full to overflowing, so I worked with W. L. "Shorty" Voegeli more and more.

Shorty Voegeli knew sales incentives perhaps better than Bill Roberts had known them. Shorty liked to gamble, gamble big, but gamble on a sure thing. He never had a loser. He was the greatest guy I ever worked for—imaginative, fair, and challenging. He didn't believe in closed-end budgeted incentive programs. He wanted our incentive programs to be open-end. He told me, "Let them go as far as they want to go, provided we make a buck off of the last sale."

## WHEN NATURE WON'T, SALES PROMOTION WILL

Human nature, being what it is, will find sales people comfortable if they're in the mid- to upper-range of their company's sales team. They know that they can make more money if they work a little harder, but what the heck. Life's too short anyway. How do you move such a guy off of dead-center? You can't, but his wife can. Dangle an exotic trip to a luxurious surrounding in front of her, and she'll get her couch potato spouse to work long hours. Show her a grand piano her husband can win if he works a little harder, and she'll explain to her husband that it is absolutely essential for little Jennifer to have a piano on which to practice her scales.

Send the announcement to her. Send the weekly standings to her. Who would enjoy a ball game if the scoreboard can't be seen?

The basic rules for incentive trips include such things as: "Don't pay for what you're going to get without paying for it." "Don't pay for things that you can't get into the cash register." "Make the rules so simple that your salesman/saleswoman will be able to quote them when he/she turns over in the middle of the night."

Over the years, we got good at dangling the carrot on the stick. Naysayers find things objectionable about incentive programs, as they do with everything else. In my book, it's all gain. The sales person gains when extra effort is invested that brings returns. The company gains by adding to corporate profits and stockholders' dividends. More business means more jobs for somebody. Dealers may cut some prices, but they get extra sales volume, and more customers now mean more parts business later. Customers gain with better prices, and earlier use of laborsaving machinery. Suppliers of merchandise or travel incentives gain because they do business that otherwise would not be done.

## MIAMI BEACH-LOS ANGELES/HOLLYWOOD

Shorty Voegeli's first travel incentive program sent winning blocks of dealers to Miami and Los Angeles/Hollywood. The block in each branch that had the highest dollar gain won. Dealers and blockmen and spouses received airplane tickets. Winners east of the Mississippi went to Miami Beach, the rest to LA and Hollywood. Dealers on the winning block that had losses stayed at home.

Departing from basics, Shorty offered points for "barnyard demonstrations" during January. That meant taking a machine out to a farm, letting the farmer drive it around the barnyard a couple of turns. We offered a tenth of a point for every dollar's worth of machinery so demonstrated. I told Shorty, "You're inviting a liars' contest," and he replied, "Yeah I know, but the bottom guys will lie more than the top ones."

Blockman George Richardson, in the roughest part of Ohio, put all of his dealers and their hired help on the most expensive machines on the lot, and they called on every farm down the road. They drove in, rapped on the door, told the man to slip into a coat, let him drive the machine a few turns, and then they would say, "Haven't got time to talk . . . be seeing you," and drove off. They piled up points like Fort Knox and won the contest hands down. After the January 31 expiration date of these "farmyard demonstrations," farmers flocked into the stores of the dealers on that block.

"What in the world was that all about? Drive it around a couple times and 'ain't got time to talk . . . goodbye?' " If curiosity killed the cat, it sure worked for George Richardson's dealers too. He was on the lousiest territory in the branch but he won. His dealers had store traffic and sales like you wouldn't believe.

## LET'S DO IT AGAIN

The Miami-Los Angeles thing went so well that just about everybody wanted to do it again. We came with a repeater that had no farmyard demonstrations, but there was an added incentive: "If last year's winners repeat, they go to the opposite coast."

There wouldn't be any repeaters. I was sure of it. I told Shorty that there was no way that a dealer who stretched himself to the limit this year could pile a high gain on top of a high gain next year. "They will have used their management skills, manpower, floor space, and trucks to the limit. It can't be done."

Then Norma and I went to Miami Beach and Shorty and Ceil went to Los Angeles. After we returned, I commented to Shorty, "I'm gonna hedge a little. Given the enthusiasm I saw, a few of those guys are going to repeat." Shorty said he had gotten the same impression at Los Angeles.

To show you how smart I was with that "can't possibly repeat" comment, every winning block in the east repeated as did every winning block in the west. Only those branches huddled near the Mississippi River didn't have repeaters. My fancy theory was shattered. I then knew from experience that there are no upper limits. Winning is contagious. It's not only possible for winners to pile high gains on top of high gains, it's almost sure to happen. How else do you suppose that General Motors and Sears got that big? The occupational hazard with incentive program repeaters is that the rest of the sales force will consider the repeaters unbeatable, and will quit trying.

**CROP CLINICS**

Bob Murphy and Jerry Curren of *Rural Gravure* came in to see if we would be interested in their Corn-Soybean Clinics. We had tried the idea at Cotton Clinics in Memphis, Columbia (SC), and Bakersfield and knew that the idea worked. We said "yes" and worked with Murphy and Curren for about eight years, holding clinics in various commodity areas—corn-soybeans in the Midwest, cotton, mid-South, hay/forage in Wisconsin and New York. We had corn clinics on the east coast, in Colorado, and in the San Joaquin Valley of California. Every February there were a half dozen wheat clinics in subzero Saskatchewan and Manitoba where it is said, "they don't use their snow until it's a year old." They told us up there, "If summer comes on Sunday, we go fishing."

We teamed up with fertilizer companies, seed companies, storage/drying people, and chemical suppliers. Each company had a half hour on the program. We split costs—

building rental, advertising, and lunch between us. Costs were about $1.15 per capita for thirty minutes of personal communication. On the way out of the meeting attendees got a pack of literature. It was the finest medium I ever found to reach *new* people. When the other suppliers on the program brought in their loyal customers, their customers were not our customers. For the most part, they were Deere and International Harvester customers. We wanted to get to those people to give them a little true Persian orange religion. We put our foot in the door and smiled. We tried to make an important Allis point or two that we hoped would be checked out by our competitors' customers before they bought their next machinery.

There was a question/answer period after each session. When we went to written questions in Rennselaer, Indiana, I read the first one without censoring it. I had the words out of my mouth before my brain caught up. "What do you do about the most common insects of all—crabs?" The crowd roared and I wanted to hide. Bob Didriksen of Shell Chemical got up solemnly and went to the mike. He said, "Sir, I would recommend that you stay home Saturday nights." One day, Bob stuck a picture of a John Deere combine into Bill Barber's photo tray. The audience saw the picture of the green combine before Bill did. When the audience reacted with a laugh, Bill looked at the screen and said, "There (pointing at Bob) is the so-and-so who did that to me. As long as he stuck that picture into my tray, let me tell you a little about this combine." He wouldn't have dared take off on Deere that way on his own, but when Bob opened the door, Bill walked in.

Wad Wadleigh of Stauffer Chemical M.C.'d some of the clinics I couldn't get to. He weighed 300 pounds and bragged about his big family. At a clinic in Ontario, someone put the question in the hat, "How can a man your size have so many kids?" Wad asked the man who asked the question to please stand up, and the stupid oaf did. Wad said, "Now, my poorly endowed friend . . . " The audience roared. The questioner turned purple.

At each Crop Clinic we had an opening door prize and a closing door prize. The opening door prize was there to get people in their seats early. The closing door prize provided incentives to stay until the fat lady sang. I can't think of a reason to give a door prize at any other time.

At Salisbury, Maryland, there was a color TV as an opening door prize. I called a name and nobody answered. I worried that the poor guy was back in the rest room a second time. When the audience kept shouting, "Call another name," I finally couldn't do anything else. Still I worried that the poor fellow had to go to the rest room for a second time in the morning. Afterward I found out what had happened. The guy's name I called was the local griper. He had chewed out the chemical man and seed man and was working on our dealer in the front hall. Those around him heard his name being called but didn't tap him on the shoulder until I called another name. Then they tapped him. They said he hit the floor, then the ceiling, then shot out of the front door. His wife is probably still saying, "you and your big mouth."

After eight years, sponsors tired so Crop Clinics died. Farmers were still coming in goodly numbers, but the clinic idea was dead when the companies with the cash departed.

At the beginning of our Corn-Soybean Clinics, the Corn Belt was in transition to narrower rows. Until the '60s, corn was still planted in 40-inch rows because that was the width of the horse's rear end, and horses pulled the cultivators that weeded the middles of the corn rows. With the horse long gone, it was time to change. We came with a 3-row, 30-inch corn head—two passes and you harvested the corn that had been planted with a 6-row planter. At the time, DeKalb brought out a single-cross hybrid, XL-45, that called for high population and narrow row planting. Our two sales stories merged beautifully. At the time, we had switched to tool bar planters, so the planting units could be spaced anyway a farmer wanted them. Without a doubt, it was our Corn-Soybean Clinics that launched narrow-row planting and consequent higher yields.

## WINNING WITH 108 BUSHELS OF SOYBEANS PER ACRE

At the end of the '60s and beginning of the '70s, Elanco Chemical Company, staged soybean yield contests. The prizes were substantial—a combine for the first prize, four tractors at the second level, and twenty-four planters at the third level. The third year of the contest (and, as it turned out, the last), we were to furnish the prizes. The presentations were to be made at a hotel in New Orleans. We heard the night before that a man from the foothills of the Ozarks would win the grand prize and that he had all Allis-Chalmers equipment except a combine. Now he had won an A-C Gleaner combine with his 108-bushel per acre soybean crop. I lay awake all night dreaming of how we would splash this thing all over the country.

Ray Wilkinson, of radio station WRAL in Raleigh, North Carolina, was the Master of Ceremonies. Ray told of his many goofs in radio, not realizing that the worst was soon to come. He introduced the winner as all the ag scribes present got out their pencils, as farm editors turned on their Sony tape recorders and movie cameras. Elanco's VPs were in the front row. The winner said something like this:

"I plowed 'er and then I disced 'er an I believe I run a drag over 'er . . . yeah, I remember runnin' the drag. Then I got out my planter and that (too hot to print) thing wouldn't work." Everyone winced because you didn't say things like that over the radio in those days. The twenty-four in the audience who had won Allis-Chalmers planters winced too because they had just won one of the planters that this man said wasn't any good. I asked about it afterward and the man told me, "It was my old Oliver. That's why I got rid of the (expletive) thing and bought yours." I came back with, "But you didn't say that!" He came back, "Oh, didn't I? I'm sorry."

The man went on to say that he had applied Elanco's Treflan and then, with a stream of four-letter words told that Treflan wasn't any good either. "Why, me and my daughter, we wore out three pairs of gloves hoein' weeds outa that patch."

Two Elanco VPs passed out. Two more needed an oxygen tent. Ray Wilkinson had his head buried under the tablecloth. Reporters put their pads away. Sonys and movie cameras were placed back in their cases. But the man wasn't finished.

"When it came time to combine, I had my neighbor do it but that (more cursing) didn't know how to run no combine. My daughter and me raked an extra twenty-four bushels outa that patch."

We delivered the Gleaner as far as the mailbox and hurried out of the neighborhood. Elanco canceled all succeeding soybean yield contests.

## CLYDE HIGHT

Clyde farmed near Moweaqua, Illinois, He bought DeKalb's narrow-row corn story and bought a Gleaner corn head to harvest it. Only Clyde wanted a 20-inch head instead of a 30-inch. He consistently raised 150-bushels of corn per acre, a miracle of sorts at that time. The world was ready to change from 40-inch to 30-inch, but Clyde's 20-inch corn was just too revolutionary a change for 99 percent of farmers to swallow. He and we couldn't get the proposition sold even though the evidence was there that 20-inch corn outyielded both 30-inch and 40-inch. *Successful Farming* magazine had given Clyde a lot of publicity, so he had thousands visit his farm. Clyde's name was a household word in corn growing areas of the country.

We took him to as many Corn-Soybean Clinics as he would go to. When Clyde was on the program, there was always a packed house, and people stayed an extra hour to ask questions. At Greeley, Colorado, it was dark before we left the hall. Clyde had an honest country manner. On the platform, he could get by with murder. At an Iowa meeting he told the audience, "Me and Larry's been over your state a couple times in the last year . . . we kinda get the impression that you're ten years behind the times." If I had said that, I would have been ridden out of town on a rail. When Clyde said it, he got prolonged applause.

## GOD PLANTS EVERYTHING NO-TILL

One of our LaCrosse engineers came with a coulter that had a rippled blade. A coulter is a sharp disc that runs ahead of the plow bottom to slice the soil for the moldboard to turn over. When our rippled coulter moved in front of the planter opener, it tilled a 2-inch width as deep as you wanted to set the coulter. Corn or beans could be planted without prior tillage, right in the previous year's stubble. I stuck this no-till bit (our copyrighted word was "no-til") into one of our clinic programs. At a clinic in Kentucky, Harry Young and some of his neighbors saw it and went right home and each bought a planter from Dealer Sam Maddox in Hopkinsville, Kentucky. No-till didn't mean anything to me until I saw Harry double-crop soybeans in wheat stubble without prior tillage. He rode a planter five minutes behind his brother who combined the wheat. Over the years, I saw Harry put 47-bushel beans behind 92-bushel barley on land I know he bought at a bargain price. Fresh-killed money, if I ever smelled it.

Like Clyde Hight, Harry's name got to be a household word in ag country. Kentucky and Virginia adopted the no-till concept without argument. In Illinois a tiff raged between George McKibben at Illinois's southern ag station and the professors at Champaign-Urbana. At Iowa State in Ames, elderly professors fought the younger ones. There was conflict in Pennsylvania. Purdue had a tiny experimental plot. The rest of the states just ignored no-till. I was amazed that the Soil Conservation Service didn't pick up on no-till and give it a ride. It was such a good conservation measure. Twenty years later, SCS got on the no-till bandwagon.

No-till was another fun thing to sell because it was so different. My speeches would start with, "When the Good Lord farmed this state all by himself, he planted everything no-till. He gets a pretty decent crop of no-till weeds in the fence rows (the area a couple of feet on each side of the fence) even today. If you plant a Christmas tree in your front lawn, you don't plow the lawn. You dig a hole about yea big and set the tree in it, don't you? Tell me then, why are you digging a 40-inch hole for a half-inch kernel of corn? Why isn't a 2-inch hole big enough?"

No-till didn't take off immediately. I suspected that the industry dragged its heels because people in the industry could see in no-tillage the potential demise of the big tractor, the big plow, and big disc harrow. Today the plow isn't extinct, but it sure doesn't have the use it once had. Those who do not go all the way to no-tillage, at least go as far as minimum tillage to conserve soil. Residue left on fields no longer carries a stigma. Residue left on fields over the winter inhibits pollution. There's less wind and water erosion. Environmentalists like that facet of no-tillage, but when weeds are not plowed down or removed by a cultivator, they must be removed by farm chemicals. That, environmentalists do not like. No-tillage and minimum tillage takes management, more management perhaps than the plow/disc harrow method of tillage.

The jury is still out!

## JUMP JACK

In the late '60s, Shorty Voegeli told me, "I think we'll have a ten percent gain in the next quarter, but I'm willing to bet $100,000 that we make it. Come up with something."

I came up with "Jump Jack." The dealer in the winners' column got his points, but he also got the points of the dealer he jumped. Points piled up real good when you jumped the dealer ahead of you. Prizes were E. F. MacDonald Company merchandise. MacDonald was one of the big incentive houses in the country.

The first month of Jump Jack limped along. The second month more dealers caught on. The third month the floodgates opened. After the close of the promotion, Shorty came into my office and said, "You went a little over budget, didn't you?"

"Yeah, a little."

"How much?"

"Branches gave out the points."

"Find out how many they gave out."

I called the branches and found that we had exceeded our $100,000 budget by $842,000. Shorty wasn't surprised, but when the news reached the executive floor, we had to call for five oxygen tanks. Shorty philosophized, "We took in eleven million dollars worth of business we didn't expect to get. We made money on that baby." The next year we came with Jump Jim. By tightening up the rules a bit, we got costs down to around a half million dollars but the sales increase this time was $15 million. As a company, we were making great sales gains during these years. But competitors knew about incentive programs too, and they made similar gains. We didn't cut back on their market penetration.

## THE GIRLS

Our standard procedure at our summer trade shows was that drivers would bring machinery through our big tent. Presenters would make a pitch to the people in the stands. A three-piece band played while the machines came in and went out. We had a twenty-minute show every hour. Then our machines got bigger. They wouldn't go through tent openings anymore. At the same time, our budgets tightened.

I attended several World Fairs and noticed that big corporations used females as trade show narrators. No one had ever done that in agribusiness. In 1970, I told Ray Dague that I was going to try. Ray had been branch manager at Syracuse, New York, branch and was now general sales manager for the division. He said he didn't think the world was ready for that yet, but added, "Go ahead . . . you've got a good batting average . . . we'll never know until we try."

Karyn Caldwell, a young married woman we had starred in films we made for our Crop Clinics, ran a talent agency. She said she knew what I wanted and she would get the right women for me. The first year, we hired Ginny Haberman who had done mike work. D. C. Berg had a black belt in karate, was a pilot with an instrument rating, had a master's degree, and a sometimes TV show. Barbara Waters had been a runner-up in the Miss America pageant.

The first day at the Wisconsin Farm Progress Show in 1970, we knew we had a winner. Those gals pulled twice the people our men ever drew, and they held them twice as long. Each of the three would come on for twenty minutes out of the hour. We ran a continuous show from 8:30 in the morning to 4:30 in the afternoon. Compared to the year before, we attracted about six times the total audience for half the money! There's always a way if you look long enough.

The second year, D.C. asked to be excused because she now had a full-time childrens' TV show, so we hired Jan Fazio who had some kind of magic in her voice. When Jan came on, the crowd doubled in two minutes. She would bring young men her age up on stage and give them a hard time.

"Have I proved to you that this tractor is measurably better?"

"No way, Sister." Then the young fellow tried to escape, but Jan grabbed him by the arm and yanked him up on stage again, as the audience applauded.

"What kind of tractor do you use?" she asked.

"John Deere." The painted-green portion of the audience cheered and Jan held her head in horror.

"John Deere? I'm going to go through this thing once more and this time, you pay attention, y'hear?" She made her one or two strong points a second time.

I asked her why she never pulled one of our customers up on stage. I found she was smarter than I was.

"If I pull an A-C owner up here, he'll either lay it on so thick that it will not be believable or he'll gripe about something. Do you want that?"

"NO!"

## BUY A TRACTOR AND TAKE A TRIP

In 1963 we caught ourselves with twice our normal tractor inventory. I don't remember if we had twisted arms or if dealers were overoptimistic, but there was the inventory. The usual way to clear decks was to wait for spring, offer a $300 rebate, take a bath in red ink, and hope you'd learned your lesson. Shorty Voegeli came into my office and said, "I think we can do with $150 worth of travel now what $300 in cash will do next spring. Let's offer a trip to the factory to anyone who buys a tractor anywhere in North America." I checked and figured that $150 just might do it, if all eligibles did not come. Shorty said that break even was 100 percent unit sales increase.

The program limped at first, but then started to pick up steam. The last two weeks a most welcome deluge hit us. We ended up with a 112 percent unit sales gain and black ink. We flew 7,100 farmers to Milwaukee in ninety-nine chartered airliners and fourteen helicopters. Eligibles close to Milwaukee went to their dealer's place of business where a chopper picked them up.

Our tractor inventory was near zero, so now we could crank up tractor production and get orders to ship.

**MARKETING MAN-OF-THE-YEAR**

At a chapter meeting of the National Agri-Marketing Association, Eli Heineman told me, "Why don't you enter the Marketing Man-of-the-Year competition? You've got a lot going for you—the largest civilian airlift for all time, the girls at the trade shows, lots more." I entered and won in Wisconsin, then at the national in Kansas City, I won again. It's hard to describe the feeling of being named best in all of agribusiness, considering that agribusiness is 25 percent of the total of American business. My family was present at Kansas City when the presentation was made, but nobody from Home Office showed up. That indicated how the wind was blowing.

## THE MEN IN THE DEPARTMENT

Out at the Sales Training Center where we prepared for trade shows, we had Lynn Laughery and Harold Fisher building our trade show displays and taking them to the various events. There were two truck trailers that held displays. Lynn did good work, in fact too good. He built displays that would outlast the pyramids of Egypt. Raised in the Depression, Lynn straightened nails. His born-again nails probably cost us ten times what nails would have cost at the hardware store. Lynn was a just-in-time deadline man. He loved to go to trade shows with wet paint. He always got there just under the wire, but never missed.

Harold Fisher had opposite traits. He wanted to be all set to go a month ahead of time. Harold built as if the displays were a movie set—a light frame, a dash of paint, and up she goes. Harold's dependability was a great asset to the department. Any boss would have liked to have had a man as dependable as Harold.

My first assistant in the office was Memphis Blockman Lewis "Abe" Lincoln. We both had swivel chairs and desks in the office, but were seldom there. Abe, as the saying goes, never met a stranger. When we started a support operation for custom cutters in the Wheat Belt, Abe ran the Gleaner Caravan. He had a semi loaded mostly with warranty parts; a portable parts department, as it were. He followed the custom cutters as they moved north with the harvest. Abe parked his trailer either across the street from the dealership or at the airport. There were eight servicemen in company cars, each equipped with 2-way radio so that contact could be kept with headquarters. Our customers appreciated the support effort, even though we could only be at one place at a time. After several years of great home office sales promotion work (I once sent Abe Lincoln out to speak in George, Washington), he asked to go back to the block again.

It was in the late '60s that Bob Dewey came in to help. Bob operated the Gleaner Caravan too. He came up with a series of Dealer/Customer meetings, using the young women that narrated at our trade shows. By this time, they knew the line as well as the men. When I retired five years early, Bob should have gotten my spot. He knew all that I knew and probably more. But he was passed over for a neophyte who lasted only nine months. Bob, too, asked to go back to the block and was sent to northeast Ohio. He worked my old block, plus what had been four other blocks in my time.

## IT'S 39 YEARS AND OUT!

Even though farm income was still on the rise and the industry, all but A-C, was doing well, my budget was cut five years in a row. Allis-Chalmers was taking its lumps. If I stayed, I would superintend a sales promotion retrenchment program. Norma and I had paid our kids' thirty-second and last college tuition bill. I wanted out and General Manager Roy Uelner helped with a push. I knew A-C was sliding but I didn't know how fast. I certainly didn't foresee the disastrous '80s that agriculture went through. It was good that early retirement got me out when it did. We headed for the mountains of East Tennessee, where we live now.

You've had only a glimpse of what happened to food production during my thirty-nine years in the business. You've met just a few of the people who made your inexpensive, nutritious, and plenteous groceries happen. These folks on the land and in agribusinesses made it possible for you to place food on your table for eleven percent of disposable income. No other country's farmers and agribusiness people have done as well. You've met little people and you've met giants, all elbowing their way through our competitive system.

You've met farmers who held out for the last dollar for their tradeins and dealers who outwitted them . . . sometimes. You've met giants and you've met garden-variety types. You've seen the competitive North American free market system at its best. It's unprincipled at times, cooperative at other times. It's a rough business, this competitive American system, but it works! The folks who tore down the Berlin Wall opted for it in place of the "social security" that had enslaved them for forty years.

It took all these people to make it happen! I'm happy to have had the opportunity to introduce you to some of them.

## THE EIGHTIES

The 1970s saw foreign sales of American farm products climb each year to a peak of $44 billion in 1980. Then the curve headed downward, hitting bottom $16 billion off the peak, in 1986. After the 1982 recession, the nation as a whole enjoyed a decade of prosperity. Not so on the farm.

During the '80s we lost twelve and a half percent of our farmers and about twenty-five percent of our small agribusinesses. The federal farm credit system had to be bailed out. The strong dollar of the early '80s priced us out of world food markets. Some of our customers were broke. Their $35 oil had slipped to $15. Four presidents in succession embargoed food shipments abroad. Overseas buyers went to somebody else's store to buy.

Adding to the dilemma, domestic sales fell as well. Self-appointed nutritionists told us that the food we ate contained too much fat, sugar, salt, caffeine, calories, cholesterol or a deadly combination of these. No less an authority than Jimmy Carter's Assistant Secretary of Agriculture, Carole Foreman, said that eating beef caused heart trouble and pork would give a person cancer. Dairy products and eggs plugged up the pipes with cholesterol, we were told. Sugar caused hypertension, possibly even criminality. We heard that bread and potatoes caused deadly obesity. Hot coffee and tea released radon gas. The "experts" told us that fruit and vegetables were no-no's because tomatoes, for instance, had more toxicity than Three Mile Island. Only oat bran and persimmon juice came in free. Mothers placed their families on a diet of Twinkies and Diet RC Cola to play safe. Per capita consumption of beef, pork, dairy products, eggs, sugar, bread, and potatoes fell during the '80s. Multiply that by approximately 250 million people and you see why there was trouble in River City, and other towns in rural America during the '80s.

When agriculture receives a blow, the pain is felt by all of agribusiness. Farmers couldn't do without seed, fertilizer, and chemicals, but they could postpone purchases of farm equipment, and they did! During the 1980s, postponement was carried to ridiculous extremes. People that could have and should have bought didn't buy. Bill Fogarty, now editor of *Farm Equipment*, said it was a case of "keeping down with the Jonses," to avoid neighborhood embarrassment.

The great industry's great production machine of the '70s kept producing into the '80s, only now there were fewer customers. Inventory piled up, and when inventory piles up in any business, prices are cut. Farm buyers of machinery had always made the industry's list prices a laughing matter. Now net prices were laughed at too. A call to Home Office got an extra ten or twenty or forty percent discount, off of net! A lot of the industry's inventory was sold at spec cost, which is direct parts and labor cost only. Still farmers did not buy. One year it got so bad that the farm equipment industry was replacing tractors on farms of this country at the rate of a new one every forty years, a new combine at the rate of new one every eighty years. The stuff just wasn't moving.

It was against this dreary backdrop that the farm equipment industry experienced "fruit basket upset" in 1985. Even mighty Deere & Company stared at red ink in the '80s. International Harvester Company, once the proud leader of the industry, was buried in paper, inept management, overgenerous labor contracts, and red ink. Tenneco's Case Company division, needed both dealers and equipment so Case bought IH's farm and industrial farm equipment business, as Cyrus McCormick turned over in his grave.

At any time in the previous thirty-five years, Ford Motor Company could have bought themselves into first place in the farm equipment business, but they did not do so. In 1985, Ford bought New Holland, the strongest shortline specialty (hay/forage equipment) company in the business, then went on to buy a 4-wheel drive tractor producer too. Ford-New Holland could have been a threat to Deere and Case-IH, but then Ford wavered. Production of Ford tractors ceased in this country. All Ford tractors sold here were imported. The headquarters office moved to New Holland, Pennsylvania. Late in 1990, Fiat entered the scene. Ford sold a block of stock in the Ford-New Holland operation to Italy's Fiat.

This was not Fiat's first appearance on the American scene. Fiat and Hesston of Kansas had a working relationship that didn't set the world afire. While I was still with A-C, Fiat bought Allis-Chalmers's construction machinery business. A-C had the big stuff and Fiat the smaller units. With Fiat's good reputation worldwide, this could have been a winner that threatened Caterpillar's domination of the world market. It didn't happen.

Massey-Ferguson should have been the biggest farm equipment business in the world. Massey had a board of directors from all over. They had plants all over the world and knew world markets well. Yet in the '80s, Massey dropped its self-propelled combine that Joe Tucker's "Harvest Brigade" made famous. They bought a rotary combine from White, then abandoned it. The name of the parent firm is now Varity.

In the '80s, Allied bought what was left of White, and added a few more short-line companies. White had once been a combination of Oliver, Minneapolis-Moline, and Cockshutt.

People ask me, "Why did Allis-Chalmers disappear?" It's personal opinion, of course, but here's how I see it:

(1) Allis was a conglomerate before the word was coined. In a multifaceted corporation, management must skip around to see which division's problems it should address today. In one-industry businesses, top management

focuses its attention on one business, the only business the corporation has. Witness the success of one-industry firms like IBM, Deere, Caterpillar, Eastman, Xerox, Ford, Exxon, NCR, AT&T, and General Motors.

(2) When there's wide diversification, such as we had at Allis-Chalmers, there are always some losers and some winners. The winner's winnings are used to cover the loser's losings. At best, the firm tends to experience mediocrity. Starting in the mid-'50s, Allis's farm equipment business prospered, and the heavy line divisions looked at red ink. That's oversimplification, since we plow peddlers had our losers too in some areas, and the heavy line division had some winners. The wartime years were profitable to all divisions. As has been mentioned, this company called Allis-Chalmers with its myriads of different businesses, received 95 percent of its net profit from one combine plant in Independence, Missouri, several years in a row. That's terribly lop-sided.

(3) When winning divisions can't use their winnings for engineering, brick and mortar, machine tools, and promotion, but must cover losses elsewhere, eventually there comes the day when red ink catches up with the winner too.

(4) The turning point, in my book, was the communist-led, eleven-month strike right after World War II. You don't give the competition an eleven-month head start and then catch and pass them. We had the blueprints for the machines farmers wanted ready, but there was no money with which to build them. What little money there was, was drained off by massive antitrust fines. People in the sales departments of General Electric, Westinghouse, A-C, and another company or two, conspired to divide up the "big stuff" business on the basis of the phases of the moon, and Uncle Sam

caught them at it. The conspiracy wasn't entered into to make a profit. The conspiracy aimed to stanch the losses that all on the big capital goods suppliers were experiencing.

There was hope of revival in the '60s. While the first national sales meeting at French Lick and successful incentive programs pumped new interest into the operation, the big guns of the industry had gotten too much of a head start. The best we could do was stay even there for a while. By the 1970s, the curve started down and ended in buy out in 1985.

(5) Finally, when outsider David Scott came to Allis-Chalmers as CEO, he bet on the wrong horse. He bet the company's money on the losing heavy line divisions and ignored the plow peddlers. He did not do his homework. He did not look to see where the black ink was coming from. Finally, we farm equipment people showed red ink too and then it was unanimous ... all of Allis-Chalmers was in trouble economically. The end was near, and Allis-Chalmers filed for Chapter 11 bankruptcy. Everything was sold off except two office buildings that still had a FOR SALE sign on them at this writing. The tractor production plant has been razed. Half of one big office building was razed to make room for a shopping center, complete with a K-Mart.

To Allis-Chalmers as I knew it, R. I. P.

In 1985, Deutz of Cologne, Germany, bought Allis-Chalmers's farm equipment business at fire sale prices. Promptly, Deutz abandoned fifty years of loyalty, on the part of customers and dealers, to Persian orange paint in order to install Deutz's bright green. For this ego trip, Deutz got not a nickel's worth of anything in return. Scott Nesbitt, editor of *Implement & Tractor*, editorialized, "Look at the fuss that arose when Allis-Chalmers went from orange to green under new ownership." Ford had wisely kept New Holland's orange and red. Case held onto IH red, and they used the word Case-IH on the side of their equipment. To me, the abandonment of Persian orange paint, with nothing received in return, spoke volumes about Deutz's management judgment. City folks find it hard to understand the loyalty that many farmers have to a certain color of paint. Many farmers consider the wrong color of paint akin to taking a prostitute into church.

Deutz dumped Allis's well-accepted big tractors in favor of smaller tractors from Germany. That's not what the American market called for. Deutz imported German implements and machines that faster-moving American farmers quickly tore up. As the Deutschemark rose in value and the dollar dropped, the imports cost more money. Five executives of Deutz-Allis bought out Deutz's interest and began to build big tractors painted Persian orange again. Is it too late? Who knows?

After yesterday's storm, there always comes the dawn. Late in the '80s, farmers realized that crops had to be sold as well as produced. Farmers began to jump over the whole marketing chain to speak directly to the consumer. The California raisin people did it best with their dancing raisins on TV. Dairy people did well, reversing downward sales trends in butter, fluid milk, and cheese. Ice cream had never slipped. Cattlemen and swine producers started to advertise and they stopped their downward slide and began to edge up again. Some smiles returned to the faces of farm equipment dealers, however the sell-through-price-cut habits of the '80s were hard to break.

The United States has a greater amount of tillable land in temperate climates than anywhere else in the world. The U.S.A. has the best Mom-Pop management teams on its farms. Our farms are better equipped than any others in the world. Our competition is not all that formidable and unbeatable. Canada's wheat fields are far from the docks. Brazil and Argentina suffer economic chaos that includes unbelievable inflation rates. Racial turmoil in the southern part of Africa limits competition from that point on the compass. Europe's little pie-shaped fields could not compete were it not for gigantic subsidies. Australia is dry. The U.S.S.R., which used to feed much of Europe, has been an importer ever since Marx, Lenin and Stalin came on the scene. There's no good reason why the U.S.A. should not lead the world in agricultural production.

With an additional quarter million people born to Planet Earth each day, there just has to be a bright future for food production in this country, and for the suppliers of inputs for that food production.